Eyes of the Heart

MĀNOA 29:1

**UNIVERSITY
OF HAWAI'I
PRESS**

HONOLULU

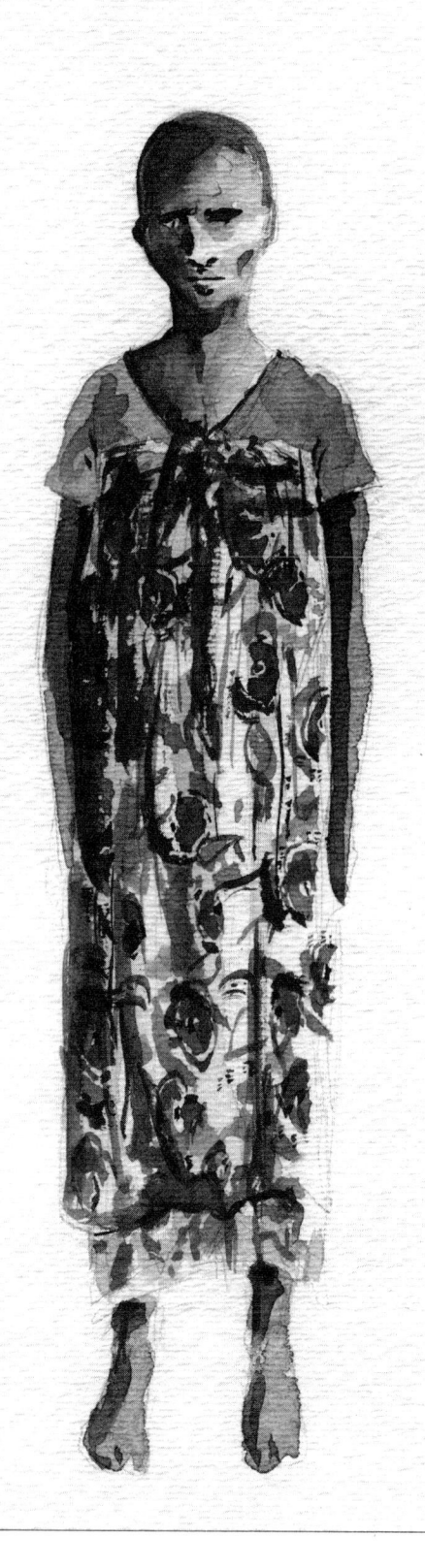

Eyes of the Heart

SELECTED PLAYS

by

CATHERINE FILLOUX

FRANK STEWART

EDITOR

ROSE
Lemkin's House
Watercolor by Camille Assaf
2005

Mānoa: A Pacific Journal of International Writing

Editor   Frank Stewart

Managing Editor   Pat Matsueda

Associate Editor   Sonia Cabrera

Staff   Silvana Mae Bautista

Designer and Art Editor   Barbara Pope

Consulting Editors
Robert Bringhurst, Barry Lopez, W. S. Merwin, Carol Moldaw, Michael Nye, Naomi Shihab Nye, Gary Snyder, Julia Steele, Arthur Sze, Michelle Yeh

Corresponding Editors for Asia and the Pacific
CAMBODIA   Sharon May
CHINA   Chen Zeping, Karen Gernant
HONG KONG   Shirley Geok-lin Lim
INDONESIA   John H. McGlynn
JAPAN   Leza Lowitz
KOREA   Bruce Fulton
NEW ZEALAND AND SOUTH PACIFIC   Vilsoni Hereniko, Alexander Mawyer
PACIFIC LATIN AMERICA   H. E. Francis, James Hoggard
PHILIPPINES   Alfred A. Yuson
SOUTH ASIA   Alok Bhalla, Sukrita Paul Kumar
WESTERN CANADA   Trevor Carolan

Advisors   Robert Bley-Vroman, Robert Shapard

Founded in 1988 by Robert Shapard and Frank Stewart.

Additional copyrights and permissions can be found on page 206.

Mānoa is published twice a year and is available in print and online for both individuals and institutions. Subscribe at http://www.uhpress.hawaii.edu/t-manoa.aspx. Please visit http://muse.jhu.edu/journals/manoa to browse issues and tables of contents online.

Claims for non-receipt of issues will be honored if claim is made within 180 days of the month of publication. Thereafter, the regular back-issue rate will be charged for replacement. Inquiries are received at uhpjourn@hawaii.edu or by phone at 1-888-UHPRESS or 808-956-8833.

Mānoa gratefully acknowledges the support of the University of Hawai'i and the University of Hawai'i College of Languages, Linguistics, and Literature; with additional support from the Mānoa Foundation.

manoajournal.hawaii.edu
uhpress.hawaii.edu/journals/manoa
muse.jhu.edu
jstor.org

CONTENTS

Editor's Note   vii

Silence of God   1
Selma '65   40
Mary and Myra   60
Kidnap Road   97
Lemkin's House   123
Eyes of the Heart   166

A Conversation with Catherine Filloux   202
About the Artist   205

The Armenian village of Sheyxalan, 1915. From the collection of the Armenian Genocide Museum and Institute Archive, Yerevan, Armenia.

Editor's Note

Playwright, librettist, teacher, lecturer, and activist Catherine Filloux has been writing plays about human rights, social justice, and individual freedoms for over twenty years. Her plays often incorporate actual people and events, but are never merely biographical. By reimagining real-life characters and situations—employing temporal shifts, dreams, hallucinations, soundscapes, and other theatrical techniques—she explores the characters' thoughts and emotions as they struggle with moral and ethical dilemmas, resist evil while searching for goodness, and react to assaults on human dignity. Her plays also question the fallibility of our collective memory, and the ways our interpretations of the past change and become distorted over time.

The plays in this volume require minimal sets, few actors, and relatively simple props, costumes, and stage business. Filloux's forceful, precise dialogue carries the plays and makes them well suited to being read on the page as well as theatrically staged.

In 2016, naming her the first Art and Peacebuilding Scholar, at the University of San Diego, the Joan B. Kroc Institute for Peace and Justice described her as a "playwright, educator and activist [who] shines a light on contemporary and historic injustice, the crises that unfold as a result of such wrongs, and individual and community quests for alternatives to oppression and violence." We are pleased to present six of her plays in this volume of *Mānoa*.

The following notes provide some historical background to the plays.

SILENCE OF GOD

Silence of God opens in Cambodia in 1998, two decades after the end of the genocidal Khmer Rouge regime, which killed nearly two million Cambodians and destroyed the country. In that year, Pol Pot, the regime's supreme leader, had surfaced in the jungle district of Anlong Veng after being in hiding since 1980.

Pol Pot was seized by Ta Mok, a Khmer Rouge commander known as the "Butcher"—a violent killer who grinned and laughed maniacally. He had turned against Pol Pot for ordering the assassination of an associate and a dozen members of the associate's family. In 1998, he offered to hand over Pol Pot to the U.S. in exchange for immunity from prosecution. If the international community

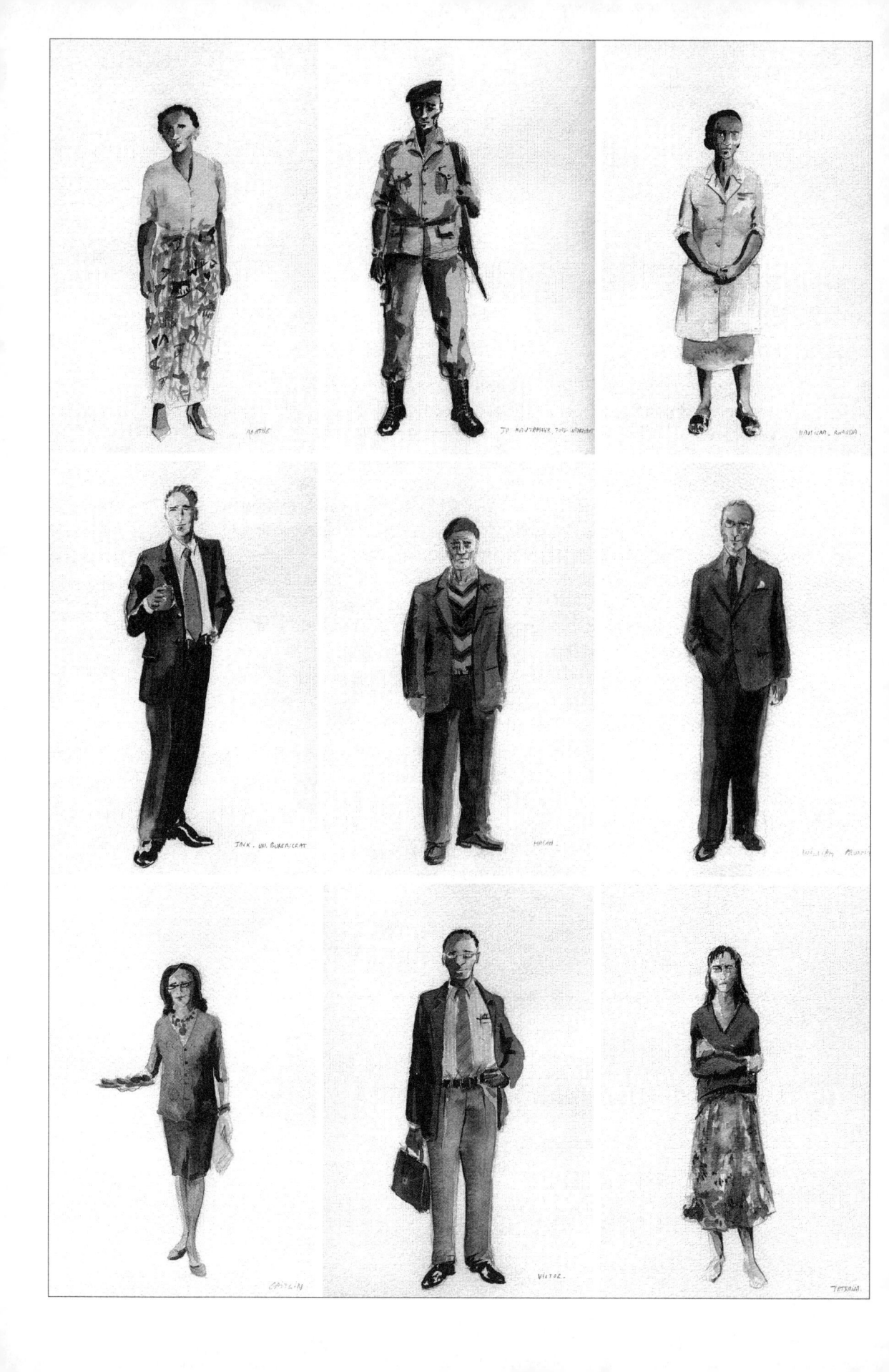
JACK. UN BUREAUCRAT
HASAN.
VICTOR.
TATIANA.

could force Pol Pot to appear in court for his crimes, some measure of justice would have been provided to his victims. But before this could happen, Pol Pot—elderly and suffering from malaria—died.

Pol Pot's brother-in-law, Ieng Sary, appears as the character named Shadowy Figure in *Silence of God*. He was also a mass murderer, in charge of brutal internment camps and genocidal killings in the name of Angka, the regime's governing apparatus. However, after the fall of the Khmer Rouge, Ieng Sary was pardoned by King Sihanouk and given amnesty from prosecution by Prime Minister Hun Sen. He also had the privilege of a diplomatic passport, a lavish villa in Phnom Penh, and the ability to send his children abroad to study.

In 2003, the United Nations agreed to help Cambodia establish an international tribunal to prosecute Khmer Rouge war crimes. After the court began operations in 2007, its mandate was weakened, thwarted, and delayed repeatedly by former Khmer Rouge leaders who remained in high positions, including Prime Minister Hun Sen, a former battalion commander. By 2017, the tribunal had convicted just three elderly men. Most perpetrators died of old age, untried and unprosecuted.

Silence of God was commissioned by the Contemporary American Theater Festival and received its world premiere at the festival, in Shepherdstown, West Virginia, in 2002. The cast members were Mercedes Herrero, Ron Nakahara, JoJo Gonzalez, and Christopher Mchale. The director was Jean Randich.

Opposite: Watercolor drawings in this volume are by Camille Assaf, costume designer for the U.S. premiere of Lemkin's House in 2006.

SELMA '65

In March 1965, Viola Liuzzo, a thirty-nine-year-old white woman from Michigan, was shot and killed while driving on an isolated Alabama road. Her killers were Ku Klux Klansmen who included Gary Thomas "Tommy" Rowe, an FBI undercover informant.

At her home in Detroit on March 7, Liuzzo had watched on television the "Bloody Sunday" brutal beating of black and white protestors as they attempted to cross Selma's Edmund Pettus Bridge. The violent images were shocking. That evening, Rev. Martin Luther King Jr. appealed to the nation's religious leaders and other citizens to march with him two weeks later, on the 21st, from Selma to Montgomery. The march would protest the beatings at the bridge, the denial of African-American voting rights, and the death the previous month of Jimmie Lee Jackson, a young Baptist church deacon. Jackson was killed by an Alabama state trooper as he attempted to protect his mother from being beaten by the trooper.

Liuzzo had participated in protests in Detroit and had thought for a long time of joining the Civil Rights Movement. After seeing the television footage, she drove to Alabama and was in Montgomery on the 25th, when the protestors reached the state capitol. Rev. King addressed a crowd of 25,000, calling the march a "shining moment in American history." Liuzzo volunteered for the carpool, shuttling Civil Rights workers between Selma and Montgomery. That evening, her passenger was a young worker named Leroy Moton. A carload of Klansmen saw them and followed.

Editor's Note

Tommy Rowe was a nightclub bouncer in Birmingham when he was recruited by the FBI in 1960 to join the KKK and work undercover. The recruiter told him that he was not officially an agent and, while he could defend himself physically, he would be prosecuted if he committed crimes. Rowe had to be a thug for the Klan while informing his FBI handlers of the Klan's intentions. His double role, and the warnings of prosecution, did not keep him from attacking African-Americans and Civil Rights workers over the next four years. He was never charged for these attacks.

When Liuzzo was murdered, Rowe was arrested along with three other Klansmen. He immediately made a deal with the U.S. Justice Department to testify against the other men in exchange for immunity. The defendants were found not guilty by an Alabama jury, but in federal court were convicted of conspiracy and sentenced to ten years in prison. For his testimony, Rowe received $10,000 from the Justice Department, a new identity in the Witness Protection Program, and relocation to California for a job as an assistant U.S. marshal.

After the murder of Liuzzo, the FBI conducted an extensive, covert campaign to cover up its complicity. The Bureau planted false stories in the national press, characterizing Liuzzo as a drug addict and a woman motivated to join the Civil Rights Movement by a perverted lust for black men. The FBI also persecuted Liuzzo's children and depicted her husband, who belonged to a labor union, as a Communist and Teamsters thug. Because of the FBI's smear campaign—and the prevalent social biases against women—many people in the country came to regard Liuzzo as an unstable, unfit mother, meddling in social issues when she should have been at home.

In *Selma '65,* Filloux has the same actor play both Liuzzo and Rowe, underlining the similarities in their backgrounds—their impoverished Southern families, their disabled fathers, their dropping out of school—as well as the stark differences in their moral characters.

The play premiered at La MaMa Theatre in New York City in September 2014, and was written to commemorate the fiftieth anniversary of the Selma Voting March. The play starred Marietta Hedges and was directed by Eleanor Holdridge.

MARY AND MYRA

Mary and Myra is based on Mary Todd Lincoln, the widow of Abraham Lincoln, and Myra Bradwell, a prominent women's rights activist, editor and publisher of the *Chicago Legal News*, and the first woman lawyer in the U.S.

When President Lincoln was assassinated in 1865, he left no will. The courts divided his estate between Mary and their two sons. But several years passed before Mary's portion of the estate was released to her, bit by bit, by the executor. She was short of funds and in debt, but as a respectable woman, she was expected to grieve quietly indoors, and to not seek an income by working outside the home. Through her friends, she lobbied Congress for a pension, but when it was finally granted in 1870, the amount was minimal. Mary was forced to raise money by other means; when she tried selling her dresses at auction, the press turned her effort to support herself into a national scandal. One newspaper called Mary a "coarse, vulgar and selfish woman who [has] cast a shadow over the life of her lamented husband." The public had never liked Mary, finding her unworthy of the beloved president. Now, the media criticized her for failing to display the characteristics of proper women: piety, purity, submissiveness, and domesticity.

The new campaign to malign Mary came at a time when she was most vulnerable. Seated beside Lincoln the night he was shot, she suffered an emotional collapse, as she had eight years earlier when her favorite son, eleven-year-old Willie, had died suddenly. Soon after her husband's assassination, Mary's teen-aged son, Tad, also died. Adding to her troubles, her remaining son, Robert, hired a lawyer and assembled a group of doctors who, without examining her, pronounced Mary insane. At her insanity trial, Robert testified against his mother. Moments after the judgment against her was announced, Mary was forcibly taken to Bellevue Place, a private sanitarium, and committed. Robert was named conservator of her estate, as he had planned.

Although not a licensed lawyer at the time, Myra Bradwell managed to have Mary released from Bellevue. Myra was unlike Mary in many ways, but both women fought the nation's social and legal discrimination against women. Myra had passed the Illinois bar exam, but the state supreme court denied her a license to practice, ruling that, while there was no doubt she was qualified, "the sex of the applicant... [was] a sufficient reason for not granting the license." It was axiomatic, they opined, that "God designed the sexes to occupy different spheres of action" and only men were "designed" to be lawyers. When the ruling was appealed, the U.S. supreme court decided against her, writing that "the paramount destiny and mission of woman are to fulfill the noble and benign offices of wife and mother. This is the law of the Creator." Twenty-three years later, just before she died of cancer, the U.S. supreme court reversed itself, granting Myra's law license retroactively.

Like Mary, Myra was publicly criticized for behaving in unwomanly ways, and had also experienced the death of a child. Myra's first daughter, named after her, died at age seven. Her second daughter, Bessie, nearly died in the Great Chicago Fire of 1871. Then thirteen years old, Bessie rushed into the office of the *Chicago Legal News* to retrieve the newspaper's ledger book, thus saving the family's publishing business. Rumors spread, however, that Myra had sent Bessie into the flaming building for the book—evidence that, by placing her career ambitions above her family, Myra was unfit to be a mother. In Filloux's play, Mary and Myra are strong willed and spirited, arguing and reconciling, each determined to have a life as a whole person despite the obstacles.

Mary and Myra was originally produced at the Contemporary American Theater Festival in Shepherdstown, West Virginia. The played starred Rosemary Knower and Babo Harrison. The director was Lou Jacob, and the producing director was Ed Herendeen.

KIDNAP ROAD

In 2002, Ingrid Betancourt, a Colombian politician and activist, was driving toward the remote town of San Vicente del Caguán with her political ally Clara Rojas. A rally had been organized to support Betancourt's bid to become the country's president. At a roadblock, the two women were stopped, forced from their car, and kidnapped by the Marxist Revolutionary Armed Forces of Colombia (FARC). For nearly four decades, the FARC guerrillas had been rebelling against the Colombian government's corruption and violence. By the time of the kidnapping, however, the rebels themselves had become ruthless, self-serving, and dictatorial.

For the next six years, FARC held Betancourt in the Amazon jungle, along with three American defense contractors and eleven Colombian soldiers and policemen. When Betancourt was kidnapped, she was forty years old, married, and the mother of two teenaged children, whom she had left in her husband's care while she campaigned against social injustice. The daughter of prominent parents, she was a high-profile person who had been elected to the Colombian senate three years earlier. As a captive of the FARC, Betancourt was outspoken, unruly, and antagonistic: she berated her captors when they were cruel, refused to answer to a number instead of her name during roll call, and attempted repeatedly to escape. After her last attempt, she was put in chains.

Like other real-life women in Filloux's plays, Betancourt was publicly criticized for not putting her responsibilities as a mother and wife ahead of her social and political life. After her release, she said, reflecting on what she learned in captivity, "When you have lost everything, when everything that you care about has been taken from you, when you feel your life doesn't belong to you anymore, there's something that nobody can take from you—the freedom to choose who you want to be."

Kidnap Road had its first public reading at the Paradise Factory as part of the Planet Connections Festival reading series in New York City in June 2015. The play had its premiere at La MaMa Theatre in New York City in April 2017 and starred Kimber Riddle and Marco Antonio Rodriguez. The director was Elena Araoz.

LEMKIN'S HOUSE

As Nazi Germany prepared to invade Eastern Europe in the 1930s, Polish lawyer Raphael Lemkin anticipated the need for an internationally recognized criminal statute that would hold nations and individuals accountable for the most heinous war crime: the extermination of entire groups of people on the basis of ethnicity, religion, or race. In 1933, Germany withdrew from the League of Nations and began to overrun neighboring countries, including Poland. Lemkin joined the Polish resistance movement, was wounded, and eventually escaped to the U.S. In 1942, he became an analyst at the War Department in Washington, D.C. A year later, he learned that forty-nine members of the Lemkin family in Poland had been murdered at Treblinka. While writing

LEMKIN.

LEMKIN'S MOTHER, POLAND
1930s.

a book that documented Nazi atrocities, Lemkin coined the term *genocide*. He would spend the rest of his life, until he died suddenly in 1959, urging nations to pass laws that would make genocide a crime punishable in international courts.

In response to Lemkin's lobbying, the United Nations General Assembly in 1948 passed the International Convention for the Prevention and Punishment of the Crime of Genocide. The Genocide Convention was not enforceable, however, until at least twenty member nations ratified it. Ninety-seven countries took that step—including the Soviet Union and United Kingdom—before the Convention was finally ratified by the U.S. Congress in 1988. During the years before its approval, Wisconsin senator William Proxmire urged its adoption in over 3,000 speeches delivered on the floor of the Senate.

However, giving genocide a name and the status of an international crime did not prevent countries from committing atrocities or empower other countries to stop them. In 1992, when Serbian nationalists began slaughtering Muslims in Bosnia, the U.N. declined to intervene; eventually, the conflict became the worst genocide in Europe since the Holocaust. Similarly, in 1994, the U.N. and the U.S. refused to intervene in Rwanda when the ethnic majority Hutus slaughtered 800,000 minority Tutsis in a matter of a few months.

Lemkin's House is perhaps the most complex of the plays in this volume. Raphael Lemkin's spirit dwells in his new home in limbo, a fixer-upper. Victims and perpetrators of genocide flow in and out of the dilapidated house. "When I was alive, I was haunted by the dead," Lemkin says. "Now I'm dead, and I'm haunted by the living." In succession, his visitors mistake him for an American general, Rwandan doctor, and Norwegian ambassador. In each case, he wants to believe that the international genocide law will prevent atrocities, but it does not.

In 2005, *Lemkin's House* was performed in the Bosnian language in Sarajevo, Bosnia, at the Kamerni Teatar 55; in Edinburgh, Scotland, at Roxy Art House; and in Washington, D.C., at the Holocaust Memorial Museum. In 2006, the play premiered in the U.S. at the 78th Street Theatre Lab in New York City. This production starred John Daggett, Christopher McHale, Laura Flanagan, and Connie Winston and was directed by Jean Randich. *Lemkin's House* received the 2006 Peacewriting Award from the OMNI Center for Peace.

EYES OF THE HEART

Lasting from 1975 to 1979, the Khmer Rouge genocide in Cambodia was led by a man calling himself Pol Pot. Almost two million people died by execution, starvation, and torture. Those who survived witnessed and experienced atrocities that left them deeply traumatized. Two hundred thousand Cambodians fled to the U.S., and a large number of them settled in Long Beach, California. In *Eyes of the Heart*, Filloux brings to light a disorder that affected about 150 middle-aged and elderly Cambodian women immigrants. Though their eyes and brains were not physically injured, the women had become blind. Initially, they were accused of faking the condition.

In the early 1980s, Drs. Patricia Rozee-Koker and Gretchen Van Boemel were among the first specialists to diagnose the affliction differently. Dr. Rozee-Koker concluded, "These women saw things that their minds just could not accept. Seventy percent had their immediate family killed before their eyes, so their minds simply closed down and they refused to see anymore."

Similar responses to traumatic suffering continue to appear in other places. The *New Yorker* in 2017 reported on children of asylum seekers in Sweden who, when they learn that their families have been refused visas and face deportation, fall into a deep coma-like state and begin to waste away. Their inert bodies must be force-fed to keep them alive. Numbering in the hundreds, the young patients have developed what is called resignation syndrome, described by child psychiatrists as "a kind of willed dying." Social observers blame the children's fear on far-right nationalists who demand tighter border control, extreme vetting, and deportation of undocumented immigrants. Sadly, *Eyes of the Heart* speaks to us more urgently than ever.

Filloux's play received the Roger L. Stevens award from The Kennedy Center Fund for New American Plays, and the Eric Kocher Playwrights Award from the Eugene O'Neill Theater Center. In 2004, *Eyes of the Heart* premiered at the National Asian American Theatre Company in New York City. The cast members were Mia Katigbak, Alexis Camins, James Saito, Eunice Wong, Nadia Bowers, and Virginia Wing. The director was Kay Matschullat.

Silence of God

TO JEAN RANDICH

All that must be done for evil to flourish in this world is for the good man to remain silent. *Edmund Burke*

Cast of Characters
Sarah Holtzman, journalist, late thirties/early forties. Sometimes when she appears with the poet, Heng Chhay, she is younger.
Heng Chhay/Pol Pot, Asian, forties. Sometimes when Heng Chhay appears with Sarah, he is younger. Pol Pot is older.
Faceless Man/Man 1/Translator/Ta Mok/Pol Pot's Guard/Heng's Brother/Brother's Guard, played by one actor.
Man 2/Male Journalist/CIA Guy/Christopher, a war crimes diplomat/Father's Ghost/Shadowy Figure (Ieng Sary), played by one actor.

Notes on the Play
Scenes are set in Cambodia, the U.S., and Thailand; locales are suggested by light and sound. The year is 1998, with flashbacks.

Act One

Scene One

Cambodia, 1998. Faceless Man is seated in a chair, holding a book in Braille. Across from him is Sarah Holtzman. She is disheveled, wearing glasses, and holding colorful sheets of paper and an envelope. She turns away from him.

FACELESS MAN When it came time to pay me, the customer took acid and threw it in my face. Then he stole my moto. I lost my eyes and my nose, my mouth, ears. Dissolved in the acid. My face. [*listens for her, unsure*] I became a member here—the Center for the Disabled—the director here nominated me for the scholarship. [*faces in her direction*] I would like to appeal to you, on behalf of all the people here, to help Cambodia's blind to have opportunities. Help us to open the door. [*Sarah turns to him; they are in silence*] You're writing about acid attacks? They use it because it's harder to get guns and grenades now—the government's made it harder—and acid is easy to find. Cheap. [*a beat*] Is it because of the acid attack on the famous karaoke singer Tat Marina that people in America want to know about me? I had six operations. [*with delight*] They trained me so well here. I can do anything other people can do! Clean, sew. Even sharpen knives! [*he seems to smile at Sarah; she takes a step, reaches out to comfort him, but then steps back and turns away; he is puzzled*] You write for an American paper. [*trying to pronounce*] Washington...?

SARAH Yes, the *Post*.

FACELESS MAN You're famous, right? You interviewed Pol Pot! [*she stares off into space; Pol Pot appears in a pool of light; he is at a stupa near a destroyed wat; he wears a costume: part black Khmer Rouge pajamas with red scarf, part orange monk's robe*] Are you still there?

She looks down at the paper she is holding and begins to read aloud, chanting.

SARAH I dream at night
    That I see you...

She moves toward the stupa, reciting a traditional Khmer "Hopping Crow" poem,* except that the words are in English. A flute plays when she recites the poem. She is simple and open, concentrating only on chanting. Pol Pot slowly transforms into the poet, Heng Chhay.

> Standing
> As you are standing the day
> You are packing your things
> For a moment
>
> I reverse it
> Look, Sarah
> As we walk to the top of the world
> And go over
> And disappear, you say
>
> And just then, in that moment
> I take the step
>
> What mistake do I make?
> What mistake?

Heng takes a step toward her.

> Glass breaks:
> The wall of time.

*Traditional Khmer poetry is usually chanted and accompanied by a wooden flute. The "Hopping Crow" form is used for laments.

Scene Two

Nantucket, summer 1985. Sarah and Heng are much younger, and she does not wear glasses. She is eating an orange.

HENG Khnhom châhng kleye jia-nek nee-pon.

SARAH *Khnhom châhng kleye jia-nek nee-pon.*

HENG Yes. "I want to be a writer." [*patiently correcting her*] *Nek nee-pon.*

SARAH *Nek nee-pon.* [*writes it in Khmer script*]

HENG This is very good. [*corrects her writing, and she tries again*]

SARAH It takes longer to write, in your language. But I like it, I like the time it takes... It's like a window.

HENG To what?

SARAH To a world.

HENG [*with disgust*] I don't know what I see anymore through this window. Of my language.

SARAH [*looks at him a moment*] Heng. Tell me what happened to you. [*a beat*] I think I need to know.

HENG No. I don't think so.

SARAH After all this time? You can't trust me still?

HENG [*going back to the lesson*] You want to be a writer. Why? *Hait ay?*

SARAH You can tell me. It hangs there. Everywhere. If you told me...

HENG Hangs there?

SARAH If you told me, you would have shared it. We could go to the next step.

HENG [*facing her*] You're young.

SARAH [*looks at him*] So are you!

HENG Old.

SARAH It will be better if you do. [*a beat*] Why?

HENG Say it in Khmer.

SARAH *Hait ay?*

HENG Good.

SARAH *Hait ay? Hait ay? Hait ay?*

HENG A question I ask myself every day.

SARAH It's what makes us human.

HENG What? What makes us human?

SARAH That you can tell me, that I can listen to you. That I am here.

HENG [*looks at her*] You are so lovely.

SARAH [*looks at him a moment*] I'm not innocent.

HENG *Hait ay?*

SARAH I've seen what it's cost my father.

They look at one another.

HENG Shall we go for a swim? It has been an hour. [*they look at one another*] When I'm here, at your family's, on this beautiful island, I feel as if I've been transported to paradise. Undeserved.

SARAH It's not paradise.

HENG Why?

SARAH You have to know, it just isn't. And you do deserve it.

HENG Do I? [*faces her*]

SARAH Yes. Now, tell me. Then we'll go for a swim.

HENG Before the swim, I will give you your assignment. Write to me, for next time, what kind of writer you will be. A poet?

SARAH Are you kidding?

HENG Why not?

SARAH You're the poet. You're Khmer.

HENG So?

SARAH Poetry in America? I don't think so.

HENG So what kind of writer? Your father has very high expectations for your writing. At the big school you attend.

SARAH He wants me to crack the puzzle. [*laughs*]

HENG [*a beat*] Which one?

SARAH Why evil flourishes. Why it can't be stopped. [*faces him, waiting for him to tell her his story*] So...?

HENG [*shakes his head, uncertain, then has a realization*] You'll be a journalist.

SARAH Of course.

HENG Of course. [*looks at her*] You say because we are human, that I should tell you...? [*kisses her*] I'll say it for another reason, Sarah. [*pronounces her name altogether differently from Americans; his own interpretation*]

SARAH Maybe I know it.

HENG [*shakes his head, unable to tell her*] Oh. [*a beat*] My wife's jewelry hidden in the hems of our black clothes so they were a little heavier when we walked. Our youngest, left, after the other son had died. I was twenty-five, finishing my studies in Khmer literature in Phnom Penh, but then Pol Pot, and suddenly I'm a farmer.

Cambodia, 1976. Two black-clad men enter, their faces covered. Man 1 is dragging Man 2, who is shackled at the ankles.

MAN 1 [*screaming*] Give me the gold, take it out! Devil!

MAN 2 *I have nothing! I promise I have nothing!*

Man 1 kicks Man 2 to the ground.

HENG [*to Sarah*] I sold my wife's gold bracelet for food. My gold, my mistake, found on this man's person. Me, in the shadows—a witness. Watching.

MAN 1 Pol Pot *hates liars!* Give it over or your feet will be cut off for following the path of Western thought!

MAN 2 My child is sick, I need medicine.

MAN 1 [*begins to hit Man 2 with the butt of his rifle*] Spies report you sell food.

Under the blows, Man 2 takes out a piece of gold jewelry from his pocket; he struggles to kneel in prayer.

MAN 2 *My boy is sick! Have mercy…*

MAN 1 *We trusted you.* Pol Pot trusted you!

MAN 2 *Please, comrade. I will do better. For Pol Pot I will work harder. My baby is dying, my littlest…*

HENG My words coming out of his mouth, Sarah.

Man 1 hits Man 2 over the head with the rifle. Blood spurts, sprays out. Heng screams.

MAN 2 *Oeuy! My beloved!*

MAN 1 Pol Pot knows your whole life history! And your future! Fertilizer for Angka. [*cracks Man 2's skull*] We don't waste bullets on traitors. [*looks at Heng and Sarah for a moment, then kneels in front of Man 2, unbuttoning the dead man's shirt; using the sharp edge of a sickle he takes from his belt, he cuts out Man 2's heart; he holds the heart in his hand, wipes some of the blood with his red krama,* and begins to walk toward Heng and Sarah*] Let me show you this. [*laughing*] The heart of Angka! Angka is all-powerful: God! [*to Heng*] Look at you holding what you have bought with your wife's jewelry, sucking the last drop of juice from your orange.

*a Cambodian checkered scarf

HENG So hungry… [*clutching his stomach*] Eating what I have purchased with the gold.

MAN 1 *Licking your face all over in your selfish greed.*

HENG [*softly*] My greed.

MAN 1 *Angka will find you.*

HENG [*to Sarah*] They find me.

MAN 1 "Intellectual." [*continues to advance toward Heng and Sarah with the heart*] It has stopped beating now. [*picks up the jewelry*] This gold bracelet, so beautiful...

HENG [*points to Man 2*] This nameless man's death, Sarah. And then my wife—killed because of her "light" skin. A chain of action.

Man 1 holds out the heart to Heng and Sarah, laughing, as lights on him fade. Sarah looks at Heng. They are in Nantucket again.

SARAH Hait ay?

HENG Maybe enough for today. Let's go. In the water.

SARAH Heng... [*he looks at her, unsure*] If I had known...

HENG You wouldn't have asked.

SARAH I thought that if you told me, that maybe...

HENG Maybe...?

SARAH I don't know...

HENG What do you want to say, Sarah?

SARAH How can that happen? Out of nowhere?

HENG Not out of nowhere, Sarah. It did not occur out of *nowhere*.

SARAH From where then?

Heng shakes his head as she continues to read from her paper, chanting the traditional Khmer "Hopping Crow" poem. The flute plays.

> Time
> Skimming
> Soft
> Wind

Heng moves back into the light of the stupa near the destroyed wat

> Over water's surface
> Coil of time
> Cannot reverse...

and transforms back into Pol Pot.

> Cannot reverse...

Scene Three

A dirt road along the Thai-Cambodian border, 1998. Sarah sits with Male Journalist, who has taken off his shirt. Despite her anxious state, she is in top form, at her best.

Both hold cellphones; their clothes are stained with sweat. Sounds of artillery shelling in the distance. Sarah hits her redial button, hears just a phone ringing.

SARAH This is terrific, just terrific. Good thing we got here at the crack of dawn, so we could sit on the side of this goddamn road for ten hours, in a sweat bath. [*Male Journalist lights a cigarette; birds chirp*] They decided to take two of us so they can leave one of us on the side of the road in some cryptic gesture of *God-knows-what!*... Did they tell you it was an exclusive, too? [*sarcastic*] You're the strong, silent type, huh? [*he inhales deeply on his cigarette*] Thanks for the review of my book. Nice how we try to help each other out in our field. Then I guess there's something about me that's different.

MALE JOURNALIST [*clears his throat; speaks in a serious, technical manner*] There were some "inaccuracies."

She turns away, closing her eyes. He stubs out his cigarette and exits. She falls asleep. Lights shift to her dream: Pol Pot enters, flanked by armed Guard and wearing black; he walks with a swagger, is sinister. Sarah opens her eyes.

POL POT Washington...?

SARAH Yes, the *Post*.

POL POT I read your book. I fear there were some "inaccuracies."

SARAH Now, let us begin.

POL POT I was not a bad student in school. I was an average student.

SARAH Would you like to sit?

POL POT No, I will stand. Did you bring the radio?

SARAH Excuse me?

POL POT I was promised a shortwave radio. And an "I-com."

SARAH Of course. The radio. It's in the jeep.

POL POT And the watch?

SARAH The watch. Also in the car. With the bicycle.

POL POT I did not ask for the bicycle.

SARAH Oh, I know. I brought it for your daughter.

POL POT [*firmly*] She rides no bicycle.

SARAH The world has questions. We should not waste time. I would not want to waste your time.

POL POT No, you would not.

SARAH During the Khmer Rouge regime, 1.7 million died. Are you responsible for these deaths?

POL POT [*looks at her a moment*] What do you think?

SARAH Yes, I think you are. Without question. *Hait ay?*

POL POT You speak very good Khmer, I am impressed. Your father was Evan Holtzman, from the famous Nantucket family, is that correct? He was in charge of the U.N. peacekeeping mission?

SARAH My father is not the subject of this interview. *Hait ay?*

POL POT He had a Khmer friend. This man taught you Khmer, he is the ghost behind your book?

SARAH Why did you kill so many people?

POL POT My goal was to save my country.

SARAH And yet you are responsible for its genocide.

POL POT [*assesses her*] Tell me, how do you know my country? Do you see its beauty?

SARAH Respond. Are you responsible?

POL POT I also saw its beauty. But could we maintain it in the wreckage of the American bombs...?

SARAH Fourteen thousand exterminated at Tuol Sleng. Barely one man, woman, or even child survived.

POL POT I did not know about Tuol Sleng.

SARAH Of course you knew. You were the top leader.

POL POT I'm over.

SARAH [*contemplates him*] You know, I've tried for so many years to meet you face-to-face. Reapplying for my visa.

POL POT Now it is my turn to ask why.

SARAH I had to know your answer to why you did what you did to people I care for.

POL POT And now what do you know?

SARAH I know more about how I have not found the answer. Is there anything you want to say to the individuals who suffered?

POL POT Sarah.

SARAH Now, before it's too late? What do you want to say?

POL POT [*stifles tears*] The way you make a man open his heart...tell them...Will you ask them...

SARAH [*nods sympathetically*] What?

POL POT Will you ask them for forgiveness?

MALE JOURNALIST [*offstage*] They're asking for you.

POL POT [*suddenly, to Guard*] Give her a heart attack.

Guard raises his gun and shoots Sarah in the chest. She falls as lights shift, and Male Journalist stands in front of her.

MALE JOURNALIST They're asking for you. Wake up. [*she stares at him, waking*] Up the road.

Sound of a jeep's engine.

SARAH [*rubs her face*] God, I fell asleep—I was dreaming.

MALE JOURNALIST Washington... They want the *Washington Post*...

Scene Four

Minutes later, Sarah is facing Pol Pot in an open-air hut in the Anlong Veng jungle. Pol Pot is gentle, wise in appearance, as if he wouldn't hurt a fly. He wears a gray-green scooped-neck shirt, which looks lovely against the jungle. He is almost in a halo of sunlight. Next to him sits a male Translator.

SARAH I do prefer to speak Khmer, thank you, but maybe your translator will help me to understand everything as clearly as possible. Since so many people around the world will read this interview. Thank you for seeing me today. I am very... honored.

POL POT [*smiles shyly; soft-spoken*] I thank you for the opportunity, you are very kind.

SARAH I realize our time is limited, so I will try to raise the important questions. One point seven million died. For the record, the world would like to know: are you—

POL POT Yes, I understand, thank you for allowing me to clarify. I came to carry out the struggle. It was not to kill the people. Even now, you can look at me, am I a savage person? No. [*Sarah looks at his kind demeanor, and he becomes more energized*] Permit me to elaborate. I am not trying to avoid responsibility. I would like to cite for you an example. We had to defend ourselves against the Vietnamese. We made some mistakes, like every other regime in the world, but there is one thing that we did succeed in.

SARAH Yes, but my question—

TRANSLATOR If you will allow him...

POL POT Yes, I understand what you are asking, but you see, Cambodia still survives today, our country has not been swallowed up. [*passes his hand delicately over his face*] When I close my eyes, if Cambodia wins, my soul is clear. [*she is drawn in as he fans himself gracefully*] I was only making decisions at the top on key points. You cannot see what is inside me. I would like to tell you a bit about my condition.

SARAH Yes, but first let me—

TRANSLATOR He would like to confide.

POL POT A few years ago, I had headaches, I was working too hard, I had some problems with this eye. [*points to his left eye*] And something with my...my... [*groping for the word, he motions to his chest*]

SARAH Yes, your heart...

POL POT Yes, you are right. Exactly. My left eye stopped seeing. It was because of my heart. [*makes a halving motion with his hand, as if to cut his body in half*] The left side of my body—

SARAH Please—

TRANSLATOR Paralyzed.

POL POT Yes, and my eye does not see. I may seem normal but, with this eye, I cannot see. [*motions toward his cane*] And that is also what is wrong when I walk. My heart was wrong—

SARAH Yes, your heart was wrong, but could we—

TRANSLATOR It was since his birth.

POL POT This is the truth. As a boy I played football, I did not know. Now I want to tell you I do nothing but listen to the *Voice of America* broadcasts on the radio... And even then sometimes I cannot stay awake...

SARAH *Voice of America*...?

TRANSLATOR He listens every night.

POL POT It is one of the rare things I enjoy—

SARAH The world, the international community—

TRANSLATOR He is very grateful to you...

POL POT [*nods at her gently*] I thank you for that. You give me the opportunity to provide an explanation...

SARAH But the question...?

TRANSLATOR This is very important.

POL POT I want you to know it was because I saw what was happening to my relatives that I joined the Communist Party. They lost their land, their buffaloes. This is what inspired me to help—

SARAH [*frustrated*] But you did not help your relatives. It was only when your own brother saw your picture in the camps that he realized you, Saloth Sar, were actually Pol Pot—

TRANSLATOR Please—

SARAH The man making him and his country suffer so. You cannot say you helped your relatives—that would be absurd.

POL POT [*a beat*] I am tired...I am very tired.

TRANSLATOR He is a sick man.

POL POT [*to Translator; softly, calmly*] Please, the next one, bring in the next one.

TRANSLATOR We must stop now, it is over.

SARAH What? No. You entered the city, you must admit, at *night* in your victory, hidden behind a *secret name*, with *no face*—

POL POT [*kindly*] Thank you.

SARAH A master of secrecy.

TRANSLATOR He would like to rest—

SARAH But I'm not done.

TRANSLATOR He is very old. Very sick. Unwell.

SARAH [*looks to Pol Pot, who tranquilly peels an orange; she mops the sweat from her face*] Could he simply answer my first question?

TRANSLATOR Come. You must come now. The interview is over.

SARAH But please—

Pol Pot eats his orange and gently waves away insects.

TRANSLATOR You must come.

Heavy rain falls. Translator forcefully leads Sarah out.

Scene Five

Minutes later. Rain falls steadily as Ta Mok, the current Khmer Rouge leader, shows off to Sarah some Communist slogans written in large white Khmer letters on a green wall. Ta Mok giggles constantly, exposing a rotten canine tooth, and limps because of an artificial leg. He's as loud and unread as Pol Pot is soft-spoken and studied. Sarah impatiently scans the wall.

SARAH "Cadres and combatants in every region must consolidate to develop national reconciliation relentlessly. Adopt the policy to have liberal democracy."

TA MOK You can tell the American people you saw these slogans. We are embracing democracy in the name of national unity. Our doors are open! The black clouds are gone. Only me and my own people right here in Anlong Veng could succeed in arresting Pol Pot! [*looks over his shoulder into the jungle; coyly*] He did not like you.

SARAH Perhaps you could speak to him. I don't think he realizes how important my newspaper is.

TA MOK [*laughs a lot*] It is not fair to say millions died—hundreds of thousands, not millions.

SARAH [*neutrally*] Hundreds of thousands… May I show you my questions, if he could agree to answer a few.

TA MOK [*lots of laughter and posturing*] But now, no more Pol Pot! No dream of Pol Pot, his hands are full of blood. Everyone denounces Pol Pot—man, woman, and child. Pol Pot is the desecration of the Cambodian people. Do you believe me? [*lots of laughter*] We are sorry we kept you waiting this morning. At least you were with your journalist colleague. [*lots of laughter*]

SARAH Right. This is not what I was promised.

TA MOK Thank you. We need people like you to play the role of intermediary with the outside world.

SARAH There are consequences—

TA MOK There is something. I don't know. I must confess we are a little confused. [*she looks at him*] We are having a problem. Perhaps you could help us.

SARAH I'm sorry?

TA MOK I don't know. We cannot for some reason seem to "connect" with the Americans.

SARAH "Connect"? I'm afraid I don't understand…

TA MOK Maybe you can help us, put us in "contact" with the right people.

SARAH The right people? [*firmly*] My paper, the United States government was made a promise.

TA MOK You see, you must understand that we have offered a deal to give them Pol Pot, but now we can no longer "connect" with them.

SARAH You have offered to give whom Pol Pot?

TA MOK The U.S. Would you please tell them we are very willing to negotiate. Pol Pot is prepared to face an international tribunal. [*lots of laughter*] The U.S. has a plan. A plane. An island. A secret island.

SARAH The U.S. has a plan?

TA MOK [*more laughing*] The U.S. is in Beijing?

SARAH Yes, the Undersecretary. He is asking China to approve a tribunal… Talking about trying Pol Pot for war crimes for the very first time…

TA MOK [*takes out a card*] Exactly. Perhaps you would like to speak to my friend. The Colonel. [*gives her a card*] Would you like me to call the Colonel on my new cellphone?

SARAH [*intrigued*] Sure, that'd be great. Thanks.

TA MOK [*checks pockets*] I do not have my new cellphone with me... I can do it for you when my cellphone is returned... There will be grave consequences for the thief.

SARAH [*matter-of-factly*] Well, Ta Mok, they do call you "The Butcher"...

TA MOK [*glances at her watch*] Ah... [*she takes off her watch and gives it to him; lots of laughter*] Rolex, gold.

SARAH Yes. [*he puts the watch in his pocket, pleased*] Well, when you find the phone, that'd be great if you could call the Colonel. I'd like to see him in Bangkok. [*smiling at him*] Can we get the jeep?

TA MOK Yes, of course. Please tell the Americans we want to accommodate them. We simply need some rice, medicine. It is my promise. Pol Pot listens to me now. [*looking into the jungle*] Your *New York Times* colleague seems to be having more luck. Perhaps he and Pol Pot are like-spirits.

SARAH Perhaps.

TA MOK [*takes out his cellphone; more laughter*] The Colonel can tell you everything about the Americans.

Scene Six

Karaoke bar in Bangkok, 1998. Sarah is with CIA Guy. She observes a woman singing karaoke offstage.

SARAH "Acid attacks"?

CIA GUY Latest method of warfare: five quarts of acid, spurned wife gets revenge with impunity.

SARAH This karaoke singer?

CIA GUY No, the famous one, Tat Marina. Beautiful. Gangrene. On the burned parts...

SARAH Don't know much about the whole thing.

CIA GUY I know too much. [*takes a hefty swig from his drink*]

SARAH So the agency has you set up in a cubbyhole as a diplomat?

CIA GUY Soon it'll be a closet, then I'll come out and join the pedophiles, Internet porn guys, and virgin traffickers...

SARAH And you're betraying the Khmer Rouge?

CIA GUY Yeah, the guys we used to pay off. Out of the blue we decided to try genocidal killers rather than help 'em. Look, basically, the Thai will assist in the capture if we get Pol Pot out of their country fast. Thailand is the nose Cambodia breathes through. And a minor caveat: China has to agree.

SARAH There is actually a real arrest warrant?

CIA GUY It's a "finding" from the President. When we have Pol Pot in custody, we take him to the Mariana Islands or Guantánamo Bay.

SARAH A Thai colonel told me Canada.

CIA GUY No, they don't "do kidnappings." Currently we're on hold over what department'll pay for his food, his incarceration…

SARAH So let me get this straight: he'll be in a jail cell somewhere in the Pacific, eating hamburgers, while the Security Council hammers out an impromptu trial at The Hague?

CIA GUY The new "war crimes ambassador" thinks we can do it.

SARAH The new appointee? I know him.

CIA GUY Look, plans are not what we're missing. We've flown over the country, looked at vectors, scrutinized the jungle, installed marshals in Phnom Penh, made up payrolls, calculated flights, smuggled our new war crimes guy into the country so the press wouldn't find out, held meetings in languages we couldn't understand because we're too afraid to bring in translators. But we're just not on the ground. One very simple thing we haven't done.

SARAH Yes. Why haven't you talked to the Khmer Rouge?

CIA GUY Too afraid we'll get our picture taken together—so cute.

SARAH Well, Ta Mok seems more than willing to "connect with the Americans." What's the problem?

CIA GUY Bottom line is "zero casualty." Face it, Cambodia's just a *sideshow*. [*a beat*] You getting the Pol Pot interview, that's quite a coup. Should make you famous, for a minute. So you tell me? How did he look? Was he up to a transcontinental trip? [*she is silent as he listens to the singer; colored lights*] I'll refresh our drinks, and we'll do one. Find a song you like.

SARAH [*looks at him a second*] "What's Love Got to Do with It?"

CIA GUY Is that your special song?

SARAH That's what the Khmer Rouge were playing. In the jeep.

CIA GUY How touching.

SARAH A friend of mine would kill me if I sang karaoke.

CIA GUY What's wrong with karaoke?

SARAH [*glances toward the singer*] "Acid attacks"?

She begins to sing "What's Love Got to Do with It?" Crackling sound of burning acid follows.

Scene Seven

Sarah continues chanting the traditional Khmer "Hopping Crow" poem at the stupa near the destroyed wat.

SARAH Im-
>Perceptible
>To me
>But loud
>To you
>To the bird
>To the ground
>To the pulse
>Please
>Reverse

Lights rise on Heng wearing an orange monk's robe and watching Sarah. His face shows love. He speaks softly.

HENG Sweet... Sarah.

It is 1998. She has just returned from Bangkok and is in Washington, D.C., in a Buddhist temple. She is holding a Washington Post *newspaper and looking at Heng, who is in the middle of packing a suitcase.*

SARAH What...? You looked different...

He continues to look at her. She goes to him to kiss him on the cheek. He quickly backs away, not without humor.

HENG You can't touch me, I'm a monk.

SARAH Oh. [*backs away, then points to a box*] I brought you some oranges.

HENG [*picks one up*] A simple orange. How it can destroy you.

SARAH Oh, I'm so sorry, I forgot.

HENG No. Thank you. The monks will like to have them.

SARAH [*showing him newspaper*] Did you see it? The paper? [*he nods*] What a joke, that he of all people ended up getting that fucking interview. He doesn't even speak Khmer. Did you read it?

HENG Yes.

SARAH Same old rhetoric. A "shadowy figure"? We've known exactly where Pol Pot was for decades. It's like interviewing Hitler in 1965.

HENG I'm sorry for you.

SARAH No, I got the real story. The interview was just a scam to get us there to make "contact." You're not going to believe what I found out—it has more than appeased my editor. Shit, I have to hurry...

HENG [*sarcastically*] You shouldn't swear.

SARAH [*looks at his monk's robe*] I thought you were going to honor your ancestors, be a monk for just a week. The seven-day plan? My mother told me. [*a beat*] I'm sorry I missed your ordination.

HENG No, don't be sorry.

SARAH She loved it. The Twinkies in the offering bowl—that really got her ... She really loved it; it's good you invited her.

HENG I was happy she was here.

SARAH What about your poetry? [*waiting*] Weren't you supposed to go teach?

HENG I'm going to Cambodia.

SARAH Cambodia? ... Wait. When did you decide that? What made you change your mind? [*before he can answer*] The U.S. actually has a plan to capture Pol Pot. Ta Mok is offering him to the Americans. It's all a big secret, though multitudes in Thailand seem to know about it.

HENG I am not interested.

SARAH [*looks at Heng*] I was there face-to-face with him. He told me about his heart condition. Got me nowhere.

HENG Where did you want to go? [*she faces him*] You're a writer, Sarah, not a sensationalist. [*facing her*] That's what you said.

SARAH When?

HENG When you first started learning Khmer.

SARAH [*laughing*] I never said that!

HENG *Khnhom châhng kleye jia-nek nee-pon.*

SARAH Did I? I don't remember. [*reading newspaper*] Wasn't what he wrote terrible?

HENG Pol Pot was "for sale." You treated him like a celebrity. He will go to his grave even fuller of himself than he was before.

SARAH He's not dead—

HENG I don't like the way you write about my country. "The smell of fear is everywhere" ... Sarah?

SARAH What is Pol Pot's legacy? People throw acid on each other now. That's the latest. The smell of fear is everywhere. We can't turn away—it's a hall of mirrors, where everyone looks uglier and uglier ...

HENG [*faces her*] Everyone. [*continues to pack his suitcase, placing some manuscripts inside*]

SARAH You just shut down.

HENG What?

SARAH You float away.

HENG I'm like a water buffalo, I move away.

SARAH You know that isn't true. It's always there, it never goes away.

HENG What?

SARAH The pain.

HENG [*looks at her*] Yes.

SARAH That's what you're supposed to say. The Buddhist stuff. But you're not a water buffalo. And you can't just move away.

HENG [*impressed*] This is better, Sarah.

SARAH What is better?

HENG You are better. You are speaking your heart. [*looks at her for a moment, realizing something suddenly*] Eyeglasses. How could I not see it?

SARAH Things in the distance got fuzzy. I tried to fake it through an eye test. I had perfect vision—eye doctors used to tell me I should have been a ball player.

HENG Very distinguished.

SARAH I don't think so.

HENG [*scrutinizing her*] Yes, they fit you well. Sarah with glasses.

SARAH Time goes by, we're not the same.

HENG [*looks at her*] This is what I want to talk to you about. Now. I must. [*a car alarm blares*] When it rains here and there's lightning, all the car alarms on the street go off at once. It's hard to pray.

SARAH Cambodia's just as loud, you know.

HENG [*a beat*] When I pray, I think to myself: perhaps now it is best to focus on the present. [*a beat*] And if you didn't get your famous interview, it may be time to stop. [*cellphone in his pocket rings; takes it out and speaks softly*] Yes, yes, I am here. [*listens to the caller*]

SARAH A monk with a cellphone?

HENG [*to caller*] Yes, it's best that you come to see me, I can help you, you must forgive. Yes, goodbye. [*putting away phone*] The older monk says you have to tame the Khmer people who come to this temple. Drinkers, gamblers, they fight with guns, impressed only by money, karaoke. Karaoke has taken over everything, replacing all that is beautiful and sacred in our culture...

SARAH Don't start with karaoke.

HENG [*intrigued*] Oh, have you tried it?

SARAH Of course not.

HENG I can't be a monk here. I'm going to give up my robe.

SARAH [*looks at him*] Why am I better? You said I was better.

HENG Yes. You said the truth. About me. Shutting down, floating away. You're right, perhaps: my country, we keep it inside. I'm happy you said it.

SARAH I thought I insulted you.

HENG No, there is nothing insulting about the truth. But you should not write about what you don't know. "The smell of fear is everywhere."

SARAH "Everyone there has their Sophie's Choice." That's what I wrote. It was in the context of an American movie.

HENG [*angrily stops what he is doing and studies her*] Yes, I know. I know the movie. I am more aware than you think.

SARAH Heng.

HENG You can reduce it down to a movie concept, Sarah, and then to a phrase. A movie title. From another holocaust, another war. Rob us of our very war. But for you, it is just "writing," the kind of writing you do for your newspaper, for your big salary, without realizing that these words may take more away than they give. This is not the kind of writer I thought you would become.

SARAH Heng—

HENG Can you truly say it so glibly? [*angrily upends the box of oranges, which scatter*] What can you do with your life when you have caused the deaths of others by your very acts and turned away from them to go on living? Why do you survive and not them? There is no life after that. That is the truth. No life. My wife was killed because of her "light" skin. You are right. You are exactly right. The smell of fear is everywhere. Even here. But do you know what it is like to survive? [*picking up an orange*] To find food to live just one more day? "Where is Buddha?" you ask yourself. Everyone has a story like mine, in Cambodia. [*sarcastically*] It's the truth. And the truth is good, I say.

SARAH [*goes to him*] I'm sorry.

HENG [*taking a moment to recover*] No, it is I who am sorry. To be so cruel to you. Please, forgive me. I don't know what came over me.

SARAH It's good that you got angry.

They look at one another.

HENG Why did you come today?

SARAH I wanted to see you. And now you're leaving again. I miss you. I need to talk to you.

HENG Even when I do not see you, I think about you, I pray for you.

SARAH You said you'd never go back to Cambodia.

HENG I have a brother. My only family.

Heng's Brother appears in silhouette, marching slowly.

SARAH [*surprised*] Did my father know that? You never told us.

HENG No, my brother was dead to me. I did not tell your father because I did not tell myself. But then not too long ago I had a dream. He was marching in a row of soldiers. I could see his neck. Slick with sweat, the soft hair of adolescence on his face... [*looks at her*] I called him a "crow." Black crow. For many years. To myself. And then he had no name at all. He was gone. But after the dream, it seemed as if my life could only, truly exist if I could see him. And see Cambodia.

SARAH [*nodding*] He was Khmer Rouge.

HENG [*nods*] Yes, after the dream I picked up the phone. He called me "little brother." He is in the government. A wife I do not know. Two sons. I went to see your father's grave to say goodbye. Burned some incense. It was a cold day.

SARAH But what about the old lady you were taking care of in Long Beach? And you'll come back to teach? Right?

HENG Ah. Now, your assignment: one "Hopping Crow" poem.

SARAH Seven lines in a stanza, four syllables in a line.

HENG Let yourself go a little. You were such a devoted pupil.

SARAH [*laughing*] Devoted? [*a beat*] I was smitten.

HENG [*looks at her a moment*] Yes. Smitten.

SARAH [*a beat*] And now you're a monk.

HENG Yes, a monk.

SARAH And I'm a writer.

HENG Perhaps. [*they stand still; a yellow halo of light appears onstage*] I will say—something is happening to both of us. Right here, right now. [*she looks at him*] We are walking up over the earth, to the top, and I can see we are about to disappear down the other side. Sarah, you wear glasses now; I don't want to be old when we decide to stay together.

He takes a step toward her. She is afraid, and laughs it off.

SARAH Another dream?

Her cruelty takes his breath away. He stifles his emotion, nodding.

HENG Yes. Another dream.

He steps back. She tries to confide, sensing a moment has passed and trying to regain it.

SARAH I wish I could go, be there with you. You'll be in Cambodia for the new year! What's your cellphone number over there?

HENG [*writes it down*] My brother's phone. Give it to your mother, too. You will tell her I wish her well on her birthday. It may be hard to call, but I will try...

SARAH And your e-mail?

HENG You know, you can have ten aliases at A-O-L dot com!

SARAH And still be impossible to reach. Who do you think will find you?

HENG Don't worry, Sarah.

SARAH It's okay, Heng. I haven't been to my father's grave. Everything in me is what he wanted for me...and now I'm here and he's not. What is there left for me to do?

HENG Have you prayed to him? Talked? [*she doesn't answer*] He can help you, Sarah. Write his name down on a piece of paper. [*a beat*] I was thinking, when he employed me, at the beginning...his open door—he was like a father.

SARAH [*teasing*] That makes us brother and sister.

HENG Yes.

SARAH I gave his Rolex away. To get the story. I had that watch for fifteen years.

HENG I will return to our wat in my village. I will rebuild the stupa. Pretend there are ashes to put in the *jchadáy** to honor my ancestors. Pray to my family for protection...guidance. You must do the same. [*she touches him, then quickly pulls her hand back, remembering*] Buddha would forgive us.

*stupa

As he moves away, she gazes at him, unable to let him go.

SARAH Buddha?

A beat.

HENG I hope your new story will help you.

SARAH When I come, you'll take me to the lake? The world of water. All the way to the horizon...?

HENG Yes.

SARAH I love you.

He begins to recede into shadow, toward the stupa near the destroyed wat. She chants the traditional Khmer "Hopping Crow" poem.

> To be still.
> In your eyes
> In your body
> In your heart

>
> Is
>
> Everything...

[*looking at him*] You never said it.

HENG You forget everything.

Blackout.

Scene Eight

Washington, D.C., 1998. Sarah is writing in her office. Christopher, a war crimes diplomat, enters and closes her door.

CHRISTOPHER We are a few days away, hold the story. Give me three more days, Sarah.

SARAH [*stands, surprised*] What are you doing? You must be pretty desperate to be here, Mr. Ambassador.

CHRISTOPHER Look, we went to the same school, we're cut from the same cloth, we stand for something—

SARAH How did you get in my office?

CHRISTOPHER International justice is a slow process. It's a matter of sufficient jurisdiction.

SARAH How did you get in here? I'm serious. [*goes to the door*]

CHRISTOPHER You don't get the big interview, so you come up with this story to save your job. The plan to capture Pol Pot can only work if it's a secret. This story is irresponsible.

SARAH I'm asking you to leave.

CHRISTOPHER This will be on your conscience. It's about impunity. Worldwide. [*rubs his face*] You know what I actually dream? [*she starts for her phone*] I'm flying.

SARAH I'm calling security.

Lights transition to his fantasy.

CHRISTOPHER I'm flying when I have this dream—

SARAH Why are you telling me this?

Pol Pot, in handcuffs and escorted by armed Guard, walks toward Christopher.

CHRISTOPHER He's just gotten off the plane.

SARAH Who?

CHRISTOPHER Pol Pot.

SARAH Maybe you need to take a day off.

CHRISTOPHER I have managed, Sarah—by brilliant calculations made in the air as I travel back and forth to the countries in which there are genocides, which are everywhere, and very faraway—

SARAH You better think about getting some sleep.

CHRISTOPHER I know the quickest route from D.C. to San Francisco to the island.

SARAH The island?

CHRISTOPHER The secret, nameless island where we're taking him. He's in handcuffs.

SARAH Since you're here, maybe you can confirm the island's name.

Christopher and Pol Pot stare at each other.

CHRISTOPHER There he is, Sarah. Right in front of me.

SARAH Guantánamo, the Marianas...?

CHRISTOPHER In the dream, my plan has finally worked—I am there at the door.

SARAH [*calling*] See me pressing the buttons.

Christopher flanks Pol Pot as Guard escorts him.

CHRISTOPHER The jail cell. I am there at the jail cell.

SARAH [*speaking on phone*] Could you please send someone up? [*a beat*] Yes.

Guard opens the cell door as Pol Pot looks down.

CHRISTOPHER He is looking at the ground.

SARAH Of course he's looking at the ground; it's your dream.

CHRISTOPHER I am standing there when he enters the jail cell. That's it. Just standing there. [*Pol Pot walks in*] A feeling washes over me. I am flying.

SARAH You said that. Security is on its way.

CHRISTOPHER I'm always flying when I have that dream. And I'm running.

SARAH That's enough.

CHRISTOPHER I'm running to make these connections so I can be there, at the jail cell. [*a door creaks*] And the door shuts. The guard closes the door. Behind him. [*the door shuts*] And the sound of the door closing. That is my dream. I am there when the door closes. He is inside. Inside the cell.

SARAH Christopher. I'm sorry to say, that's stupid.

CHRISTOPHER This is what's in my heart. I thought you might have an allegiance.

SARAH To what?

CHRISTOPHER Cambodia. To the 1.7 million dead you always write about.

SARAH Sorry, I'm not in the business of keeping government secrets.

CHRISTOPHER There are individuals and governments who will pull out of the plan if this is published.

SARAH There aren't any national security issues here.

CHRISTOPHER This is Hitler.

SARAH We could have captured Pol Pot in the early '80s. But you were too busy signing treaties with the Khmer Rouge.

CHRISTOPHER That wasn't my administration.

SARAH It's not real enough to withhold the story.

CHRISTOPHER You could say you're not ready to publish. What's the goddamn rush?

SARAH A friend went back to Cambodia. He has a brother there. What do you think he'll find?

CHRISTOPHER A better world.

A security guard enters.

SARAH For decades the editorials are filed like clockwork. "Bring Pol Pot to Justice." Each time we break out the Tuol Sleng photos, and you see the victims staring out at you. Writing moralistic op-eds is the best we've ever been able to do. You keep secrets. Make vapid plans. Frankly, I don't make the stories, I just write them.

CHRISTOPHER That's right, you just write!

SARAH It's too late, Christopher. It's on the front page. The world's moved on to other genocides.

Christopher exits, followed by the security guard.

Act Two

Scene One

Anlong Veng, 1998. Night. Pol Pot sits hunched on the side of his bed in shadow, listening to Voice of America *on a shortwave radio. Guard in Khmer Rouge uniform stands at the hut door.*

VOICE FROM RADIO Leading the news on *Voice of America*: *Washington Post* correspondent Sarah Holtzman reports that plans are currently in progress by top Khmer Rouge leaders to hand over Pol Pot, to be tried for crimes against humanity. The dying Khmer Rouge movement hopes to receive food and aid in exchange for their former leader.

POL POT [*speaking softly to Guard*] I do not have the strength...

VOICE FROM RADIO After nearly two decades on the run...

POL POT To escape again.

VOICE FROM RADIO The man said to be responsible for the deaths of millions of his countrymen may be near apprehension. Sources in Thailand and the U.S. ...

POL POT [*reaches out and turns off the radio*] We are surrounded.

GUARD Baat.*

*yes

POL POT [*tenderly*] It is fitting you are here with me tonight. [*Guard nods deferentially; Pol Pot motions for him to approach*] Come, tell me. When did you join the revolution?

†friend

GUARD [*moves in*] I was twelve, Respectful Uncle.

POL POT Please. Call me Friend. And did you know how to read and write?

GUARD No, Respectful Uncle. [*correcting himself*] No, Friend...

POL POT You see, I want you to know, what I tell you is very important: all I did, I did for you.

GUARD Baat.

POL POT I only wanted to help the poor. When I joined the movement, I was living in a country where half the people were illiterate.

GUARD Baat.

POL POT Now you and I must draw a lesson from this report by Sarah Holtzman of the *Washington Post*. [*puts his hand on his heart, motioning to Guard*] Would you pour me a bit of whiskey? [*Guard locates a hidden bottle and pours; Pol Pot points*] You will gather for me those two bottles of pills. Yes, right there. When they are writing the book, you will know how to explain exactly why. [*taking the pills*] Good. Thank you. [*gesturing to Guard*] You should write.

GUARD Baat. [*takes paper and pencil*]

POL POT You see, I will face any court. But to give Mok this victory—never. A man whose mind has never been in the least connected to his mouth—who would kill to keep a wristwatch. A *thief*. This I despise. Write. [*pours pills from container*] For malaria. [*dictates to Guard*] One *single mistake* I made. The photograph of the assassination of my former Defense Minister. Mok used this photo to name me a *traitor*. You see, there must never be a face to the act. Never a face to the act. Why did I order the assassination? Because I'd just been betrayed by my brother-in-law, with whom I studied in Paris—my own brother. Brother Number Three. He had joined the puppet government. Lesson: could I be betrayed again?

GUARD Never, *Mit*.†

24   *Mānoa* . *Eyes of the Heart*

POL POT [*pours pills from another container*] Valium. [*turns to Guard*] For the little children assassinated with the Defense Minister, I am sorry. And the men shouldn't have run over the dead bodies with a truck. You see I am Mok's last playing chip. He needs me, of course, to save himself. Final lesson: look, my hands are clean, Friend. I never killed a man. [*to himself*] Besides myself.

GUARD [*writes as if he is putting an epigraph on a tombstone; with pride*] He has a large spirit of union, deep and firm confidence, likes to live in the calm. In silence.

Pol Pot calmly pours a glass of water from a pitcher. He sits hunched in shadow as Guard comfortably lays a robe around him.

Bright, wonderful sunlight. Nantucket, 1985. Sarah and Heng are swimming.

SARAH You swim like an eel. Who taught you?

HENG Myself! I jumped in, became a fish, catching fish, eating fish, dreaming fish, flying fish, falling fish, taming fish, holding fish, loving fish, and loving water, currents, rising and falling. The color, the sound, the brightness at midday, the descent into darkness, the moonlight. The soft fluidity. No one had to teach me. The lakes are shallow in Cambodia, you can stand. And you?

SARAH My father.

HENG Yes, what a good teacher!

SARAH His hand under my stomach, my legs and arms wriggling like a lizard, totally and absolutely hopeless. Land born. I couldn't learn...

HENG But now you are such a strong swimmer.

SARAH I could always feel that he would hold me up.

HENG Love. The true patience. This salt stings. Your Nantucket ocean. The lakes were sweet. Sweet-watered.

SARAH [*looks at him*] You're sweet, the way you repeat the words over and over. The same way. The way you write the letters so carefully. I can't believe the way you do that! It's the hardest language in the *world!*

HENG I made a promise to your father. I must keep it.

SARAH Sweet.

HENG Is that good?

SARAH Was the water in the lake good?

HENG Yes, the water in the lake was good. [*a beat*]

SARAH Thank you for telling me what happened. [*a beat*] I'm so sorry.

HENG Okay.

SARAH You'll help me?

HENG I'll help you in any way I can. Because I love your father. For what he did to give me a new life here. But I would warn you to be careful. What you are entering is very black.

SARAH If I speak Khmer, then that will be one key.

HENG Yes. "Lake" in Khmer: *beung*. I'll tell you about the lakes in Cambodia. Tonle Sap. Water all the way to the horizon. An occasional fisherman living a life of fish.

SARAH I wish there was another kind of land. A land of water. We could live—

HENG I don't think so. [*facing her*] I will promise to help you in any way I can.

SARAH I always wear my suit in the summer. Ever since I learned to swim. I put it on first thing in the morning and I wear it all day. So I'm ready...

HENG I went naked, and so I was always ready.

SARAH We could do it at night. Naked. Just the waves.

HENG [*they begin kissing*] We could do it anywhere, it would not matter. [*they make love*] What will I do to you?

SARAH Don't think.

HENG A luxury you might have. But not I.

SARAH Heng, your skin.

HENG [*touching her*] Your skin.

SARAH I could bury myself in it...

HENG Bury myself.

SARAH Don't be afraid.

HENG You never are?

SARAH Always.

HENG Of what?

SARAH So many things. That I'll fail, that I won't arrive. That my parents will die. That you'll think I don't understand, that I have too much privilege, that you'll want me to cook for you, that I can't be what you expect...

HENG [*extremely amused*] Cook for me?

SARAH Khmer women do.

HENG I don't care about that.

SARAH What are you afraid of?

HENG What I will do to hurt you...

SARAH *Shhshh.*

HENG What I won't do.

SARAH I love you.

HENG I don't believe...

SARAH You don't believe in...love...?

HENG I don't know. We should return. They will think we have drowned.

SARAH We have. [*they go underwater, caress each other, come back up*] Say it in Khmer, I'll listen.

HENG *Bong sra-lanh own.**   *I love you.

SARAH You can cry. It's just tears. And there's so much water out here already. A world of water.

Lights shift. Washington, D.C., 1998. Sarah on the side of her bed peers into the night.

SARAH Heng told me to write your name, Father. On a piece of paper. I can't visit your grave. Cement is so lonely. [*lights a cigarette and smokes; self-deprecatingly*] At least smoke is rising to the heavens. For you.

She stands and looks into darkness, seeing a man's faint shadow.

FATHER'S GHOST Cultures are remarkable. The individuality, the idiosyncrasy. They must be saved, nurtured at all costs.

SARAH In the morning there's a stillness, Father. Running, I think I see you—my eyesight is gone. I see figures in the distance—I see then that they are you and Heng. I'm running, gasping for air, but where am I going? Off the shore? Straight into the river?

FATHER'S GHOST Billions of dollars—and the country wrecked.

SARAH You think your peacekeeping mission in Cambodia failed.

FATHER'S GHOST Go see Heng. Try.

The shadow fades as Sarah goes to sleep.

Lights rise on Heng sitting on the side of his bed and holding a cellphone. He no longer wears the monk's robe. Lights also rise on a man in a military uniform wearing gold jewelry and facing away from the audience. He holds a golf club.

HENG My brother
    Wrapped in his wealth
    The shell of corruption
    At the expense of the poor
    So apparent
    Everywhere
    I look at him.
    My brother.

Lights out on the man in the military uniform.

> No.
> I love my country
> Its people.

[*asking for forgiveness*] Save my country, save my country, O Lord, give the dead a proper resting place. *Tee bonh choh tee-et. Tee bonh choh tee-et.**

*a proper resting place

Heng carries an effigy of Pol Pot, then watches it go up in flames and burn.

SARAH [*agitated, talking in her sleep*] No. Stop. You can't. Wait.

Pol Pot hisses and whispers. He sounds brainwashed, obsessed.

POL POT [*voice-over*] I want to reply: mistakes were made, fighting, like every movement in the world... I don't like the way you write about my country, Sarah. [*pronounces her name as Heng does*]

SARAH No.

POL POT [*v.o.*] It has been written in the book. Lesson number one: rob us of our very war.

SARAH No.

POL POT [*v.o.*] Your assignment: save Cambodia.

SARAH No.

She sits up, wide awake. Smoke rises from the effigy. Man 1 holds the heart that he cut out from Man 2's chest and begins to eat it.

POL POT [*v.o.*] Even God is silent.

SARAH [*to Man 1*] What is inside the heart?

Frozen with fear, Sarah takes heart, begins to eat it. Heng looks at Sarah's bloody mouth. Lights out.

Scene Two

Sarah is jarred from sleep by the ringing phone. Breathless, she answers.

SARAH Yes? Who is it?... Yes?

Lights up on Christopher, standing in a pool of light; talking to her on his cellphone.

CHRISTOPHER Happy?

SARAH Who is this?

CHRISTOPHER He's dead.

SARAH Who is this?

CHRISTOPHER Pol Pot. He died today. Are you satisfied now?

SARAH [*realizing who it is*] Christopher... Wait...

CHRISTOPHER Dead.

SARAH How did he die?

CHRISTOPHER The day your article came out and you revealed the plan was the day we were going to take him into custody.

SARAH How did it happen? How did he die?

CHRISTOPHER You played right into his hands; he fooled you.

SARAH I was on deadline, I wrote the truth.

CHRISTOPHER You robbed Cambodia of its only chance for justice.

SARAH The public had a right to know.

CHRISTOPHER No punishment, no crime.

SARAH You know he was impossible to capture.

CHRISTOPHER I want you to know I will count it as the biggest failure of my professional career.

SARAH I did what I was paid to do.

CHRISTOPHER Over. [*hangs up*]

Sarah stares into darkness, holding the phone. She takes out a piece of paper, then dials a number. Lights rise on Heng sitting on his bed and holding his phone.

SARAH Heng, I dreamed Pol Pot was whispering in my ear, the devil in the most beautiful disguise. Is there a devil inside of me for seeking him out...?

HENG Come with me to the village: we'll rebuild the stupa.

SARAH I talked to my father. Wrote down his name.

HENG What did he say?

SARAH He told me to try.

HENG We'll pretend there are ashes to put in the *jchadáy*. Free my family's spirits.

Heavy artillery echoes in the jungle.

Scene Three

Cambodia, 1998. Sarah stands with Ta Mok, who holds a cellphone.

TA MOK His wife came to tuck in the mosquito netting around his bed, and found him dead. It was 10:15 in the evening.

SARAH On April fifteenth, right? And what was the cause of death?

TA MOK [*laughs*] He died of heart failure. I did not kill him. He was right here, in his hut.

SARAH He died in his sleep?

TA MOK [*lots of laughter*] Yes. Exactly... "in his sleep"... His heart was very bad. He listened to *Voice of America* at 8, then went to bed, as usual...

SARAH [*looking at him*] He listened to *Voice of America*?

TA MOK Every night. He heard he was going to be captured, and perhaps he had a shock. Shock of the heart. Who knows?

SARAH You can confirm he heard he was going to be captured on *Voice of America*?

TA MOK Yes, your report was on the news! We warned him earlier this week he might have to go "abroad." He and his family had to hide in that trench, right there, because of fighting with the traitors. He dyed his hair black to disguise himself, but everyone will always know Pol Pot! Right?

SARAH You know he heard the broadcast?

TA MOK We are more connected than you think!

SARAH There wasn't a chance in a million we could have captured Pol Pot. It was a fairy tale.

TA MOK [*laughs, tickled*] But you Americans like fairy tales! [*pouting*] Don't you?

SARAH The government has requested that his body be handed over for an autopsy.

TA MOK Later today he will be cremated.

SARAH To establish cause of death.

TA MOK Heart attack. Bad heart. Black, black heart. [*laughter*] His death is good for the Khmer Rouge. I feel no sorrow.

SARAH May I speak to his wife?

TA MOK She is in mourning.

SARAH And your movement? Did your forces kill innocent people on the outskirts of Phnom Penh?

TA MOK I am very tired.

SARAH There are reports you met with the Cambodian government for the first time yesterday.

TA MOK I am not going to be a running dog of Viet Nam like Pol Pot's right-hand man, Brother Number Three. You tell the world community it was all Pol Pot.

SARAH He was alone when he died?

He has been sketching something for her on a scrap of paper.

TA MOK This is the model of the satellite phone. I want a good one. One that I can use to call anywhere in the world. Collapsible.

SARAH Allow an autopsy.

TA MOK I would like to invite you to be the witness. I want you to see him burn.

Pol Pot is bathed in red flickering light as we hear Jay Leno's monologue: "Pol Pot died with his head down so he could see where he was going. What were his brothers' names? 'Crack and Crock?'" Sound of canned laughter and then a Buddhist prayer chanted in Khmer.

Scene Four

Cambodia, 1998. Sarah and Heng kneel in front of a beautifully sculpted stupa amidst the rubble of Heng's family wat. Heng writes on pieces of paper.

HENG Sarah, the names of
    My wife
    My mother
    My father
    My two sons
    Ashes to put in the *jchadáy*.

Together they place the pieces of paper in the stupa and burn them.

    Smoke rising to the heavens
    Air
    Fire
    Earth.

SARAH Water.

HENG [*takes her hand, chanting a prayer in Khmer*] Som thai rehk-sa yung.

SARAH Please, take care of us...

HENG I pray my family will give me the strength to love you.

HENG / SARAH [*praying*] Som thai rehk-sa yung.

HENG Protect us, ancestors.

SARAH Oh! *Kúhn bon ba-roh-may!** **Protect us, ancestors!

They light incense and put the sticks in the ground.

HENG There's a prediction people tell each other, here in the countryside. "Pra-put tomnyay, 'Kra-lap make.'"

SARAH "Buddha foretold, 'The sky will be turned upside down!'"

HENG *"Kapúh lang pong luh phnom."*

SARAH "Shrimp will lay eggs on top of mountains."

HENG *"K'ike k'mau punreay play lewier krop kuh-lein."*

SARAH "Black crows will spread figs on the land."

HENG *"Mul-tau luh-áh kongcrau ru-luy kan knong."*

SARAH "Beautiful on the outside, corrupted inside."

HENG [*turns to her*] When I came back, Sarah, Cambodia had been dusted by a cloud. It was as if I was looking through a kaleidoscope that made my eyes red and my head ache. I couldn't adjust, couldn't see straight. The future, when I tried to adjust my eyes, slipped away, turning back into the past before the war, after the war...

SARAH [*nodding*] It's like when I look at you.

Sounds of rain.

HENG *Plee-ing hai...*

SARAH The rain...

HENG *Sadáp, somlaing yum.*

SARAH Listen to the sound of crying. Souls. [*closes her eyes, feeling the rain*] Water all the way to the horizon...

HENG Sweet water.

SARAH A world of water.

HENG [*holds out his hand*] Sarah? [*she opens her eyes and looks at him*] Marry me? Live with me, try.

SARAH [*takes his hand*] *Zha! Zha! Zha!** My mother will be so glad.

HENG I will tell my brother. I need to forgive him—his children are good...

SARAH [*looking upward*] My father will be disappointed he wasn't here...

HENG [*whispering to the sky*] *Samto.*† Sarah, I'll buy some silk from the women at the curve in the river... After, we'll go to the lake, I know a place... The rain!

SARAH [*looks around at the destroyed wat*] The wat is beautiful, your family village. We'll have the ceremony here...

HENG [*shocked*] Beautiful?

SARAH Through your kaleidoscope, I can see it is.

HENG Yes.

SARAH We're all wet! Let's go down the road—celebrate! Sing some karaoke!

HENG Never.

---

*yes
†sorry

SARAH Yes! What song will you sing?

The rain falls on them. He holds out his arms, lifting his face to the rain. She does the same.

HENG [*singing*] Somewhere in the smile she knows
 That I don't need no other lover
 Something in her style that shows me
 Don't want to leave her now...

He takes her in his arms, and they dance in the rain.

Scene Five

Phnom Penh, 1998. Heng is at a government function with his Brother, who is wearing a military uniform and gold jewelry.

HENG I must talk to you, Brother. I have good news.

HENG'S BROTHER First there is someone I want you to meet...

HENG I am not one for these types of gatherings...

HENG'S BROTHER The man I work for.

HENG The gold jewelry makes me uncomfortable.

HENG'S BROTHER You are from America, this is impressive. You don't want to know for whom I work? Help yourself to whiskey, cognac, or brandy... Are not these buildings still as striking? The good news is now the French don't own them.

HENG Yes, yes... I want to tell your family something, your children. Could we have a moment before the meal?

HENG'S BROTHER Where is the American journalist?

HENG Here in Phnom Penh. That is what I must speak to you about. I was hoping you could meet her tonight. We're going to be married.

HENG'S BROTHER Married?

HENG Yes.

HENG'S BROTHER Well. Tonight, I will not have the time, I must play golf.

HENG Golf?

HENG'S BROTHER But tomorrow, we'll go to the restaurant across the bridge, remember? Yes, of course, not all has changed, there is the restaurant across the bridge. [*Heng notices in the crowded room Shadowy Figure holding a cocktail glass with his back to the audience; Heng's brother is trying to get Heng's attention*] Beautiful, on the roof, we have the whole roof, you bring her with you.

HENG Who is that man?

HENG'S BROTHER You know who that man is. It's Ieng Sary.

HENG [*in disbelief*] But Ieng Sary is Brother Number Three.

HENG'S BROTHER Just Ieng Sary now.

HENG Yes, I thought I was imagining things.

HENG'S BROTHER [*pointing in another direction*] There is the man I work for, over there. Come and meet him.

HENG Why is Brother Number Three at this party?

HENG'S BROTHER He is no longer called by that Communist name, and this is not a party, it is a meeting.

HENG He's still Brother Number Three.

HENG'S BROTHER My boss works for him. Let me introduce you.

HENG Works for him?

Heng's Brother brings him to Shadowy Figure. Heng's face is seen over Figure's shoulder.

SHADOWY FIGURE [*to Heng's Brother*] Hello, a pleasure to see you. [*to a waiter offstage*] Can you refresh my drink? [*to Heng*] What can we bring you?

HENG'S BROTHER [*to Heng*] He lives with his wife off Norodom Boulevard. And his wife's sister Ponnary—remember Ponnary?—she lives very close.

HENG Ponnary?

HENG'S BROTHER Yes, you know: she was a teacher at the high school we attended.

HENG And Pol Pot's first wife.

HENG'S BROTHER Now let bygones be bygones.

SHADOWY FIGURE Exactly. [*taking out a wallet and speaking to Heng's Brother*] May I show you pictures of our new grandson?

HENG'S BROTHER Of course! My brother has come from America to see me. [*looking at photos; to Heng*] Look, he is a very serious boy.

Heng glances at the photo, tries to smile.

SHADOWY FIGURE Very serious, already wearing glasses at such a young age.

HENG Like his grandfather.

HENG'S BROTHER A true compliment.

SHADOWY FIGURE Eyesight was not always our forte. [*showing photos*] And this is the rest of the family.

HENG'S BROTHER [*showing Heng*] So many!

SHADOWY FIGURE Yes, a very large clan.

HENG'S BROTHER How are your efforts to secure the land for the hotel?

SHADOWY FIGURE The land by the river is ours—the most beautiful part!

HENG'S BROTHER Congratulations! This is wonderful news!

HENG Hotel?

HENG'S BROTHER He is building the nicest hotel in the city. At the curve in the river, you know? [*to Shadowy Figure*] When do you start to build?

SHADOWY FIGURE So many luxury hotels ahead of us, we may have to pull a few strings, for I am impatient. I am not young.

HENG'S BROTHER You are not so old.

Heng starts to go.

SHADOWY FIGURE Your brother is very quiet.

HENG'S BROTHER Will you please excuse him? I am very sorry, he is tired, from his...airplane trip, he is not himself. [*crosses to Heng*] Brother, what are you doing? Mr. Ieng Sary is in the middle of showing you pictures of his grandchildren.

HENG I do not want to see them. [*feels as if his head is spinning and sounds are slowing down; in shock*] I must go. [*to himself*] No air...

HENG'S BROTHER You must be respectful of this man. He is high up in the government, powerful.

HENG [*stares at his brother, aghast*] Do you not remember?

HENG'S BROTHER What?

HENG He was Pol Pot's right-hand man. Do you not remember?

HENG'S BROTHER I don't know what you are talking about.

HENG His children? What about my children? [*walks away*]

Scene Six

Phnom Penh, 1998. It is extremely bright and sunny on the white, dirt street. Sarah rings a buzzer at an ostentatious black gate. As she waits, she inspects a piece of silk she has purchased. Guard in crisp uniform enters.

GUARD You are the woman who called? [*reading from envelope*] Sarah Holtzman?

SARAH Yes. I'd like to see Heng. He's staying with his brother.

GUARD [*hands her a letter*] Please read and return. I am standing here. I am waiting for you. And watching.

SARAH [*takes the letter, confused*] May I speak with Heng?

GUARD The letter. Read the letter. [*shuts the gate, takes out an orange, and begins to peel it*]

SARAH Is Heng's brother home?

GUARD Read the letter.

Sarah stares at the letter. She opens it and unfolds the colorful sheets of paper. Heng appears.

HENG Sarah, while I was with my brother a strange thing happened. I was introduced to Pol Pot's right-hand man, Brother Number Three. I learned he has now purchased land to build a luxury hotel on the most beautiful part of the river. [*Guard eats the orange, watching Sarah*] There are many ways to try a killer. Gather all the evidence in a stack on the floor. And there are piles and piles of evidence. [*writes on paper*] Take a piece of paper and write "Pol Pot is guilty." And "There was a devil." Gather the people who lost their families in whatever court is brave. Take the piece of paper and post it on the court wall. Or I'm afraid there will be another Pol Pot. I cannot live with the shame. I honor those who can. [*looks at her*] I do not deserve happiness. I do not feel worthy of you. Perhaps I believe that we are too strange for each other—that our fantasy of seduction is better left just that. For when you are real, you suffer. I am from a small, faraway country that has destroyed itself. And you from a country that many believe helped destroy mine. It's hard to live out each day, but with you I thought I could. [*Guard is holding up orange, which has turned into the bloody heart*] I have died a thousand times already. [*pours a glass of water from a pitcher; holds out to Sarah a handful of pills*] Malaria and Valium.

SARAH A known combination.

HENG [*downs the pills*] The only paper I can find is the receipt from an Internet café. I leave this letter with my brother to give to the woman whose name is on the envelope. Sweet Sarah.

She starts to double over as Heng suddenly disappears. She is back on the bright, white street. Guard, wiping his hands with a handkerchief, walks toward her. He looks toward the house behind the black gate.

GUARD My employer would like the letter now. He had no choice but to show it to you. He knows who you are.

SARAH [*dumbly*] Who?

GUARD *Washington Post.* He knew you would dig until you found out the truth. And that could do damage. [*reaching for the letter*] This is personal information: the letter belongs to him.

SARAH I must speak to him now.

GUARD Let bygones be bygones. The letter.

SARAH [*tries to get past him to the gate*] I have to speak to Heng's brother.

GUARD On the phone you said you had an appointment. At three o'clock? You will be late. [*reaching for the letter*] After your appointment, you said, you leave for Bangkok? Is that correct?

SARAH There are some things I need to know.

GUARD *Washington Post*. [*reaching for the letter*] You do not understand.

SARAH More than you can imagine. [*starts to leave*]

GUARD [*threatening*] You *die* when you *write* it down on a piece of paper.

She hurries away.

Scene Seven

Cambodia, 1998. Faceless Man is seated, holding a book in Braille. Across from him is Sarah, disheveled, holding the colorful sheets of paper. She turns away from him.

FACELESS MAN When it came time to pay me, the customer took acid and threw it in my face. Then he stole my moto. I lost my eyes and my nose, my mouth, ears. Dissolved in the acid. My face. [*listens for her, unsure*] I became a member here—the Center for the Disabled—the director here nominated me for the scholarship. [*faces in her direction*] I would like to appeal to you, on behalf of all the people here, to help Cambodia's blind to have opportunities. Help us to open the door. [*seems to smile at Sarah; she takes a step, reaches out to comfort him, then steps back and turns away; he is puzzled*] You write for an American paper. [*trying to pronounce*] Washington...?

SARAH Yes, the *Post*.

FACELESS MAN You're famous, right? You interviewed Pol Pot!

She stares off into space. Heng appears in a pool of light. He wears a costume: part orange monk's robe, part black Khmer Rouge pajamas with red scarf. By means of light and sound, he alternates between being himself and Pol Pot.

HENG I am the devil...

She looks to the faceless man.

FACELESS MAN When I first became blind, I became a masseur.

She looks at Pol Pot.

POL POT And a poet, a killer angel.

She sees Heng.

FACELESS MAN I wondered why people would entrust their bodies to me. [*moves to her and slowly begins to massage her back*]

HENG I am guilty of everything.

FACELESS MAN In my hands, they said, there was magic...

Heng becomes Pol Pot.

POL POT I've killed no one.

FACELESS MAN My hands could heal them...

HENG But the blood of all is on my hands.

FACELESS MAN They became my friends...

POL POT There are hundreds who should be brought to trial.

FACELESS MAN A man like me, given chance after chance...

HENG I am solely responsible.

FACELESS MAN The opportunity to feel useful.

POL POT The best of intentions.

FACELESS MAN When I am old, my hands will be tired...

HENG The worst of reasons...

FACELESS MAN I will need to read with my hands...

POL POT This pitiful country swallowed up by her enemies...

FACELESS MAN To educate my children...

HENG Write it down on a piece of paper.

Sarah sees only Heng.

FACELESS MAN To write. Write it down on a piece of paper. [*she looks at Faceless Man; lights out on Heng; she stands and puts her arms around Faceless Man; she hugs him tightly to her; he holds her, comforting her*] Bong sray, kum prooy men ay tay...*

*There, there... It's okay...

†Please, take care of us.

Scene Eight

Cambodia, 1998. Sarah writes Heng's name on a piece of paper, kneeling at the stupa near his destroyed family wat. She places the paper under a small flame.

SARAH For the afterlife. [*lights incense*] Som thai rehk-sa yung.† Hait ay? Why? [*takes out a piece of paper*] I cracked my father's puzzle. Remember? Why does evil flourish? Here is the article I've written. "Heng Chhay was a poet. Together we lived in a world of water. This is a world where you float. So beautiful and...bottomless. You might ask yourself how many teardrops or raindrops or drops of fresh morning dew would it take to fill the ocean, to fill the lake, and I would tell you not as many as you think, and what you see at night in the water—the glistening, bending light, the reflections—is the magic of love, and also your own suffocating drowning. That's the world of water. You can go under the surface and slowly motion to the one you love, and he will answer with his hands. You might ask yourself, 'Are we fish, not human?' and I will answer that we are human, but we don't always do human things, and that is all I can tell you, for there was so much I did not let myself know, and so much I will never know. Heng Chhay, the man I was going to marry, wrote me a letter the day he died. He said while in Phnom Penh he met Pol Pot's right-hand man, Brother Number Three, who had just purchased land for a luxury hotel on the most beautiful part of the river. There are many ways to try a killer. Write his guilt down on a piece of paper. And so I am. The luxury hotel will sit on the bones of Heng's family, open to the green-brown water upon which shadows fall like tempests. Storms leave you altered, barely swimming."

HENG *Khnhom châhng kleye jia-nek nee-pon.*

SARAH I want to be a writer. That's what I always wanted. I owed you an assignment. I didn't do the rhyme scheme. [*chants the traditional Khmer "Hopping Crow" poem; a flute plays; she is simple and open, concentrating only on chanting*]

> Look, you said
> As we walk to the top of the world
> And go over
> And disappear
>
> And just then, in that moment
> I take the step
>
> Glass breaks:
> The wall of time.

[*facing him*] Heng, I love you more than the shadow.

HENG And I love you. With it.

Sarah watches as lights go out on Heng.

Acknowledgments

I have been assisted by many people to whom I am grateful. Nate Thayer was especially helpful with his knowledge and with letting me view the videotapes of his 1997–1998 interviews with Pol Pot and the Khmer Rouge leadership; David Chandler for his help on Pol Pot; Elizabeth Becker for her insights, having interviewed Pol Pot in 1978, and for reading my plays; Craig Etcheson for his instructive e-mails.

Selma '65

TO BRIAN RICHARD MORI

The stories of Viola Liuzzo and Gary Thomas Rowe are part of the historical record. Selma '65 is a work of dramatic fiction created as a one-person play. The play is dedicated to Selma 1965 and is a creation of my imagination.

Cast of Characters
Viola Liuzzo / Tommy Rowe, a white woman and white man; one actress plays both roles.

Prologue

Viola is beside a tree, wearing 1960s-style cat glasses and talking directly to the audience. She smokes a cigarette.

VIOLA I am always walking past *this* tree. I'm barefoot, holding my father's hand. He only has one. He lost his hand in the coal mines. I love that hand of his, cracked and soft at the same time.

He tugs mine suddenly.

[*sees something*] Darkness. The lights go out. I don't know where I am. My heart leaves my body.

[*her accent becomes more Southern as she reminisces*] What happened, Daddy?

No, I want to look.

Wait, I can't see. What was that in the tree, Daddy?

Why? I don't understand. I want to see. [*her Southern accent fades*]

I always wanted to see—just that kind of person. But the mind is like a clean piece of paper, and certain things they're like ink on a press, they leave their mark. The mind is innocent until it's not. Memory's written like a dark, black message. There are things I need to erase. What I did to Leroy.

This road in the Lowndes Swamp is *lined* with trees. As I'm driving, the nightmare of the first tree seems to go on forever—I see an explosion of trees. Tree, tree, tree, tree. [*singing slowly*] "We shall overcome, we shall ohhh..."

[*finds a rock*] My daddy was a coal miner. He knew rocks that light themselves on fire. "Make a trail of rocks if you get lost," my daddy told me. Make a trail of rocks if you get lost. Coal.

[*sets down the coal and finds another rock, holding it up to the light*] Have you ever seen smoke trapped in a rock? Smoky quartz from the Lowndes Swamp earth.

[*sets down the quartz, trying to make a trail of rocks*] I'm lost in limbo.

That march was the most beautiful day of my life.

Images appear on a screen, and a voice-over of Martin Luther King Jr. at the end of the Selma Voting March: "Now, it is not an accident that one of the great marches of American history should terminate in Montgomery, Alabama."

It is 1965. Viola is driving her car, speaking to Leroy Moton beside her; she puts away her cigarettes.

To see Martin Luther King speak today, Leroy. "It is normalcy all over Alabama that prevents the Negro from becoming a registered voter." First, Bloody Sunday, then Turnaround Tuesday, and finally today, the Selma Voting March made it to Montgomery. Three times a charm. All of us marching together today, singing—the children lining the road, the American flags. What will *your* dreams be tonight, Leroy?

[*laughing*] Voting, yes. Please, I said, call me Viola.

Don't worry—I want to make one more trip to Montgomery to get the last of the marchers. Everyone's so tired, but I won't sleep tonight. You know those times you feel you're being called? I know what it means, Leroy, a white lady like me and a young black man like you, but we have to live by our actions. What an action, when you think of it: just two people sitting, driving in a car. I've never been happier than tonight.

You're not a big talker, but the way you dedicated yourself to the marchers these past few days. What makes you so brave?

When I was eighteen, I didn't have half your integrity—to see that in someone your age, it cheers your spirits. I hope my sons grow up to be like you. I'm sorry *I* talk so much.

There's nothing to be afraid of. After we get back to Selma, I'll have another cup of coffee and start the long trip home. Drive straight through. I got down here in two days and four packs of cigarettes. I never smoke in the car, unless I'm alone. I want to respect your air rights. You'll come visit me and my family in Detroit? You need to meet my best friend, Sarah. I'm not black, but I consider you and Sarah my people, Leroy. I'm volunteering with her at the NAACP when I get back. What about you?

People love pizza. My husband's Italian.

[*stops at a red light*] Do you see what that lady's doing? [*to the lady in a car beside her*] You want me to play your little game? [*sticks out her tongue*] You happy now, lady?

See, she drove away, Leroy. Not giving us any more trouble. I'm sorry—you don't deserve to live like this every day. I want a better world for you. There's really just a fine line that divides us; that's why I'm here.

This morning after finishing work at the first-aid station, I climbed to the top of St. Jude's to see the crowds of marchers. You feel on top of the world. I had a premonition that Martin Luther King was going to die. I ran back down and I prayed. I became a Catholic for my husband, but I left the church because my baby couldn't go to heaven, he wasn't baptized. I still prayed. Then I took off my shoes and marched barefoot the last four miles to Montgomery. I'm originally from the South...

Transforming into Tommy Rowe, she puts on a cotton hood similar to a Ku Klux Klan hood, but without the pointed top.

TOMMY I'm originally from the South. Gary Thomas Rowe, Tommy.

I'm wearin' this 'cause I'm in Witness Protection, Senator. I want to tell the intelligence committee I was a big starred-and-striped American flag, flyin' at full mast for the FBI. The FBI recruited me to infiltrate the Ku Klux Klan. I thought the Klan was nuts. I never thought a guy had to disguise himself in a stupid bedsheet to have a good fight. My handlers told me I'd been known from the start as a kind of rowdy, wild type—I'd worked as a bouncer at certain clubs. Let's just say I had a kind of standin' as a man who thrives on adventure. The FBI did some background checks on me and considered that in a situation of pressure I'd deliver to them what they were lookin' for. It all started with the "Freedom Riders," Senator. I would do *anythin' in the world* for my handlers. My first handler was Barry.

[*takes off the hood and speaks to his handler, lighting a cigarette*] Barry, I tell ya, the police is givin' the Ku Klux Klan *fifteen minutes* to beat 'em up when they arrive at the Greyhound Station.

Why don't you take off your hat and relax, Barry? Have a cigarette. At the Klavern meetin' the Exalted Cyclops is talkin' about how many blacks and Civil Rights workers they can kill in *fifteen minutes*. There's about sixty KKK men ready to meet the bus. It's a "Fiery Summons"—the biggest call to action in their *so-called* Klan rules. Everybody's obliged to go. It'll be Sunday in the mornin' at the Greyhound Station. It's Mother's Day, and most of the police are *supposedly* at home with their mothers.

Yeah, you better order some flowers, Barry. The cops on duty will stay out of the bus station for *fifteen minutes*. The Ku Klux Klan has free rein to beat 'n' pummel as many of the people comin' off the bus as we can. They'll be equipped with guns, bats, pipes. After *fifteen minutes* we disperse or get arrested...

I said, Sunday at ten o'clock, Barry. I've been told to wait at a phone booth in the

Greyhound Station for Police Sergeant Cook to call and let me know exactly when the bus is arrivin'. Cook's assigned a pay phone at the station for me. You want me to go?

A pay phone rings. Tommy picks up the phone.

Why the hell not? [*listens, then puts down the phone*] The Greyhound's not comin', guys, we need to get the hell over to the Trailways Station. Haul fuckin' ass.

In the Trailways Station.

Okay, they're comin' out of the bus. Just in time...

[*bending down*] He's in his Sunday best, poor thing, like he's goin' somewhere special... Get him. Hold down that nigger. Beat the fuck out of him.

A camera flashes.

Fuckin' photographer. Grab that camera. Smash it. Get that film!

[*looking at a photo in a newspaper, talking to his handler again*] Barry, yeah it's *me* in the photo, but my back's to the camera, no one's gonna know. I don't care if the Old Man has a shit fit, I'm here because I love the FBI and my country. I told you 'bout the *fifteen minutes* more 'n once—the police was givin' the Klan free rein. Y'all allowed it to happen.

I know the police was part of it. You wanted me to stand off to the side, twiddle my thumbs and *watch?* This was my first big test with the Klan. Who do you take me for, a moron?

[*touches his throat*] Went in deep. We went back out to beat up more people comin' off the buses, didn't know the black man had a knife. Found a "doctor," stitched me up, no anesthesia.

[*looks at the photo again*] We broke the camera, Barry. I don't know how the photo got out.

It's not Cagle. I told you, it's *me!*

Oh, right... it *could* be Cagle.

Okay, it is Cagle.

It's Cagle—I got it, Barry.

Oh, Jesus. "To the day I die," it's Arnie Cagle in the photo.

You told me to go through with it. I was *leadin'* it, for God's sake.

[*referring to the photo*] This other guy with the lead pipe? He's part of Fields's group.

Yep, those Nazis were there. We tried to get Dr. Fields and his guys to leave.

Yeah... sure, that's right, it was all *their* fault. They planned the whole thing.

Yeah, I wasn't even in the bus station.

Right, I was outside with some others doin' a peaceful demonstration. [*laughing*] It was Dr. Fields and his men who caused it.

Relax, Barry, I wasn't even part of the fightin' at the Trailways Station.

[*referring to his throat, laughing*] And this is a shavin' cut.

Hundred-twenty-five-dollar bonus?

Hey, how'd your mother like the flowers?

For your *wife,* that's elegant, Barry—a dozen.

Nothin', I moved out.

I know the rules, I was gonna tell you I left her. Look, Barry, the FBI is my life. I'm married to *you*. Fighting Communism. I'll buy you two dozen red roses.

VIOLA [*driving, speaking to Leroy*] It *is* quiet, Leroy. I didn't think the road would be so deserted. Just this afternoon the march seemed like a celebration that would never end. So many more marchers than expected.

No, it's too late to turn around. Montgomery isn't far. Those marchers are waiting to get picked up—we can't abandon them. We're fine. You'll be back home in Selma very soon, and I'll be on my way back home to Detroit. Just two weeks ago I was home watching *Judgment at Nuremberg* with my husband and oldest daughter when a live report interrupted the program. My younger kids heard the screaming on the TV and came out of their rooms.

[*watching TV*] They were just trying to walk peacefully across the bridge, darling. You three need to go back to bed.

People are being beaten, honey.

Yes, black people. Like Sarah.

You can ask her tomorrow, she's probably watching it, too.

Jim, it's terrible what's happening.

They're asking for the right to vote, darling.

It's *tear gas*, honey.

Right, because it makes you cry.

The police are spraying it so people can't see—and move forward.

This is important, Jim—the right to vote belongs to all of us.

They're chasing them away on the horses.

It's late, sweetie, I don't want you to have bad dreams.

It does look like war.

This is not my fault, Jim. It's on national news. Writing a check isn't enough. "The appalling silence of the good people."

I will not turn it off. She's a grown-up, she can finish watching. *I'm* the one who is saying she can stay up. It's up to me, okay?

You're not her father. *I'm* making the decisions.

I don't know if the movie will come back on.

Okay, it's a commercial, sweetie. I'll bring you some milk.

A Lifebuoy soap TV commercial plays on the screen. A man in a suit reads the paper at breakfast as a woman in a nightgown pours him coffee. The woman smells the man. Viola mouths the commercial voice-over as she moves back behind the steering wheel—driving her car, staring out at the night—and the footage continues.

"This man just showered with a new kind of soap, new Lifebuoy Mint Refresher, a soap so loaded with mint, so tangy, so frosty it drives wives... 'wicked.'"

Music plays as the image ripples; devil horns appear on the woman's head and Viola's head. The woman in the commercial murmurs seductively, slinking down the man's body.

"Every bar of new Lifebuoy Mint Refresher contains the essence of 125 mint leaves. Soap has never smelled this good before and neither have you. New Lifebuoy Mint Refresher drives wives... 'wicked.'"

[*driving, speaking to Leroy as the TV footage fades*] I *am* wicked, Leroy. Horns grow out of my head regularly. My house is always a mess. That's why I hired Sarah when I started college. Do you think a white woman hiring a black woman as a housekeeper is wrong?

Sarah didn't want to come to the march. And she didn't want me to postpone my finals; she thought I was crazy. My mind, I get wound up too tight; she says I go in a million directions.

Once when I was working in a lab, I stole a microscope on purpose so they would arrest me. I wanted to make a statement that women don't get overtime, or severance. It backfired—the police just made me return it. Sarah says I need to relax, take it easy.

Images appear and a voice-over of Lyndon Johnson endorsing the Voting Rights Bill, saying, "The time for waiting is gone."

When I heard Martin Luther King and President Johnson were organizing a peaceful march after Bloody Sunday, I knew I had to come.

[*arguing with her husband on the phone*] This march *is* my business, Jim. I'm a mother and that's why I'm going. This is not another Lucille Ball episode. It's good they fired me because now I'm in college.

You're right, taking them out of school was a bad mistake. You want me to kneel down and say *mea culpa* a thousand times? [*starting to kneel*] I'm not kneeling, I'm not a Catholic anymore, Jim—*I* get to decide what heaven is. A mother knows it's a safe place, not limbo. We're not living in Dante's *Inferno*. I won't be able to live with myself if I don't go, people from all over the country are going.

I went AWOL because I had to clear my mind, something in my body felt wrong, the medicine. And you know I've been doing much better after the hospital. I don't want to go against your wishes, but Sarah has promised me she will take care of the children. You go against my wishes sometimes. Do *I* gamble away our money?

I don't smoke as much as you drink.

Sweetheart, I love you. Why are we fighting? You get to do your work at the union, why can't I do this?

A special surprise? Okay, my love, you can trust me. I'll wait for you to get home to decide.

[*driving in the car with Leroy*] I didn't wait, Leroy. I threw clothes in a brown paper bag and drove a thousand miles alone. I like to drive fast. Don't worry. I was supposed to come with a group of students from Wayne State, but everyone canceled. I completed the Selma Voting March today against everyone's will. [*looking in rearview mirror*] Finally, another car on the road.

My birthday's next month. Jim gave me a rock-polishing machine last year. It makes it look like the rocks are underwater, permanently. He says he has something even better this year. You know, there's something about rocks.

Yes, rocks.

Well, I don't know. It's hard to explain. I wish I were a poet. But I'm not. I'm a realist. Actually, I don't know what I am. I'm also a dreamer. You have the eyes of a dreamer, Leroy. I bet people tell you that all the time. I have a sixth sense about things like that.

I fall in love with people. Not romantically. Well, with Jim it was romantic. He's the love of my life. My husband. This is his old car. It's easy to drive. You barely have to put your foot on the gas. But there's a place where you think you should be, and you try to get there, a world that you want—that's all you can do, keep trying. You'll see when you get older.

[*drives in silence for a moment; looks in the rearview mirror*] Wait . . . Is that Chevy following us? The road is so dark.

TOMMY [*puts the hood over his head*] Darkness. The lights go out. I don't know where I am.

Ohhh, my God!
I'm watchin'
Through the window of the car.
In my soul that's what she's sayin'.
Her mouth is completely open.
She's seen you, you better stop.

Holy shit, that lady is crazy, goin' ninety, more 'n that.
Bullets poppin' into the asphalt like bubbles.

[*catching himself*] Sorry, I'm fine, Senator. This hood. Brings back memories I need to erase.

Well, you see, the way it worked is the FBI asked me to infiltrate the weekly Ku Klux Klan meetin's.

Tommy takes off the hood as a scene is projected from the silent film Birth of a Nation *in which a "black man" is chasing a white woman.*

[*speaking to a Klansman*] Yeah, it's a good film, man. A classic. I love the part where the nigger is chasin' the white woman and she jumps off the cliff. [*laughing*] Lands like a sack of potatoes.

Oh, I can't wait to see it again.

Each time? Better?

Thanks for gettin' me the bridal silk. That was nice of your wife to stitch it up. And this patch with the drop of blood...

"Give your life for the Klan." I'll thank her myself.

Fine, you thank her.

The silk feels good. On.

Crossburnin'? I work at the Dairy 'til five.

Yeah, pick me up at five—I'll pack my robe in my trunk.

A gun?

Yeah, okay, I'll tell him the Wizard sent me. It's not exactly huntin' season.

[*laughing*] Always huntin' season, sure. Okay, the gun—and the bats, too.

Karate? The men want it now, really? Well, tell 'em to gather 'round. [*showing him his hand*] Broke my hand so many fuckin' times choppin' up bricks, doctor told me to stop comin' back.

[*begins his karate demonstration*] All right, guys, you wanna learn to break a neck?
On your right leg. Sidekick to throat.
Any volunteers? What, you men scared?

Palm strike to throat. Grab and crush. Crack to skull. Attacker dies unless given immediate medical attention.
Okay, come on up. Go slow learnin' this...

[*speaking to his handler*] Barry, I had to teach 'em somethin', they keep askin' me. Don't worry, these guys are the biggest sissies.

You know what it's like to watch the most horrific three-hour film you've ever seen in your entire life? Over and over. And pretend you like it? I swear to God I feel like I'm goin' crazy there in the dark—I try to fantasize 'bout other stuff.

Don't ask.

[*laughing*] What all guys fantasize 'bout, Barry—I'm rescuin'—

No, not a kitten in a tree, Barry, I hate cats.

Different kind of pussy. I'm rescuin' damsels in distress—"well endowed and unholstered," if you know what I mean.

Anyway, these *Birth of a Nation* filmmakers are psychos. Didn't even use real black people...

[*takes a paper from his pocket*] Here's the receipt for the robe. It's like little boys playin' dress-up. *Boo!*

I'm savin' the best news for last: I was just elected Klokan Chief. To be honest, I was the only one runnin'. I'm joinin' the inner circle.

They're talkin' 'bout the blacks who ride at the front of the bus. We'll be takin' a couple cars, boardin' the buses, and beatin' 'em up.

That's it.

You sound disappointed. You think I'm holdin' somethin' back? *There just isn't a lot goin' on at these meetin's.* If you don't believe me, go fuck yourself, Barry.

Yeah, I'm all right, my daughter dropped by the Dairy. She said, "I want you in my life."

Such a pretty girl, smart.

[*speaking to his daughter*] I love you, baby, but I got a job to do. Now, I grew up in the South and I know the Southern Way is here for a reason. Integration of schools, interracial marriage, they're never gonna work. You see, me and the U.S. we're together fightin' Communism. Martin Luther King's a Communist, honey, 'n' a sexual pervert. Someday you're gonna know what I done and you'll be proud of me.

How's school? You haven't lost the honor roll?... Good.

[*takes out some money and gives it to her*] Buy somethin' new. Don't tell her, she'll want all five of you to get the same. Here, honey. Get your hair done... Please, look at me. Take it.

[*speaking to his handler*] I walked her to the bus, Barry... *I never got past junior high, my daddy dropped out when he was twelve.*

Protectin' our country, keepin' it safe, that's what's important to me.

[*a beat*] You think you could help me move up, Barry? Somethin' in law enforcement? Police?

[*a beat*] Well, maybe someday... Okay.

What do you mean? You're leavin'?

Why didn't you say anythin'? Shit, is it because of my picture in the paper? Did I put you through hell gettin' caught in that photo? You had to lie. I know that took a toll, but I din't have a choice, I told ya. You're my handler. If you din't want me to go to the bus station, y'all should've stopped me.

What am I gonna do without you, Barry?

Mac? He's even more nervous than you. I don't wanna work for Mac. His bowties, forget it.

I don't want to switch handlers, why didn't you tell me anythin'? If you go, I go. This is for you, Barry, I do it for you. We have somethin'. Shit.

I'm not cryin'.

[*takes something from Barry*] What is this, Barry?

For me? What did you get me, Barry, two dozen red roses?

[*looks at a ring in the palm of his own hand*] Ruby-red rock in it, color of blood.

VIOLA [*holds out a ring*] Here, honey, your birthstone. You got married—a mother wants to know. On my way home from Selma, I want to stop by and meet your new husband. I know I had no right to take you out of school. Please, look at me. Take it.

[*adds the ring to the trail of rocks; bright headlights are behind her as she drives*] I can't wait to get back to my kids, Leroy. One of my daughters moved out. Such a pretty girl, smart. I yanked my kids out of school to fight a law allowing children to drop out at sixteen.

Now I see I overreacted, I was taking some medicine. *I* never got past junior high, my daddy dropped out when he was twelve—he lost his hand in the coal mines.

A rock fell from the pit roof and crushed it—they removed it at the wrist. There were no unions like Jim's then, my daddy had no rights. I had to leave school, help my mom, he never forgave me; my daddy was a good man—I loved him. You hear how my Southern accent comes back? My children were out of school for forty days, my daughter lost the honor roll. She didn't even tell me where she was going; she told Sarah.

Oh. Those headlights *are* really bright.

They warned us: the National Guard and the Army were going to be pulling out. [*changing the subject to calm herself*] You know, the woman I'm staying with in Selma, I told her I'd take in her daughter Frances so she could finish school. Frances just had a baby, the cutest little girl. Sarah says, "Viola, you are always taking in strays." I loved Sarah right away. During the war, they were rationing and I went into a store to get some pepper—the owner tells me they haven't had any pepper for months. Sarah's at the cash register, she says, "Yes, we do have pepper, Miss, my boss keeps it right here behind the counter for the special people," and gives me some! We picketed the tear gas at the Sojourner Truth…

Yes, in Detroit.

I had her over for coffee—we started talking about everything. We were both from the South. She took care of Jim and my babies when I went back to college.

Jim's my third husband—three times a charm. Then I hired her full-time as my housekeeper. We're like sisters, we went to New York last year for a Civil Rights conference—she wanted to see the Statue of Liberty. I almost fell off a cliff.

[*walks down a cliff, finding a rock and calling to Sarah*] Sarah, it's a black rock with bubbles. I went too far down the ledge—I can't get back up.

Yes, you can.

Sarah, don't be mean.

It's the first time this has happened. Don't tell Jim, please.

You're right, it's happened before. Where are you going?

[*examines the rock*] It comes in on the Gulf Stream with drift seeds. At least I didn't fall off the ferry. I never thought New York was like this. You feel on top of the world...

[*calls out*] Yoo-hoo! Thank you, gentlemen, I'm sorry to inconvenience you.

Collecting rocks.

Yes, rocks.

[*holds out her arms to be helped up*] I lost track of how far down I went.

Thank you so much, sir.

May I give you one as a...?

Okay, goodbye.

This pumice is for you, Sarah. You always get me off the ledge.

[*places the pumice in the trail of rocks as the headlights behind her get even brighter*] Those headlights! What are those people doing?

TOMMY [*puts on the hood, showing a ring*] Senator, my first handler, Barry, gave me his college ring for a present when he left the FBI. Barry knew I admired it, and he was born with a silver spoon in his mouth. Barry's college ring is the closest I ever got to high school. My handlers *loved* me—that's just the way it was. We had a bond. Mac was next after Barry. Mac wore prissy little bowties. All different colors. And patterns. But it's easy to fall out of favor, a tightrope to walk, really. My handlers were always pushin' me to get in deeper with the Klan, and by the same token spittin' out warnin's like "don't get caught."

Well, you see, Senator, I was never givin' the FBI *enough* information, or the information they *wanted*. And they were always goin' out of their way to say, don't you *ever* call yourself an "agent," you're just an informant.

[*takes off the hood and smokes, reporting to Mac*] The cops found the guns in our cars 'n' arrested us, but there's something else...

Machine guns, bazookas, boxes of buckshot...

Relax, your ulcer actin' up or somethin'?

The police gave us the thumbs-up later, erased it all. No record whatsoever. Come on, loosen that tie. That is quite the tie, Mac. Are those little golf clubs on it? Cute.

Well, the Klan is planning to stab Reverend Shuttlesworth when he's at the Dobbs House Restaurant.

Yeah, Dobbs House at the airport. I'm supposed to shoot one of Reverend Shuttlesworth's bodyguards.

I tried to tell 'em it was too risky, but the guys are friggin' out of control. If I don't show up, I'm dead meat, Mac; it's givin' me nightmares.

[*having a nightmare*] Imperial Wizard, I'm writin' your FBI report real nice 'n' makin' my handwritin' better.

Mac, I swear I'm gonna kill Reverend Shuttlesworth's bodyguard. Fuck, I don't know if I'm the guy behind the sheet or the guy reportin' to my handler...

My girlfriend says, "Tommy, you're havin' a nightmare. You look possessed starin' into the dark like that. Did you fall off a cliff in your dream?"

I say, "Shit, Muffin, I'm keepin' too many secrets. One of these days I'm gonna fuck up and disappear in the swamp."

[*imitating his girlfriend*] "Oohh, let me kiss you, baby, let's take a shower. I'll soap you up with that mint soap that makes me 'wicked'—just like in the commercial!" [*laughing*]

[*to the committee, laughing*] Senator, I had lots of girlfriends to talk me off the ledge. After three marriages I knew I liked the more temporary approach, if you know what I mean? Yes, Mr. Senator, I alone saved the life of Reverend Shuttlesworth. My handler, Mac, warned the police chief and the mayor, so the integration at Dobbs House went off peacefully with no deaths. I'm the reason he's still alive. But then the Klan drags me up to face the Wizard. Jesus Christ, you'd laugh if it wasn't so goddamn dangerous...

[*facing the Wizard*] There I am, the Wizard's blue fuckin' eyes starin' me down, gun in his hand. Just a wiry psychopath piece of shit who likes to stuff bats with lead. A little cottage industry he has goin' in his garage. My heart leaves my body. So I grab him by the neck, his Adam's apple is throbbin' under my palm.

[*grabbing the Wizard by the neck*] "I am not F-B-fuckin' I and if you don't believe me, go screw yourself, asshole. How dare you question me after everythin' I've done for you. You two-faced motherfucker, I'm a far goddamn better Klansman than you are!"

We are watchin' each other, eye-to-eye, man-to-man. The big test. I'm chokin' him to death.

"I-I know you're loyal, Baby Brother," he finally whispers. I let the Wizard go. My stomach was about to explode, lost my dinner in the car. Beef stroganoff. After that, the Wizard was always my biggest fan.

Well, okay, I'm gettin' there, Senator. 'Round that time, the Klan wanted to kidnap and lynch some Negro students who got into the university. And we were bringin' back Dynamite Bob into the Klan. A guy called Sister White was teachin' us how to make bombs at the meetin's, keepin' our stash in the swamp.

I am not avoidin' the question about the Sixteenth Street Church deaths, Senator, I just can't tell you anythin'. I wasn't there. And I believe you want me to get to the point. On the last day of the Selma Votin' March, I told my new handler, Neil, the Klan was goin' to Montgomery.

[*ironically*] Three times a charm, Senator. My third handler, Neil, was so finicky he had me callin' in all the time. The Klan wanted me to do a little missionary work, harass the marchers, "break up some of those sex orgies goin' on in the churches." Honestly, I do not know how many actual *orgies* were truly occurrin'…

My handler, Neil, told me to go, Senator. I put on my holster and gave him the description of Gene's car—'63 red-white Chevy. We were four in the car. The temperature that day was very high. I was on guard—Neil knew that—the place was *crawlin'* with clergy. And with a certain type of *white person,* Senator, who was attracted to these kinds of Civil Rights demonstrations, as if this was an occasion for them to let their hair down, sleep outside, go barefoot, play the guitar, expose their "hippie side" if you will—"white kooks"…

VIOLA [*looks in the rearview mirror at the bright headlights*] Yes, that Chevy is pushing its luck now, Leroy. I'm going to try to get a little distance, we'll be fine. Once we make it over the hill, we'll see the lights of Montgomery. It's the trees lining the road that make it darker.

[*to herself*] Sarah, if something happens, you'll take care of the kids for me, right?

[*looking in the rearview mirror*] They will not let us go.

[*to herself*] I am a white woman and I won't allow Sheriff Clark and his officers to beat down those protestors, Sarah.

[*to Leroy*] The Air Force base is too dark, there's no one there. It's more dangerous to pull off.

[*to herself*] I am not looking in the wrong place, I'm looking for justice.

[*to Leroy*] The Lowndes Swamp. It's starting to rain. I'll turn on the windshield wipers…There.

[*to herself*] You should have come with me, Sarah. I wish you and the kids could have come. Jim would never allow it.

[*to Leroy*] They are just not giving up. What is wrong with these people?

[*to herself*] What's wrong with leading with your heart, Sarah? I don't think a heart can ever be too big.

[*picks up speed, concentrating*] It's okay, Leroy. I'm going to have to outrun them. [*beginning to sing*] "We shall overcome… [*singing more slowly, with Leroy*] We shall overcome…"

Who sang it real slow?

Lucille Simmons? I never knew it's her song.

TOMMY [*crouches down in the backseat, holding a gun, looking at the car next to him*] Gene, the guy sittin' next to her in the front seat doesn't look like one of Martin Luther King's top leaders to me. You been drinkin', Gene. Cop just gave you the ticket for the muffler, there's a record you're on this road, don't be stupid! This place is crawlin' with Army, National Guard, we'll get caught. Let's go back to town, find someone else.

I *got* my gun out, kid. Headlights behind us, lay off, Gene. It's over—lost our chance, waste of time. If you have to skin a head tonight, let's go back to Selma. Slow the fuckin' car down, you're gonna kill us. Gonna get pulled over for speedin'. She's seen you, you better stop. Holy shit, that lady is crazy goin' ninety, more 'n that.

VIOLA [*on the tree-lined road with the trail of rocks*] My daddy told me, "Make a trail of rocks if you get lost."

TOMMY [*at a phone booth in the dark*] I'm at a pay phone, Highway 11. It's rainin'. Need to talk to Neil right away. Have him call me here and make it fast.

[*hangs up, takes out a flask, and drinks while he waits*] Fuck. Fuck. Fuck.

Oh, God, I was shooting at the road.

Did they see?

What am I going to say?

[*lights a cigarette; the phone rings; answering*] We got to talk. I was in the Chevy with Gene, and the other guys.

Okay, yeah, the parking lot.

[*talking to his handler in a dark place*] I'm fine, Neil. No, we just had some beers in the afternoon. Sorry I got you out of bed. Are those your pajamas? Mac always wore bowties, even in the middle of the night.

He did.

Long, long day.

Yeah, I can tell ya now. There were three others in the car: Gene, Wilkins—a kid, babyface—Eaton, bald, problem with his heart, they call him Curly.

You do know these guys.

Come on, you've seen 'em around, I know you have.

Okay, I know my nerves are shot.

[*takes out his gun and shows it*] No, I didn't use it, I swear.

[*waits a moment to see if his handler is going to inspect it; puts it back in his holster*] Wilkins is on probation, he didn't have a gun. He used Gene's.

The Pettus Bridge. That's where we first saw 'em.

VIOLA [*on the tree-lined road with the trail of rocks*] My daddy told me, "Make a trail of rocks if you get lost."

Coal that lights itself on fire.
Smoky quartz from the Lowndes Swamp earth.
Ruby birthstone for the one you loved who left.
Sarah's pumice, with bubbles, drifting in on the Gulf Stream.
[*finding a rock*] Galena, the rock they pack tight into bullets.

Bright lights overpower her. Sound of static. On the screen is dreamlike footage of a contemporary blonde newswoman—Martha on Fox News Live—*watching Viola.*

What are you doing, trying to conjure the dead?

Martha announces, "There is a voting controversy that's going on now in South Carolina that's catching a bit of attention. The Palmetto State's Attorney General saying more than 900 of the voters in the recent elections were actually dead people. And you might wonder, 'How do those dead people find their way to the polls?' That's what we're wondering." The caption below Martha reads MORE THAN 900 "DEAD" VOTED IN RECENT ELECTIONS.

VIOLA [*facing Martha and bright TV lights*] Well, I'm the patron saint of dead voters—you've come to the right place. *Fox News?*

[*pulls some bullets from her back*] I'm sorry, I had a few bullets shot through my spinal cord. Why were there more than 900 dead people...?

[*looks down at her dirty bare feet*] Oh, we walked barefoot the last four miles. The greatest march ever. Alabama, Selma.

Your name is...Martha? Here's a rock.

[*tries to hand her a bullet; shoes are offered to Viola from offstage*] Maybe not good to dirty your pretty shoes, I never had time to clean up. After their autopsy, I actually never got my underwear back.

Oh, this is *national news?* Then let me tell you what really happened. They checked my body for semen because there was a young black Civil Rights worker sitting in the front seat with me. His name was Leroy. They lied and said I was braless, and without underwear.

[*looking at her arms*] Said I had needle marks in my arm. You can find it in the FBI report.

[*taking out a cigarette*] I *am* a smoker, but I wouldn't even know how to shoot up with a hypodermic needle.

Poor Jim, he did start drinking too much after. That was partly because my FBI report was thicker than four phone books. Most of the report was redacted. The FBI tarnished my reputation to save theirs, and they turned Jim into a "Communist" because he worked for the Teamsters. They only gave him my wedding ring back eleven years later. He was going to surprise me with a cabin in Grayhill for my birthday. Waking up to the dark-black branches, the fog—dawn sitting on the mountains and the yellow grass.

TV lights on Viola begin to go out. Sound of static.

[*looking at her bare ring finger and talking to herself*] I meant to put on the pearl necklace sitting on my dresser before I left.

I left the bottle of holy water there, too.

Nine births, four babies didn't make it; one exiled from the Catholic Church because he died before the baptism, baby in limbo.

Is he still rotating around the planets like an unwanted shame?

Housewives take trips to my grave, to kick the tombstone.

HOUSEWIVES [*overlapping voice-overs*] I'm here because I wanted to see the tomb of a woman who abandons her children and husband for the right to vote. Demonstrations are nothing but publicity and the urge to get in with the mob. I turned on the TV but I became so disgusted with the way things were going, I turned it off. Marching up and down a backwood road for some stupid cause, how could she? There are enough causes in our backyard to fight for. Each guy looking after his own keeps everybody safe. I'd march for my children but not for some... If we were invaded, then I think we'd fight. It would mean getting killed for protecting our families, not for someone to vote or things like that.

VIOLA Dead people can't vote. Why would anyone make up that story? *Who* needs an ID to vote?

In Georgia, I saw a black man hanging from a tree. I was a little girl, holding my father's hand. We were walking past the tree, and my father tugged. His hand was cracked and soft. Comforting. My heart left my body. What happened, Daddy?

No, I want to look. Wait, I can't see. What's that in the tree, Daddy?

Why?

I don't understand. I want to see.

I saw the man hanging. People circled 'round. My daddy told me the man had talked to a white woman.

"What was wrong with that?" I asked. My daddy didn't answer. Serious. I walked *past* that tree! I thought about him, that man, his last moments, what happened to his body. He had a family, probably a daughter just like me.

I put Leroy's life in jeopardy driving with him in Lowndes, but he survived! He was all bloody from *my* blood, but he laid his head on the lap of my dead body and pretended to be dead until they drove off. He got out of the car, ran down the road, and got away. Then they actually accused him over and over of having sex with me.

He was eighteen years old. I was just another white woman who put a black man in jeopardy.

See, I'm lost in limbo like my own unbaptized child, trying to find my way out.

The last person I saw was Tommy Rowe. Didn't know him from Adam. When he looked in my eyes... Tommy Rowe... When he looked...

TOMMY [*speaking to his handler and smoking*] A white woman drivin' a blue Oldsmobile, Neil, with a Negro sittin' next to her in the front seat. Gene tells us to "Crouch down. Let's burn a whore. They're goin' somewhere to have sex." We follow 'em across the bridge. It's about eight. Gene gets his gun, hands it to Wilkins. The chase goes into the Lowndes Swamp. Bullets poppin' into the asphalt like bubbles. She stares over at us. Her mouth opens. Wilkins fires at her head. His second shot goes through the glass, straight in, and gets her in the face.

Suddenly a bright light floods the stage, as if an angel is appearing. Tommy stares in surprise as a phone rings.

Yes, I'm Tommy Rowe.

Wait a minute, Mr. Director, am I dreamin'? You put the fear of God in people, but it is a great privilege for *me* to talk to you, sir. How are you doin' tonight?

I am glad to hear it.

No, you didn't interrupt. I couldn't sleep, I was watchin'...

VIOLA Tommy Rowe was watching me. And he was watching them, the guys in the car.

TOMMY [*talking on phone*] You are welcome, Mr. Director. It has been my great honor to serve you. I can't tell you how much your phone call means to me.

Witness Protection, I understand, sir. I haven't been with my family for a while now. I've dedicated myself to you. Still, my children need to be safe.

Thank you, sir. I appreciate that. It will be hard to leave.

VIOLA I grew up in the South. Tommy Rowe grew up in the South.

TOMMY [*talking on the phone*] Everythin' I know is here, Mr. Director, but I'll do anythin' to further the cause.

Good night, Mr. Hoover.

[*to himself*] Did he call me, or was it just the CC and Seven? Does it even matter since it all gets redacted?

VIOLA [*speeding in the car, talking to Leroy*] Leroy, crouch down.

[*to herself*] The premonition I had at the top of St. Jude's Church: it's me who is going to die...

Sarah, you'll take care of my littlest...?

In surreal lighting, she finds a rock and shows it to her youngest child.

Granite is my favorite, sweetie. Speckled like a spotted animal.

[*laughing*] Good! Like a leopard. It makes monuments, strong like you.

[*suddenly defensive*] Who said that, sweetie? You're normal. When you were born, I was taking medicine.

Remember how I said I lost your baby brothers?

Yes, in the cemetery. I needed more strength in my body. Like granite, to have you. You needed a little extra-special care—you were such a cute baby. You're always better when you come through a storm, sweetie.

[*sings a song, which she makes up for the child as she goes along*]
A mother will find you, wherever you are
She'll hold you within her, no matter how far
You cannot lose her, you're her star.

[*puts the granite in the trail of rocks*] They're pullin' up to us. This is one ledge you can't rescue me from, Sarah. There's just a very fine line that divides us...

TOMMY I'm a very good actor, Senator, an informant needs that more 'n anythin'—I should've gone straight to Hollywood, but who cares who I am—right, Senator? I was just their *snitch*, and they swallowed me right up for their machine, just like you're using me to clean up your tarnished FBI, Senator. They put me and my family in Witness Protection...

The more I testified at the various murder trials for Viola Liuzzo, the less I could please anybody, and after Gene and Wilkins got out of jail, they turned 'round because they could and accused *me*—they were celebrities after they killed her. It's free rein in the South, it's the white man's word, and she was a "white nigger," which is probably worse than a black man.

Sound of rapid series of bullets.

VIOLA This road in the Lowndes Swamp is *lined* with trees. As I'm driving, the nightmare of the first tree seems to go on forever with the bullets.

As I go down, that's what I see: an explosion of trees.
Tree,

Tree,
Tree,
Tree.

[*singing slowly*] "We shall overcome..."

TOMMY I don't feel sorry for the white woman, Senator; she got what she deserved. Big fancy ceremony with all the famous people at her funeral, her kids bawlin', her Hoffa-lovin' husband, eyes red from what I'd call shame. He was a crook for the Teamsters, he had *that reputation*. And she was a drug addict. Why'd he let her out of the house, leavin' five children alone? When I saw her drivin' on the Pettus Bridge with that black buck next to her, I thought to myself, she will not survive the night.

The Lowndes Swamp was a very long, dark strip of road, Senator; she knew that. And the cameras were off by then, everyone had gone home. No one was watchin'...

VIOLA Crouch down, Leroy. It will be okay. Crouch down. "We shall ohhh..."
I am looking at him.
Tommy Rowe.

TOMMY Ohhh, my God!
I'm watchin'
Viola Liuzzo turns to look at me
Through the window of the car
In my soul that's what she's sayin'
Her mouth is completely open,
Ohhh...

VIOLA I am looking at him
His gun is down, he is shooting at the road.
Bullets poppin' into the asphalt like bubbles.
His eyes meet mine,
Through the window of the car
He is saying, "Ohhh, my God."
He wasn't *that* good an actor.
His mouth is moving, "Ohhh, my God!"
I am singing,
"O-ver-come..."

TOMMY I just never wanted to worry you with my undercover work, Momma. I'm sorry, all I ever wanted was to be a police officer.
Wear the uniform.

VIOLA [*finds more bullets*] "Now, it is not an accident that one of the great marches of American history should terminate..."
Lowndes.
I am not lost.
[*lays the bullets in the trail of rocks, which extends into the audience*]
The trail ends here.

Acknowledgments
Hilton Als, Christie Brown, Kia Corthron, David Cunningham, John Daggett, Paola di Florio, Michael Frierson, Patrick Harnett-Marshall, Maria Jacobson, Samantha Leigh, Charles Lewis, Gary May, Diane McWhorter, Cassandra Medley, Brian Richard Mori, Natalie Osborne, Megan Pries, Heather Raffo, Mary Stanton, Monica Trausch, Glory Van Scott, JoEllen Vinyard. The voice-over of the housewives is inspired by an article in *Ladies' Home Journal* 82 (July 1965): 42–44.

Mary and Myra

TO ED HERENDEEN

Cast of Characters
Mary Todd Lincoln, fifty-six; widow of President Abraham Lincoln; has a Kentucky accent.
Myra Bradwell, forty-four; America's first woman lawyer; prominent figure in the Woman Suffrage Movement; comes from a sterling New England background.

Setting
Bellevue Place, a private insane asylum in Batavia, Illinois, in the year 1875.

Act One

Prologue

Mary Todd Lincoln is bathed in red light as she enters her small room, wearing long widow's weeds, an intricate veil/bonnet with flowers, and a large ribbon at her throat. The door slams and she rushes to try the door, which is now bolted shut. From above come the horrifying shrieks of a woman. Mary hurries to the barred window, clutching herself. A slot in the door slides open, and eyes watch her from the other side. Mary ducks as the red light fades.

Scene One

July 29. It is afternoon as Mary dusts a black bonnet; she hears loud, consistent pounding on the ceiling. Her room has a ragtag writing desk, a bed that appears higher than usual, and an unusual number of carpet-covered footstools. The set is framed and constructed with steamer trunks.

MARY TODD LINCOLN [*calling toward the room above*] Mrs. Wheeler, I can hear you! There's nothin' I can do. The nurse'll bring you some chloral, but I'd be careful! Better perhaps to accept the Bellevue remedy... Mrs. Wheeler, dear, I can hear you...

There is a knock on the door. Before Mary can open it, Myra Bradwell, statuesque and elaborately coifed, storms into the room carrying her briefcase.

Pray God! My dear Myra, never has a soul been happier to see you...

MYRA BRADWELL My poor, dear girl, how are you? How are they treating you?

MARY [*starts to kiss Myra's face, then begins to hit her*] Why have you not come earlier? I have written and written. Where have you been?

MYRA Your son, Robert, forbids all visits, intercepts all letters.

MARY [*anguished*] What has happened to my son?

MYRA Robert has taken the popular recourse of Men of our Age. He has locked you away so you won't annoy him. A deep injustice has been done to you. James and I know you are not insane, and we will get you out.

MARY Oh, how is your dear and *gentle* husband, James?

MYRA Occupied at the court today, but I assure you he will help in any way he can.

MARY [*acting the hostess*] I do apologize. Sit, there is not one acceptable chair. Do you know they had the audacity to give me a rocker? [*softly, to herself*] Red. [*looking at Myra's dress*] You are beautifully arrayed—the fallin' leaf color was the rage of the Continent. Shall I ask my attendant to bring a small collation?

MYRA We hardly need a small collation in an asylum. Now, look at me. Dr. Patterson has allowed us only ten minutes. [*trying to look at Mary's eyes*] Be still.

MARY [*embarrassed*] Oh, *my great bloat!* I am quite an exuberance of flesh. [*hides*]

MYRA Come out of there. I only worry that you are on fire in that wool dress. Are they giving you medicine?

MARY I have ordered a lawn dress from town. The crepe... [*finds a fabric sample*] Feel, abysmal...

MYRA Mrs. Lincoln, am I speaking to a woman under the influence of strong medicine?!

MARY No, rest assured, I accept nothin' but "the Bellevue remedy."

MYRA "The Bellevue remedy"?

MARY Eggnog with two teaspoons of whiskey. [*looking to the slot, lowering her voice*] But I hear Dr. Patterson killed a patient with one hundred and ten grains chloral hydrate. I never go near it!

MYRA Very wise.

MARY At most, a little beer...

MYRA Your eyes, they do not look well.

MARY I blink too often. [*rubbing her eyes, red from crying*] You stopped writin' to me long ago, Myra. You ceased to invite me to your illustrious dinners.

MYRA Now, let me tell you my plan!

MARY Did you not hear me?

MYRA I will induce the public to have your case reopened! The way your son conducted the trial is illegal and I will make him pay. Now, you must quickly answer my questions so I can build your case. Dr. Patterson is watching the clock...

MARY The "Patriarch."

MYRA [*taking a newspaper from her briefcase*] Yes, after you smuggled your letter to me, I came here immediately. The "Patriarch" would not let me in. I was forced to write an anonymous article in a local paper, discrediting the doctor.

MARY [*prepares to clip the article with her blunt scissors; reading*] "No One Allowed to See Widow. Remarkable Interview with Her Physician and [*emphasizing*] Jailer." You are clever!

MYRA I have no choice. Now, these doctors at the trial who declared you insane—when did they examine you?

MARY They never *examined* me. They don't even know me.

MYRA They never examined you?!

MARY They are Robert's friends. [*confidentially*] I try to be on my best behavior with Robert and the Patriarch, but it's *killin' me*. At the dinners—which the doctor's wife insists I share because I am, after all, famous—the Patterson son speaks only of gynecology.

MYRA What?!

MARY They are all so proud of his new specialty. He's the first gynecologist in the land.

MYRA Your propensity to wander is especially trying, Mrs. Lincoln. I am in a deep crisis at the paper.

MARY Oh my, you still own that paper?

MYRA Every lawyer in the country reads it, and I have already written about you in it.

MARY [*in anticipation, picks up her scissors*] You wrote about me in your paper?

MYRA Yes, I will not let the public forget you.

MARY Do you have a copy?

MYRA [*gives her the paper*] Yes. *Now* I will report in my column that Robert chooses doctors who do not *see* patients before diagnosing them!

MARY Oh, bring me a copy of that, too!

MYRA Now *why* did your lawyer call not one single witness for you?

MARY Because he wasn't *my* lawyer. He was chosen by Robert so I wouldn't get it into my head to find some mischievous lawyer to make trouble.

MYRA [*holding out her hand*] I am she.

MARY Pardon me?

MYRA I am your "mischievous lawyer."

MARY But you were denied the right to practice—you're a woman.

MYRA Women have been admitted in other states. My law journal has acquired such dimensions I have little time for a practice, and I do not need the title of Attorney to know I *am* one.

MARY A woman's sphere is the hearth and home, Mrs. Bradwell. Our raisin' money together for the wounded durin' the war was ambitious enough!

MYRA I fear this is not a good topic for us. Now, I came to your hotel directly after your trial. I was turned away by guards. To think that it was then that you tried to… [*stops herself*]

MARY Tried to what?

MYRA Take your own life, my poor darling queen.

MARY I never tried to take my own life! Who in God's name told you that?

MYRA [*takes a newspaper clipping from her folder, reading*] "Another Sad Chapter for the Demented Widow. Mary Lincoln Attempts to Poison Herself."

MARY Let me see this paper! My Heavens, the *Chicago Inter Ocean*?

MYRA Are you absolutely sure you did not go to three different pharmacies trying to get opium?

MARY I think I would remember, Mrs. Bradwell, if I went to get *opium*… Had I planned to kill myself, it would have been long ago. You know Robert's former law partner *owns* the *Inter Ocean*.

MYRA Oh, my Lord, he is more evil than I imagined. What could you have done to the boy?

MARY I have done nothin' to the boy. You hardly seem to be the one to talk—

MYRA That's enough. We will not stray from the course!

MARY And who, pray tell, charts this beauteous course? *You?* [*goes to window and holds bars; outside is a net*] They say I am here until my reason is restored, but I never lost my reason, so I wonder how long I'll stay.

MYRA [*making a note*] The bars on the windows—I will speak to the doctor.

MARY Robert has all my money 'n' deludes himself thinkin' this is a country club, though it's clear it's *third class*. He invents my suicide in this paper. [*pointing down*] But sends me to a place where there's a net down below to catch me!

MYRA I must ask you strictly as a formality, Mrs. Lincoln: how is your mind?

MARY I am bent with sorrow. Hacked to pieces with neuralgia. Famished by the bland diet—the doctor believes spice excites the nerves—they don't even know how to make a proper griddle cake—I'm longin' to buy a new bonnet—all mine are soiled from dust—

MYRA *Answer the question!*

MARY But I am not insane... I have simply not talked to *anyone* in so long. We lost touch, Myra... [*a woman screams; Mary hyperventilates*] Oh, Heaven! Listen! Mrs. Munger? Last night she stole a carvin' knife from the kitchen and... stabbed herself below the navel. When I went down this mornin', they were cleanin' the... [*cannot continue; the room is faintly washed in red*] In the water closet, all over. [*whispering*] Red... The attendant told me it was Mrs. Munger... [*looks to the slot in the door*] I pay an additional price for a private attendant, but she spies on me through the slot for the doctor.

MYRA Unlawful.

MARY I try to appear *normal* to Dr. Patterson, sayin' politely hello, but sometimes I try so hard I say hello three times in five minutes, and he certainly must think I'm bizarre... [*picks up some turnips*] He's fixated on the vegetables in the garden and seems to think you show high "moral character" if you pick some for your own dinner.

MYRA That is his treatment? [*looking around the room*] Why are there so many footstools?

MARY I hoped to have a séance, but this place has proved surprisin'ly free of mediums—or spirits...

MYRA I strongly urge against any talk of *spiritualism*.

MARY This hateful room turns all the spirits away...

MYRA In the minds of these doctors, spiritualism is one with insanity. They call it "theomania."

MARY Oh yes, the Patriarch accuses me of both "theomania" and "monomania." Couldn't you perhaps help me to arrange a séance?

MYRA Absolutely not. You are exasperating!

MARY Tell me, how is your home? Is your poor daughter, Bessie, doin' better?

MYRA What do you mean is she doing better?! She is a valedictorian at school.

MARY When I think you had two...

MYRA Now, at the trial, what your family doctor claimed you said about *the Indian* rearranging wires in your head? I need to hear *your* side of the story.

MARY [*looks in a trunk*] I have beautiful Chantilly curtains for Bessie, bought but never used.

MYRA Yes, I read about all the curtains you are buying for the home you do not have.

MARY How do you know what home I have? You've failed to contact me for more than a year.

MYRA *Mrs. Lincoln!* The family doctor—

MARY [*sees a* carte-de-visite *in her trunk*] When Tom Thumb and his new bride visited the White House, the Great One leaned down to shake the Dwarf-General's hand…

MYRA Wires in your head. *Who was the Indian?!*

MARY *You* remember—Pinkie, our spirit guide?

MYRA *No, I do not remember Pinkie! You are infuriating!*

MARY I see that your aggressive nature has only accelerated, Myra. It is a true shame… It simply *feels* as if durin' my headaches strings are bein' pulled through my eyes. I did not truly believe there was an *Indian* doin' the maneuverin'.

MYRA Again, I beseech you not to discuss spiritualism with the doctors, nor with your son.

MARY Aren't you a spiritualist, Myra?

MYRA No, I am not.

MARY But we went to so many séances together. Remember how we'd park the black barouche on a side street and pray no one recognized us?

MYRA No, I do not remember.

MARY Didn't you say, "How insignificant all worldly honors are when we are thus so severely tried—

MYRA Do not start!

MARY [*continuing litany*] "If we could only realize how far happier they are now in Heaven than on Earth—"

MYRA Soon you will make me lose my reason, and then we will *both* be *raving maniacs.*

MARY [*stops cold*] Please, you may leave now.

MYRA You are not listening to me.

MARY *Go!*

MYRA [*a beat*] You are right, my child had died. I took comfort in the séances, but I always knew it was the mediums disguised as spirits coming out of the little cabinets...

MARY But you spoke to little Myra on the Other Side, I was there...

MYRA Please, I would ask you not to say her name.

MARY Little Myra's name? But it is your name. *Myra.*

MYRA Now you have said it twice.

MARY Myra, your little girl was a bein' far too precious for Earth...

MYRA [*firmly*] Now promise me not to mention Pinkie or any other Indian. The Voices you heard outside your hotel room?

MARY Pinkerton detectives Robert hired to follow me...

MYRA So you would not further humiliate him... [*a knock on the door*] These are the rules of the game.

MARY What game?

MYRA One: you must be consistently pleasant to your son.

MARY *Oh, I want to choke him!*

MYRA Second: to everything the doctor says, you answer, "I think this fair and right." Repeat.

MARY [*in disbelief*] I think this fair and right?

MYRA Fine. Third: nothing will be said about Robert's invention of your suicide.

MARY *Why would he do it?!* I've given him all the income of the house where you and I were once neighbors—First Lady of the Land, then a boarder in roomin' houses. I've also given him loans for his crooked investments. [*catches herself*] Shhhshhh.

MYRA In your letter you mentioned these crooked investments.

MARY [*jumps*] If he knew I wrote to you, he would *blast* me...

MYRA What are these investments?

MARY Sanctified information.

MYRA Tell me. If we could cast doubt on your son's integrity, it would help... Mary?

MARY [*pretending*] I'm afraid I didn't hear.

MYRA This is no comedy. I am in need of ammunition. [*Mary is silent*] I'll find out the secret myself.

MARY No, you won't.

MYRA Your son represents the most influential men in Chicago. I can beat him, but you must help me.

MARY [*playfully picking up the turnips*] "Oh, Dr. Patterson, I so love to harvest my own vegetables here at the asylum..."

MYRA Hold my hand.

MARY You have a fine perfume.

MYRA [*taking a perfume vial from her briefcase and giving it to Mary*] Your fight for your pension, the sale of your old clothes, your obsessive concern for your son's safety have all *humiliated* him. Stop, it only proves to make him meaner.

MARY How d'you know this?

MYRA The papers told me it every day, Mrs. Lincoln. Everyone knows.

MARY The Great One and I lost our mamas when we were small—we wanted so much that our children not have miserable childhoods, we let 'em play *free*...

MYRA We will launch our own counterattack. When does Dr. Patterson visit his office on Doctor's Row?

MARY Every single Saturday...

MYRA Good. A reporter friend will come to interview you. You have a sister in Springfield, do you not? I will write to her... [*packing her briefcase*] And now, my dear girl, I must run to the depot...

MARY Won't you stay...?

MYRA [*opening to a page of a legal brief*] What do you see on this page? Are there *words*?

MARY No, it is blank.

MYRA Exactly. The printers in my legal-brief trade demand to be paid for *blank pages*, as well. I have fired them all and called the *Times* for non-union men. [*proudly*] I must go—even during the Great Fire, my paper got out...

MARY Ah, the Fire! Standin' together, you and I, in Lake Michigan, watchin' Chicago burn. To think your poor Bessie ran into the flamin' buildin'.

MYRA I will ask you *never* to mention the Fire.

MARY *You* just did. I'm very worried, Myra. There seems to be a bevy of topics I'm not at liberty to mention...

MYRA [*putting on her hat and gloves*] I would not want to miss the last train and be forced to stay in this primitive, little town. Please forgive me, I meant no harm...

MARY [*looking out the window; night is starting to fall*] At night there's a different Order which descends here. I'm so thoroughly chilled. My limbs.

MYRA Tell me goodbye.

MARY The perfume will make me think of you. *You will go straight home and not return to the office.*

MYRA I will return to the office or my paper will not come out.

MARY You spend too much time away from your home—James and Bessie suffer. Do you still have the cats? *They* must suffer. A few days here in the country would do you extreme good.

MYRA Yes, eggnog and whiskey. It is a perpetual Christmas! [*there is a loud knock on the door*] Oh no, I hope he did not hear!

MARY When will you return? Promise me it will be in a few days. Write to me, tell me exactly *when*. Tell me everythin'. Collect every single newspaper with my name in it. They give me no privacy.

MYRA Do not worry. [*taking Mary's hand*] I am your "mischievous lawyer." I hold that above all else.

MARY My son Tad's spirit has stopped comin'. My All hovers, but I do not see him.

MYRA *You do not listen!*

MARY [*looking in the mirror as she puts on a strange jacket*] Robert has always wanted me to be someone I'm not. I can only be who I am.

MYRA But you can make small adjustments to attain what you *need*.

MARY [*looking at Myra in the mirror*] And one day the small adjustments are so big you're no longer who you are, Myra.

MYRA Hush, what is that you are wearing?!

MARY My gardenin' coat. I'm forced to dig up potatoes so the doctor will think I'm well. Will you please bring me some fabric samples?

MYRA Yes...

MARY Now go and do it quickly or I will *scream*. Too long in this bin and you start to do what everyone else does. [*Myra leaves; Mary goes to a trunk, taking out a stuffed eagle and other items, using a byzantine but logical filing system*] Tad's military costume?... Purchased in sixty-two? How he loved the regalia!... Ah, here!

She unwraps a gun as lights fade.

Scene Two

Eight days later: August 6. There are all sorts of vegetables in the room: corn on the cob, eggplant, carrots, beets, etc. Mary is going through her trunks, occasionally adding a small accessory to her mourning costume.

MARY [*trying to say it convincingly*] "I think this fair and right. I think this fair and right. Yes, sir, I think this fair and right." [*hears pounding on the ceiling; calls upward*] *Give her some chloral and let her sleep, for God's sake!* [*goes to the barred window and puts out her arms, as if to fly*] Like a child. Into the White... Like a cloud... [*jumps into the air as Myra enters, holding her briefcase, a lawn dress, a suitcase, newspapers, etc.*]

MYRA What are you doing?

MARY Not one thing. [*begins to hit Myra as in Scene One; Myra raises her briefcase to shield herself*] You have stayed away *eight days*. You have not written.

MYRA I passed a patient. Mrs. Johnston? [*showing her wet shoe*] She urinated on my shoe with the explanation that God imposes higher duties than cleanliness.

MARY Yes, Mrs. Johnston's angry. Her husband's put her here...

Mary gives Myra a cloth to wipe her shoe.

MYRA [*looks to the window*] They have not removed the bars? [*giving Mary a letter*] Excellent news: your sister responded. She agrees that you can live with her when I get you out. Here is the lawn dress you ordered in the village.

MARY It is a *horrid* color.

MYRA It is black.

MARY When you have lost a husband and three sons, you come to know Black. I insist on the *blackest*.

MYRA Why not try it on? Right away.

MARY No, I shall return it.

MYRA [*handing Mary a stack of newspapers*] My column about your son's choice of quack doctors is on the top! [*Mary gets her scissors*] The doctor just told me you insist on corn bread every morning, leave it untouched, and call for rolls. You order griddle cakes for supper but call for corn bread...

MARY To everythin' the doctor says now, I answer, "I think this fair and right." It is *ravagin'* me...

MYRA *Try harder.* [*putting down some fruit*] The strawberries are from my friend Belva Lockwood.

MARY Strawberries are pleasant for invalids...

MYRA Belva's been rejected to practice law. The justices say barring women from the Supreme Court goes back to the days of England, so I am writing a bill asking all male attorneys to wear gowns and periwigs. [*looking around*] It is *dismal* in here.

MARY It is dismal because it is a *nuthouse*. [*looking out the window*] Sometimes it feels as if fallin' into that white net would be my redemption. Myra, I *am not mad but soon shall be!* I assure you I have strange leanin's...

MYRA Perhaps we should keep the bars.

MARY [*returning to her trunks*] I'm still searchin' for the curtains for Bessie. I'm confused as to their placement...

MYRA I have received some very distressing news.

MARY [*taking a book from the trunk and offering it to Myra*] "Into each life some rain must fall." There is no doubt that Longfellow is a spiritualist... *New-England Tragedies*.

MYRA None other than *you* paid for the Pinkerton detectives who followed you all these years and for the doctors who certified you Insane.

MARY I never paid a cent.

MYRA You did not know you paid, but your son took the money from your estate.

MARY *This cannot be true.*

MYRA [*showing Mary the paperwork*] I wrote to the executor. *You* paid thousands.

MARY [*becoming violent, hitting furniture*] Why should he do this to me?! I don't understand! What have I done to so upset the boy?

MYRA Please, stop at once, you will bring the attendants. [*Mary pounds on the window bars; Myra tries to restrain her*] That is enough, Mrs. Lincoln.

MARY Let me go...

MYRA You are not improving.

MARY I'm deterioratin'!

MYRA [*wrestling Mary to the floor*] You are no match for me, Mary, I'm twice your size and younger.

MARY [*punching Myra*] Leave me alone or I'll bite you!

MYRA [*pinning Mary's arm behind her back*] Stop moving or I will spank you. If you want to get out, you must make *no fuss! Do you want to get out?! Answer me!* [*Mary calms down*] I will expose your son's illegal use of your money in my next column. I will bring you a copy.

MARY [*lying facedown on the floor, sobbing*] I nursed him. I washed him. I sewed all of his clothes. He was a cross-eyed boy. Now he's *a big fat pig!*

MYRA [*lying next to Mary on the floor*] *Shhshh*, do not speak. It will be easier... [*ironically*] For everyone...

MARY I want to speak. I want to *scream! I'm so angry!*

MYRA [*putting her hand over Mary's mouth*] Are you finished? [*appeasing her*] I will force Robert to give us immediate reimbursement. I told Bessie about the curtains. She would be pleased to have them.

MARY White lace curtains blowin' in the wind, the smell of balsam and pine... To think poor Bessie went into that flamin' buildin', it's a wonder she survived!

MYRA *Mrs. Lincoln, that is none of your business.*

MARY James said he tried to hold her back but she ran in to please you—

MYRA James and I do not discuss the Fire!

MARY A husband and wife must discuss everythin', I told you, that day in the shops—

MYRA I will not listen...

MARY Myra, I tried to warn you, Bessie is sufferin'...

MYRA Please!

MARY I simply want to help...

MYRA I cannot discuss this.

MARY Since that day, you have treated me as a *stranger*. And now suddenly you are here... You're shakin'.

MYRA [*looking around the room*] Is it wise to keep so many vegetables?

MARY Here, they are the crownin' mark of sanity. Won't you answer me?

MYRA Is she watching us through the slot?

MARY Pay no attention. You must start by givin' up your work at the paper.

MYRA How can I give up my work at the paper? I *am* the paper. I told the men I would not allow dictation by the union, and they came crawling back.

MARY You are so strong-minded it's a wonder James finds you attractive *in the least*...

MYRA He finds me *very* attractive.

MARY Oh!... You are a wicked girl.

MYRA Did your "Great One" find you so?

MARY He could not help himself.

MYRA It must have been hard to kiss such a *God*.

MARY He said the Todd women were *somethin'*.

MYRA He had more than one?

MARY He accompanied my sister to a few balls. I fortunately do not know the particulars. [*sensually*] My husband was a slow man in all things.

MYRA Well, James always finds me attractive. No matter how late at night I work, he's always ready.

MARY Why did the good Lord make you so fortunate?

MYRA Why should he not? I am not like one of those strident, unmarried suffragettes. [*taking fabric and ribbon samples from an A.T. Stewart package*] Tomorrow Mr. Wilkie, our reporter, arrives on the eleven o'clock train. If you promise you will behave, I will show you the samples.

MARY [*exuberant*] Oh, I cannot overcome my weakness for velvets! [*holding a sample to the light*] This tarlatan lights up beautifully! It is to be flounced, *qu'en pensez-vous?* I will enjoy it because it's a variety not figured... [*making a pile of samples*] I would be grateful for four black widow's caps made of this heavy mournin' silk, richly trimmed with black crepe myrtle—very *distingué* lookin'. This exact shade or I do not want it. Help me measure my head with this string... [*Myra measures Mary's head, as Mary's fabric frenzy builds*] One cap should be adorned with this Mary Louise blue ribbon, most bewitchedly piquant—but they must not ask me over five dollars for it. One black watered silk and a bertha point of lace trimmed with swans' down. Oh, this bombazine and this merino with tiny flowers would be just sweet enough to eat—and this black illusion *à la vierge!* For the veils, the very finest 'n' the blackest 'n' the lightest. [*checking a trunk*] Oh, an ermine fan with silver spangles would go nicely with my chinchilla set, sable cape, cuffs, and muff... I must look for my shawl pin ball and chain!

MYRA I have never known a woman quite so resourceful.

MARY My grandmother Jane wove her weddin' dress from weeds. As a girl, I made hoops for my skirt from willow reeds. [*pulls out a huge, white hooped skirt from a trunk*]

MYRA [*gets papers from her briefcase*] Franc Wilkie arrives in the morning, we have work.

MARY [*getting out her money*] The name sounds familiar—the War days?

MYRA You met him at the White House. He was at the *Times*.

MARY Yes, in sixty-two. I met him once for a minute. I met so many men. Here's the money for the caps. [*taking back a few coins*] I cannot part with the pennies; I've a weakness for My All's profile. [*trying to give her money*] Now, I've always been very careful about money matters. You never accept anythin' from me, why?

MYRA Mr. Wilkie will be interviewing you.

MARY Have you cleared it with the Pater? You should know that I am the one who pays for your sins *after you leave*.

MYRA Mr. Patterson—I refuse to dignify him as a doctor—will be absent. He leaves on Saturdays.

MARY I'm expectin' a visit from General Farnsworth. He was a dear friend of my husband's. You gave me no notice of your arrival, I can't always be at your disposal...

MYRA May I at least open a window?

MARY They're locked shut. General Farnsworth was there on The Night. You know, the rocker in which my husband sat That Night? The curtains? The fabric in the box? It was all red. Like the inside of a doll house.

The room is faintly washed in red. Myra looks at Mary, who is lost in her reverie.

MYRA When does General Farnsworth arrive?

MARY [*returning to her trunks as the red fades*] The General is an ardent spiritualist. I'm hopin' he will recommend a medium in the area.

MYRA Mrs. Lincoln!

MARY You're not the only friend I smuggled letters to. [*taking out porcelain*] Have I shown you the Haviland Solferino plates?

MYRA Yes, of course! Many times. I love them.

MARY You've never seen the plates. Lyin' does not become you. Perhaps it was a "White Lie"?

MYRA *No, it was a real lie.* You must put on a fresh dress for the General—with your reputation for fashion. How can you bear that wool?

MARY I am cold.

MYRA You are cold, in August? [*Mary takes the strawberries and gets into bed*] What are you doing? You are fully dressed. Get out of the bed instantly, it deviates from *Mr.* Patterson's notion of "moral behavior." *Out!* [*pulls Mary out*]

MARY [*holding up the stuffed eagle*] The bird's missin' a foot.

MYRA [*reading aloud from her writing paper*] "Occasionally some word has come up to the great busy world, concerning the condition of the *lady* in whom all American people feel a kindly interest. The Lady whose 'afternoon of life' is filled with such a Chilly Atmosphere—"

MARY Afternoon of life?! Is that from Whittier?

MYRA [*continuing*] "Recently, a representative of the *Times* in quest of scientific facts by means of Personal Observation—"

MARY What are you doin'?!

MYRA I am writing Franc Wilkie's article. I am a journalist, I will fight your son with what I do best—in the *press*. I will also choose the print date. When we are finished, your son will *beg for mercy*.

MARY *This* cheers me up...I was worried about you as a "lawyer."

MYRA What did you say?

MARY The Supreme Court invoked the Law of the Creator, forbiddin' you to practice.

MYRA I passed the bar exam with the Highest Honors, Mrs. Lincoln. I did better than *any man.*

MARY The *Supreme* Court of the Land must be right, Myra. Not to mention the Creator. [*points upward*] I was worried to have a lawyer-that-isn't-a-lawyer representin' me.

MYRA I *am* a lawyer! In other states I could practice, so what is the difference?

MARY The difference is the *law.*

MYRA *So get another lawyer!*

MARY Truth is I need whoever I can get. And if you are a non-lawyer, so be it, you are after all a Journalist of *Some* Repute.

MYRA And you have criticized me for that as well!

MARY This is certainly not an attractive side. You have changed...

MYRA *You believe a woman should not work outside the home.* Have you given these ancient canons any real, sensible *thought?*

MARY My only real, sensible thought is *I'm angry at my son. So angry I'm thinkin' of the unspeakable.* Forgive me, if I hurt you. Let's write the article!

MYRA When does the General arrive?

MARY *He does not arrive. I lied*—A Great Sin—but still only a "White Lie," as he may have come since I invited him...

MYRA Your mind, Mrs. Lincoln, is something quite hard to fathom...

MARY I lied *to make myself seem more popular.* All right?

MYRA In a mental institution, you wanted to seem more popular? You fail to see the large picture...

MARY *Carry on with the article.*

MYRA [*writing quickly*] "The *Times* representative visited the institution of Dr. Patterson and, whilst there, was introduced to Mrs. Lincoln by..." [*pointing to herself*] Me. "A mutual..." Nameless... "Friend who happened to be there..."

MARY Friend?

MYRA Tomorrow you will come down to meet Wilkie. Make *no reference* to him as a newspaperman—simply treat him as an old friend. Invite him up to see the view and we will stay here "in conference" for about two hours. Is that understood?

MARY [*removing keys hidden in her petticoat*] I would like you to take these keys and hide 'em.

MYRA What are they?

MARY Keys to all my trunks at Robert's. Should anythin' happen to me.

MYRA You must keep them. When you get out—

MARY He will block me, I know it! *He's young in age but old in sin!*

MYRA Please, be calm. I will stay with you here tonight, I have already received permission from your doctor.

MARY *You are stayin' here tonight?!*

MYRA Yes, we see Wilkie in the morning.

MARY [*hugs Myra*] Hooray! You are an angel. I adore you...

MYRA [*extricating herself*] Excuse me...

MARY Thank you, thank you. I'll try to behave.

MYRA [*scribbles*] "The lady appeared in very good spirits and her mind was clear and lucid."

MARY "Clear and *sprightly*."

MYRA "Clear and sprightly. She invited the gentleman to her room to obtain a view of the pastoral landscape..."

MARY *Hidden behind bars!*

MYRA [*putting her off*] Later... "Concerning Mr. Lincoln, she related anecdotes illustrating his extreme good nature..."

MARY He tended towards melancholy...

MYRA "And conversed about the assassination..."

MARY General Farnsworth was present at his bedside That Fateful Night...

MYRA Where did you go with Tad in Europe?

MARY France, England...

MYRA "Her visit to England was alluded to and *thoroughly discussed*. Tad was with her and she alluded—"

MARY That's "alluded" twice, dear...

MYRA "To the child now dead but whose memory is very dear to her..."

MARY "She showed all the warmth and affection a fond mother might be expected to exhibit..."

MYRA "There was, however, *not a sign of weakness*." We will make that a headline. "Or any abnormal manifestations of mind visible..."

MARY [*opening her desk drawer and taking out the gun, showing it to Myra*] I plan to kill my son when next he visits. I told you I had leanin's.

MYRA *For Heaven's sakes!* Where did you get that gun?

MARY I bought it from Gus Gumpert's store in Philadelphia to go with Tad's military costume.

MYRA Is it loaded?

MARY [*hasn't thought of this*] Well, aren't most guns? At least in Lexington, Kentucky—where I was born—guns were loaded.

MYRA Give it to me. [*exploding*] What is Wilkie going to say *if he sees you have a gun?!*

MARY People regard me as crazy. If I say the moon is made of green cheese, they heartily agree.

MYRA Give me that. You are ruining my case.

MARY Ah, so now it is *your* case!

MYRA If the doctor sees it, he is going to send you up to the *very top* and you are never coming down.

MARY My son and Husband's friends have forgotten that despite their *power*, the Great One stays the man I love and the father of my children. They cannot take that away from me... I know I'm not an easy person, I have my foibles.

MYRA I had not noticed...

MARY Why wouldn't he just leave me be and let me live my little life?

MYRA Because men like Robert are used to *getting their way*. [*trying to take the gun*] You are making me hyperventilate.

MARY That happens to me...

MYRA Trust me with the gun until I go.

MARY What would *you* do, Mrs. Bradwell, if your own child saw you suffer through the deaths of your three Sons and the shootin' of your Husband? Put you on trial for Insanity and sent you *here*? [*looking around*] Is this the kind of place to send someone you care for...?

MYRA Put your arms around me, Mary.

MARY This is how I know he doesn't love me... What if your firstborn little Myra had done this to you?

MYRA Please do not say her name, I asked you not to...

MARY Oh dear, I am such a *fool*.

MYRA [*holding Mary*] I love you, my pet, and I will care for you. I promise. [*Mary cries in her arms as Myra takes the gun*] Thank you.

MARY As a boy, Robert used to try walkin' in his father's gigantic boots. He's been tryin' it all his life, poor thing...

MYRA [*unloading bullets from the gun, taking a deep breath*] What would you like to do if you could do *anything at all*?

MARY [*thinking a moment*] I would like to jump on this bed.

MYRA [*a beat*] Then do. Is it a good mattress?

MARY I bought my own mattresses... I would like for you to jump with me.

MYRA [*cynically*] Of course.

MARY Take off your shoes. They're stained anyway.

MYRA You make things worse for yourself.

MARY *I always have.* [*takes off her shoes as Myra puts away the gun*] You did say "anythin' at all"?

MYRA Yes, I sadly did. [*Mary gets up on the bed*] Wait. [*covers the slot in the door with the gardening coat*]

MARY I am waitin'.

MYRA I would rather not.

MARY Promise is a promise. I'll make a scene.

MYRA Alas. [*takes off her shoes*]

MARY [*begins jumping*] It's not a bad mattress. Has a certain give. [*puts out her arms as she jumps*]

MYRA What are you doing?

MARY Somethin' *you* never seem to feel the need to do. *Let go!* [*Myra gets up on the bed, as Mary jumps, holding out her arms*] You're as still as a corpse. [*Myra begins to jump tentatively, then gets caught up in the action; the two women laugh*] A serious newspaper lady. What would your subscribers say? Or those *tough union men*?

MYRA Please, do not tell them.

MARY You'll see, once you start it's like a ball of yarn unravelin'! [*jumps higher, encouraging Myra*] Higher... higher... Unknit that threatenin' brow! [*hoots gleefully*] Yahoo! You are spendin' the night!

MYRA At Bellevue with the Lunatics! [*Mary throws a pillow at her*] Don't.

MARY You began it.

MYRA [*hitting Mary with a pillow*] *You* began it.

MARY You continued it.

MYRA You are hurting me.

MARY With a feather pillow?

MYRA Stop!

MARY You stop! Such an important lady, jumpin' on a bed!

MYRA And a First Lady!

MARY A former First, now a Beast of Yore. My ankles feel like twigs. It's a wonder they hold me up at all.

MYRA My stomach hurts.

MARY Mine as well. I feel a bit indisposed.

There is a knock on the door.

WOMAN [*offstage*] Ma'am, Mrs. Lincoln? Is everything all right?

MARY [*calling out*] Perfect!

MYRA [*under her breath*] Delightful.

MARY [*gets off the bed; touches Myra*] I could never fire a gun. They do give you a sense of control. [*going to the door*] Please excuse me, you know I have a weak bladder. [*exits*]

Myra holds her stomach, unsettled. She begins to rifle in Mary's desk drawers, searching through letters and papers.

A wild scream. Myra rushes to the window. She shivers, gazing at the light through the bars. Sound of a train whistle. It slowly fades. She heads back to the open desk drawers, snooping, as Mary reenters.

MARY You will find no investment secrets.

MYRA You scared me with that gun. You must trust me in the future... [*Mary goes to the window bars and looks out at the night, as Myra writes*] "There was some light through the bars to which she called the attention of the gentleman. She said they seemed to menace her with the idea that she was imprisoned..."

Another scream.

MARY They're force-feedin' Minnie Judd.

MYRA They force-feed patients?

MARY Tiny Minnie weighs less than eighty.

Mary joins Myra, who stops writing.

MYRA "She was apprehensive that the presence of insane people in the house, whose wild cries she heard, might affect her mind... so as to unseat her reason."

MARY [*all business as she dictates to Myra*] Write: "Mrs. Lincoln 'specially dwelt on her friendship with MR. SEWARD." In capitals. In Wilkie's day, the *Times* was a Seward paper. In your article we must speak highly of Seward. [*dictating*] "It was the habit of the Secretary to dine with the Lincolns three times a week." I *despise* Seward, but this will help our cause. And in my visit to England we must mention

Mr. Motley. "Mrs. Lincoln told how badly she felt when Motley was removed by President Grant as Minister of England." Motley was Charles Sumner's choice and this will show my deep allegiance to Sumner, and *give a good jab to that small specimen of humanity, Grant!*

MYRA [*impressed*] "She keenly described the characters she met abroad, showing great powers of analysis."

There is a knock on the door, and a tray is thrust through the slot. Myra takes a plate stacked high with vegetables, another stacked with corn bread.

MARY *I asked for griddle cakes!*

MYRA *Take the bread.* Remember what I told you?

MARY *Return the plate!*

MYRA [*opens the door and hands back the plate*] I am sorry, Mrs. Lincoln is not hungry tonight.

MARY *I'm famished.*

MYRA [*listens to the person outside; to Mary*] She would like to know if you want anything else.

MARY God forbid.

MYRA [*thinks, then speaks to the person outside*] Uh, please, if you would be so kind as to bring the patient, um, *one generous cup* of "the Bellevue remedy." That will suffice, thank you very much. [*closes the door*] *If they give you griddle cakes, take griddle cakes.*

MARY They did not give me griddle cakes, they gave me corn bread!

MYRA Just accept everything pleasantly.

MARY Do you know how long I've been here? Seventy-eight days.

MYRA Are you here for the cuisine, Mrs. Lincoln? Take whatever is needed to get out.

MARY I will get out on my terms, Mrs. Bradwell.

MYRA On your terms? From an asylum?

MARY [*takes the china plates from the trunk and puts the vegetables on them*] Shall we eat on the Haviland?

A knock. Myra opens the door, taking a plate stacked high with rolls, and a large cup.

MYRA [*listens to the person outside; to Mary*] She is asking if you would like anything else.

MARY Simply my small glass of ale before bed, thank you.

MYRA Two ales, please. [*closes the door*]

MARY [*looks at the plate*] Rolls?! [*Myra downs the cup of the Bellevue remedy in one desperate gulp*] Halt, that's *whiskey!*

MYRA Ahhgghh.

MARY You scare me...

MYRA Now, listen carefully. When I return to Chicago, I will visit Robert at his office—our final maneuver...

MARY [*hands Myra a plate of vegetables, showing her the china*] The gold border with the two lines signifies the union of North and South.

A knock on the door. Myra flings it open, grabs the two glasses of ale, and listens to the person outside as Mary returns to her trunks.

MYRA [*to Mary*] Your "bedtime ale." [*listens again to the person outside*] She wants The Key? [*Mary hands over the key, shutting the door*] What was that for?

MARY To lock us in.

Sound of the click of the lock. Myra takes a swig of ale. Mary finds a pen in a trunk.

MARY This is the Pen my Husband used to sign the Emancipation Proclamation...

MYRA Would that it sign ours! [*downs the ale*]

MARY I would like you to take the Pen for your dear husband, James. I have never seen you drink.

MYRA I do not.

MARY The ale is for bedtime.

MYRA [*drinking*] I am afraid I am quite overcome suddenly.

MARY A woman at night should always be fresh. This kind of harsh overwork is akin to devil worship.

MYRA I will pretend I did not hear that.

MARY Be nice to James. Please take the Pen.

MYRA I will meet Wilkie at the station, you will make *no reference* to him as a newspaperman.

MARY Let me give you one of my peau de soie nightgowns.

MYRA [*changes for bed, staying in her undergarments*] No, thank you. [*under her breath*] We are not quite the same size...

MARY There is one small problem I failed to tell you about.

MYRA I am not particularly surprised.

MARY I usually leave the place next to me in the bed for the President.

MYRA [*a beat*] Oh, of course.

The two women prepare for bed.

MARY Let me contemplate this for a moment...

MYRA [*having finished her ale*] May I have a bit of your ale?

MARY Leave me a swallow. [*touching the side of the bed where the spirit of the President usually sleeps*] I suppose I could talk to him... I am sure he would understand if this once he relinquished his place.

MYRA Especially if he knew how *tired* I was.

MARY Would you like to speak to him yourself?

MYRA Perhaps it would be better if it came from you.

MARY Yes, you are right, as always. [*goes to window and communicates with the spirit of the President; Myra looks at the pen*] He is in agreement. He sends you his deepest regards. He always liked you.

MYRA I liked him... Is this the correct side of the bed?

MARY Yes. Oh dear, my ale has completely disappeared. You are worryin' me, dear Myra. I thought you practiced temperance.

They get into bed.

MYRA I did. When you come downstairs tomorrow to greet Wilkie, what will you do?

MARY I'll say it's nice to finally see a *newspaperman* who can tell the world the truth.

MYRA *You will greet him as an old friend!*

MARY But that's a lie... You know, my husband refused to even say, "I am delighted to see you," if he wasn't *in fact* delighted. One mistruth leads to another.

MYRA Just say hello. Ask him up to see the view.

MARY Has the eggnog gone to your head? [*Myra covers her face with the sheet*] Do you mind if I glance quickly at my sister's letter?... Goodnight. [*reads the letter as a bell is heard in the hall; the slot opens and eyes look through; Mary lies down, and the lights go out; suddenly there is the drawn-out sound of a gunshot; smoke and red light slowly wash the room; the red rocking chair appears as Mary stares*] Red, on red. [*looking at her hands, soaked with blood*] Oh...

MYRA [*wakes and sees Mary sitting and staring at her hands*] What has happened to you, Mary? [*tries to take Mary's hands in her own*]

MARY [*a beat*] Stop, I will soil you... the blood...

Myra takes Mary's hands as the nightmare fades. Mary continues to look at her hands. She gets out of bed and goes to the window. She looks out at the moon. Myra joins her.

MYRA Do you have these memories oft?

MARY [*a beat*] It was seein' the blood—downstairs in the washroom—that's made it all come back. After Mrs. Munger used the knife... *And* all of our reminiscing... [*they look out the barred window*] The moon is red.

A piercing scream from the room above as lights fade to a red moon.

Act Two

Prologue

Mary sleeps, dressed in a black peau de soie nightgown. Suddenly, a light floods the foot of her bed. The spirit who appears to her is a vaporous cloud. Mary gets up.

MARY Tad, is that you...? My sunshine, my darlin' boy? I thought this *despised room* was repellin' you all. My heart bleeds at the return of these anniversaries... [*searches through a trunk and finds some stockings*] I offered Mrs. Wheeler's boy a pair of your stockin's today. I told the boy I'd bought 'em 'specially for him. The Patriarch reproached me. Lies are forbidden as part of his "moral treatment." I asked him if he'd ever heard of a *White Lie*. "It's a lie so Light and Lovely it pleases." He no doubt passed it off as *Insanity*... Not one great sorrow ever approached the agony of losin' you. You who in your tender treatment reminded me of your beloved father—My All. [*another spirit appears at the foot of the bed*] Come closer... Willie, my sweet son? You cannot dream of the comfort this gives me, to see you. I am bowed to the earth with great sorrow... [*takes a dress from a trunk*] I wore these black flounces at the White House ball, but they were for *you*; as you lay dyin' 'n' God was punishin' me for my Worldliness. Only the Grave can soften this Grief. [*replaces the dress in the trunk, and a dusty cloud bursts forth*] Oh, I have such a terror of moths... [*the net outside the window billows and another spirit appears*] Little Aleck?! My precious lamb, you were too young to fight. Lord, this is quite a *showin'* tonight! [*sound of a woman emitting a long, low wail; the spirits instantly disappear; Mary rushes to the window*] The New Patient? [*whispering*] I need to get out... Eighty-nine days... [*looks at the window, where the bars have been removed; turns, seeing eyes spying on her through the slot*] Hide me, O my Savior, hide me! [*ironically*] Yes, this is the epitome of Restful.

Lights fade.

Scene One

Eleven days later: August 18. It is late afternoon and raining, as Mary stands at her open door, still in her black peau de soie nightgown, her hair down and tousled. She addresses someone who has just left.

MARY How dare you go on vacation! You forgot Tad's anniversary! You are a dirty dog, Robert! A dirty, dirty dog!

Items from the trunks are spread on the floor around the room. Mary gathers some feminine objects and exits.

After a moment, Myra, exhausted and looking slightly less polished, hurries in, carrying an umbrella, her suitcase, newspapers, and a bouquet of flowers. She looks for Mary, adjusts her hair in the mirror, and wipes her brow. She finds something to put the flowers in, then straightens the unmade bed as Mary reenters. Myra hands her a lawn dress.

MYRA It is nearly evening. You are not dressed. What has happened to you?

MARY I find no reason to get dressed anymore.

MYRA You went out in your nightgown? That is against the doctor's "moral behavior."

MARY What does he know of "morality"? I brought the New Patient some trinkets to lift her gloom...

MYRA *Stay away from the patients.* It paints you in a poor light. [*looking at the disarray*] Why are you emptying your trunks?

MARY *Inventory.*

MYRA [*trying to wrestle Mary out of her nightgown*] You cannot stay in your nightclothes. Downstairs they are saying you are *capricious.*

MARY I don't care if they're sayin' I'm a limb of Satan lopin' down the broad, high road. It's a sanitarium, I'll *rest* if I want to. And if I want to dance 'round the garden in my nightgown in the rain, I will do so.

MYRA Please, do not dance around the garden!

MARY Have you no imagination, no *wit*?

MYRA [*gets the nightgown off*] You are less plump...

MARY The logical result of *starvation.*

MYRA You must really wash, Mrs. Lincoln. Do you not want to get out of here?

MARY You are insultin', Mrs. Bradwell. *I have heard nothin' from you in eleven days!*

MYRA Let us tie your corset, quickly. I am on my way to Wisconsin to meet Miss Goodell...

MARY [*deeply hurt*] *Wisconsin?!* Did you truly say Wisconsin?

MYRA Yes, the state has denied Miss Goodell the right to practice. She needs me.

MARY *Pray then, go! Go to Wisconsin! Do not waste another minute! I'm releasin' you as my lawyer—or whatever you are. Please depart!*

MYRA [*referring to a recent newspaper*] I accuse Mr. Patterson in my column of denying your postal rights and threaten a habeas corpus.

MARY [*stares at Myra as she ties Mary's corset*] You look unwell, Mrs. Bradwell. The dark circles under your eyes? Oh, these new steel-busk'd corsets are hateful.

MYRA Have you tried the health bustle? Less heating on the spine.

MARY I've tried nothin'. This is no fashion show. Are you gettin' enough rest?

MYRA I have just been appointed to the convention in Chicago. Susan B. Anthony came to me yesterday...

MARY Ah, your *great* friend!

MYRA She is miffed because I have chosen to go with Lucy Stone and the moderate ladies. I gave Miss Anthony a seat on the platform to assuage her. I barely fit you in. [*getting the dress*] Come, we are wasting time...

MARY Your time is far too precious to be spent with Minions like me! There are *bigger* women who need you more. [*frisbees Myra's flowers out the window*]

MYRA Why, the bars have been removed.

MARY Conveniently. I may simply be one of your causes, Myra, but I pray you to remember I *reside* here. Every mornin' I wake to the knowledge that I'm *locked up*. *Chained.* You suddenly arrive like the Archangel. I can feel your body radiatin' with the world outside. It pains me.

MYRA [*holding out her arms*] My dear girl, embrace me...

MARY Absolutely not. You're all artifice. A carefully orchestrated instrument of manipulation.

MYRA [*trying to get the lawn dress on Mary*] I met with your son...

MARY Yes, he was just here.

MYRA At his office, he accused me of being a high priestess in a gang of spiritualists. I convinced him *no*. Your son has threatened to destroy my paper.

MARY [*looks to the door*] He says my sister's suddenly *too sick* to receive me...

MYRA He *made me a promise* you could go to your sister's, but then he heard I brought *Wilkie* here. He wrote me a lethal letter. Your son is very vindictive... His waistline has certainly expanded...

MARY Yes. When the Patriarch learned that Wilkie was here, *I* was put in solitary quarters. He threatened to send me *up to the most cramped of attic garrets*. To a place where *"a woman cannot even stand up straight—even a short woman."* I withheld that we also *wrote* Wilkie's article.

MYRA We simply drafted it. I *saw* your sister in Springfield: she invites you, and you will go! *Robert is lying.*

MARY He says *my* lyin' should be put down to Insanity. He's left *for vacation* with his family, *to Rye!*

Myra finishes arranging the lawn dress and brandishes a piece of silverware as Mary escapes to her trunks.

MYRA Do you recognize this *silver spoon*? You had a séance before your trial and gave the rest of the service to a *clairvoyant*?

MARY Yes, I gave it to her with *extreme and utter satisfaction.*

MYRA Robert *adored* the service. He has the spoons.

MARY I could not care less if he has the *nut picks* ...

MYRA You will tell me who is this clairvoyant and I will return the service to Robert to appease him!

MARY I *will not!* I see my son has manipulated you well. [*Myra physically forces the name out of Mary; it comes out in a peep*] Mrs. Farwell.

MYRA Your hair, let me brush it ...

MARY Lookin' at yours, I would prefer not. [*going through a trunk*] I can't find the Chantilly curtains for Bessie ...

MYRA Robert *returned* them. He returned *all* the curtains you purchased in Chicago.

MARY Impossible! I am beyond *loathin'* ...

MYRA My daughter will not mind.

MARY I'm not thinkin' of Bessie! Oh, my Lord, he brought those curtains back to all the shopkeepers? If I had committed murder in every city in this blessed union, I could not be more vilified.

MYRA [*fixing Mary's hair*] If I may be so bold, Mrs. Lincoln, what were the *myriad of curtains* for?

MARY You may be so bold. I planned to purchase a cottage in Wisconsin. Finally unpack my things, settle there.

MYRA [*surprised*] In Wisconsin?

MARY Yes. Where you are going. [*Myra takes a pin from her own hair and puts it in Mary's*] To Clear View.

MYRA The spiritual camp?

MARY I liked the mountain air, my windows open to the smell of balsam and pine—white lace curtains blowin' in the wind. A home. That's all I ever wanted. [*with deep anxiety*] What have I done?

MYRA [*showing Mary herself in the mirror*] Here, see how much more respectable you look.

MARY [*raw*] I am sad.

Filloux . Mary and Myra

MYRA [*understanding*] So the curtains were not for some imaginary home after all...

MARY No, they were not. Please send my deepest apologies to your poor daughter, Bessie. No one likes to get their hopes up, especially her...

MYRA You will not bring Bessie up again. I will say it once and for all: I sent her into no burning building.

MARY Myra, your whole family is sufferin'. James told me Bessie bravely entered the *Legal News* to retrieve your subscription lists. *To get your love.*

MYRA James knows perfectly well I would never have sent her in. She went to the paper with him—there was no fire in that part of the city. I asked them to get the lists without knowing it would spread!

MARY This is what I tried to say that day in the shops, out of respect, love. Bessie would do anythin' for you because you have never shown her the love you showed... [*starting to say "Myra"*] that one... the unnamable daughter...

MYRA *Stop.*

MARY You fail to see what's right in front of you. Bessie, the people who love you—

MYRA What do *you* see? I am fighting tirelessly to protect you, but you continue to behave as a selfish, impetuous lady, lost in the dust of her memories.

MARY You must know you've kept a special place in your heart for little Myra.

MYRA You are one to speak—with a son who hates you so completely.

The two women look at one another. Mary draws the blinds, takes a book, and gets into bed.

MARY You must have more important cases.

MYRA [*storms out; after a moment, reenters*] Mary, the secret about his crooked investments? Is there not something we can use? Think about all the terrible things he has done. Would it not please you to make *him* suffer a little?

MARY No, it would not please me. I am his mother. Together, he and I have been through hell. I know what it's like to be maligned by the press. I will not sink so low. He's suffered enough.

MYRA By putting you here, your son has chosen the cheapest way to manage you until the day he gets complete control of your estate. And you are protecting him?

MARY A good mother does.

MYRA I am simply being just. Do you know the Chicago Bar Association, which I myself founded, will not let me in? *And now your son is after me.* [*quickly putting items back in the trunks*] Bellevue, by the way, is going bankrupt. That is why the doctor is so scared of bad press.

MARY I suppose they'll dump us into the garden and leave us to live off the *grass*. Please, close the door on your way out.

MYRA Mrs. Lincoln, after we print the Wilkie article, I promise *the public* will rally to your aid...

MARY The public despises me.

MYRA Nonsense. And I told the press your release can be obtained without appeal to the law. Which is a direct threat to your son. I also said Patterson signed your certificate of recovery.

MARY Your techniques are disingenuous.

MYRA *Any deceit is permissible if the ends are noble.*

MARY [*watching Myra put away her things*] *Please, you are upsettin' the order of my trunks!*

MYRA The *order?*

MARY Yes, there is a *great and infinite order.*

MYRA Your sister confided that you and Robert's wife have a bitter misunderstanding, which is at the source of Robert's anger.

MARY I don't wish to speak ill.

MYRA I must know, so I can help you.

MARY I loved Robert's wife, but *entre nous* she is enamored of the "flowin' bowl."

MYRA The "flowin' bowl"?

MARY Liquor.

MYRA Are you certain?

MARY At her home, I picked up a wrong cup. That cup is always by her side. I said somethin' only because she's havin' a second child. How might a "little life" feel, trapped inside a mother's stomach, showered day in, day out with champagne?

MYRA It might feel very nice—but that is besides the point...

MARY She's not addressed me since.

MYRA She was always a quiet sort.

MARY Oh yes! Robert prefers *quiet* above all else. His wife briefly broke up housekeepin' after I mentioned the *wine*. He has such a horror of bein' talked about! My son now blames me for her sin as well as all my own sins, which are infinite.

MYRA Well, she did play the harp divinely.

MARY Are you here with us at all? What could a *harp* possibly have to do with anythin'? I'm dyin' inside, Myra... I love my son.

MYRA Then it would have been best, Mrs. Lincoln, not to say the truth.

MARY You are just like my son. *A lawyer.*

MYRA Well, that secret will not help us much.

MARY Shouldn't you be goin' to the depot? What about Wisconsin?

MYRA Yes, I will ride all night. Please tell me your son's investment secret, for our sake...

MARY No.

MYRA Have you had recurrences of the kind you had the night I slept here?

A beat.

MARY Since The Red Night, for ten years I have always had the dreams...I do not believe they will ever disappear...Myra, there are memories that cannot be forgotten. That leave an *imprint* on the mind. [*goes to the window; it is twilight*] And love as deep as the sea...It is *I* who approved my Husband's bodyguard. I made no investigation of him. He was drinkin' at the bar The Night the President was shot.

MYRA You are not responsible.

MARY Every joy in my life has been followed by a sorrow. I was too happy in the White House...Willie died...The war was won...Mr. Lincoln...My pension finally came...Tad.

MYRA It only appears this way in times of grief...

MARY *One song* was dedicated to me...

MYRA A polka, was it?

MARY A *funeral march*...By Sousa the Elder. A *dirge*. [*begins to hum the funeral march as she takes steps, walking backwards across the room*]

MYRA I will go; Miss Goodell is such a *brave soldier*...You must be seen downstairs...Mary, why are you doing that?

MARY Mammy Sally told us walkin' backwards at twilight would help the dead to return...When we were children...

MYRA Please, stop.

MARY [*finds a candle in her trunk and lights it*] Last night, for Tad's fourth anniversary, he and Willie appeared at the foot of my bed. They brought with them my half-brother, Little Aleck, killed in the Confederate Army...

MYRA I promise you, you will be free. If we must, James and I will call a court hearing. [*picks up her suitcase*]

MARY The truth, is I envy you your freedom to go, Myra. [*taking out a piece of jewelry*] Pass my imperfections lightly by, and excuse so miserable a production. Durin' my midnight watches, I have searched for this. It's a bracelet... Abraham gave it to me for my birthday. I was forty-four. Set with a pearl... *You* are forty-four...

MYRA No, no, keep it...

MARY It will give me great happiness to think of you wearin' it... in Wisconsin. Would that *I* were that age...

MYRA No, adieu. [*goes to kiss her*]

MARY Get out and never come back.

MYRA Mrs. Lincoln...?

MARY You are a hateful woman. An *ingrate*...

MYRA I am rushed...

MARY You are cold. Cold as ice. Impenetrable. I feel sorry for your husband. I feel sure the picture you paint of domestic bliss is false.

MYRA You are a fool. I have thought that for a time, but I never said it. You conduct yourself as a clown. Your actions show no forethought.

MARY Ah yes, forethought! For you, all is a refined calculation. How sad to live one's life that way...

MYRA How sad to live one's life *this* way. Afraid to go out, abandoning the very standards of cleanliness and femininity...

MARY *I am far from afraid to go outside!* I simply have no reason to go. What would be the purpose?

MYRA The purpose would be to show the staff that you are well, so this case can be won.

MARY Why should I have to prove I'm sane?

MYRA Because you have a history of eccentric acts. Bombarding congressmen with letters for your pension?

MARY What was I to do? I deserved one, and now I have set a precedent for other poor First Ladies.

MYRA Selling your old White House fineries?

MARY Empress Eugénie did it in France to grand success.

MYRA Sending your son telegrams, believing he was dying.

MARY Everyone else has.

MYRA You are not a logical person.

MARY And you are too logical. Your heart must have shriveled to the size of a pea while your manly mind has swollen to a pumpkin.

MYRA You are a vain woman. You say you despise the press, but you scour the papers for your name!

MARY Yes, that is a morbid flaw...

MYRA You regularly disobey the rules.

MARY If I had not *smuggled* a letter to you, you never would've come.

MYRA I came repeatedly. I was turned away. I kept coming and coming until I saw you. On July twenty-ninth.

MARY You know the date. To what end did you come?

MYRA To make you *free*.

MARY To make a name for yourself as a lawyer. I was your callin' card.

MYRA I will leave now, I have nothing more.

MARY Please, wait, you *have* helped me. I'm too sharp-tongued...

MYRA You have no vision. You are a woman who drifts.

MARY [*self-deprecatingly*] I have been called a wanderin' woman, but never "a woman who drifts"...

MYRA Sometimes I ask myself if you *are*...

MARY Crazy? You may say it... "Sanity" is not easy to define, Myra. It is a vast territory with the tallest of mountains and the lowest of caves. [*Myra exits; after a time, Mary throws the bracelet far out the window; she turns and blows out the candle, then begins to walk backwards like a little girl, completely lost*] Every Friday the jaybird goes to hell to tell the devil our doin's... And what shall he say of me? I am low-down. I only hope all who died will lift me. [*sound of children playing*] My mother, dead when I was six. In childbirth. How she must have suffered. She made such a good home. Searchin' for her in Heaven—"white against the evenin' star." [*light shines on a footstool*] And then Mammy Sally, a slave. My true mother. Taught me how spirits can return... in night's softest drafts.

The net billows. Light shines on another footstool. Mary stands with the spirits of her mothers, gaining some peace.

Lights fade.

Scene Two

Twenty days later: September 8. The room has been tidied. Myra's suitcase and a large bouquet of roses sit on the desk. Mary is well groomed and wearing the lawn dress as she clips articles from fresh newspapers. Myra hurries in, brandishing a folder. She is perspiring and worn, a different woman from before.

MYRA *When in God's name did they make you see this McFarland?! Just when I'd finally succeeded!*

MARY [*holding up the front page of a paper*] The Wilkie article turned out beautifully, if we don't say so ourselves! Word for word as we wrote it...

MYRA [*enraged*] *When did you see Dr. McFarland?!* I just heard he was here.

MARY [*holding up other articles*] Dr. Patterson says, here, I can go! The public says, "Let her be released!"

MYRA [*going to Mary*] I am serious: I will find a sharp instrument and I will harm you with it!

MARY Myra, you worry me. [*confused*] When you say a sharp instrument...?

MYRA [*seeming to turn into a wild beast, all her polish gone*] When did you see him?!

MARY Oh my! I saw him yesterday. Your dress is soiled, your hair usually so coifed...

MYRA *You know McFarland is the man who locked up my client Liz Packard?* He's the former president of the Association of Medical Superintendents of the American Institute for the Insane.

MARY Anyone with such a title must be mad!

MYRA [*hits Mary with the folder*] What—I shudder to hear—happened when he saw you?!

MARY He began by sayin' it is not often he meets First Ladies! I said, well with the way they are treated, he'll doubtless meet *more* and *more*. He assured me he was here in the *strictest secrecy*, and I graciously told him there was no need, since the entire nation knew when I so much as *passed wind*. He asked me the Date—which I couldn't remember, since I stopped countin' long ago. The Day of the Week, I didn't happen to know, either. When he asked me the State I lived in, I said, "An Anxious One," and when he asked me the Country, I confidently threw out, "China." For the Planet I told him Venus, and he stopped before Galaxy and Universe!

MYRA [*reading from the folder, she loses control*] "He doubts the safety of your visit to Springfield, fearing a desire for further adventure will take possession of your mind. There are features of your case that give him grave apprehension..."

MARY Are you breathin' sufficiently?

MYRA "Unless the utmost quietude is observed for the few ensuing months, beyond which *all reasonable hope of restoration must be abandoned*." [*takes the bouquet of roses and drops them out the window*] Your son is downstairs now, arranging a *second visit* from Dr. McDill—superintendent of the *Wisconsin* State Hospital for the Insane...

MARY Sit, before you faint...

MYRA *You* paid three hundred and forty-one dollars for your little *divertissement* with McFarland, not to mention what I have paid. You have nullified all that I've done, all that I am.

MARY Rest a moment...

MYRA After what you accused me of at my last visit, I would never have returned for *you*. Your son has threatened to destroy my journal. *I will retaliate.*

MARY I hit bottom at your last visit. There was perhaps one advantage: I could go no lower. I feel surprisin'ly better now...

MYRA You are mad! Only a madwoman would have done what you did. McFarland is a *fearsome* enemy. I know it firsthand. Do you know how he diagnosed Liz Packard as insane? *He took her pulse!*

MARY You should've seen his red face. He's quite a well-fed individual...

MYRA [*going at Mary with the blunt scissors*] Do you know how many women have been placed in asylums? Isabella Hooker, Sophia Vanderbilt—after she gave her husband twelve children—Anna Dickinson. *It was one of the injustices I aimed to correct!*

MARY [*speaking with great dignity and simplicity*] I am finished playin' their game. I don't care. There is a niche for my coffin next to my Husband's. That's all I hope for...

MYRA *Don't speak to me about your husband!* Who could this Great One possibly have been? Certainly not a Human.

MARY If these machinations that you insist on playing must be done with my son—my own blood—I want no part of it. Let me rot away here in this house. It seems more sane to me than outside.

MYRA It has nothing to do with you anymore. It is *my* case and I *will win it*. James and I will think of something.

MARY Ah, your James, so devoted a man.

MYRA Be quiet. Don't talk to me. [*goes to the window*] It has been the most atrocious of days... [*Mary returns to her newspapers*] Since I chose to go with Lucy Stone, I've had a great falling-out with Miss Susan B. Anthony. Miss Anthony has told me that in her great *History of Woman Suffrage*, I will be left out. In the Table of Contents the tips of readers' fingers will pass from B to C, without a mention of Bradwell. In a hundred years, Myra Bradwell will be a woman no one has heard of... *A blank page...*

A beat.

MARY You know, sometimes when you run, Myra—you run away... I believe you mean well with your causes. But you fight so often with the opposite sex, you've become it.

MYRA I have fought endlessly for justice, placing the law ahead of myself on every occasion, and they have ignored me, trampled on me, placed obstacle after obstacle in my path. *I am furious.* Give me the secret about your son.

MARY No, I can't...

MYRA Please, Mary, I beg you. Do it for our sake, for our dignity.

MARY No...

MYRA Your son has not been kind. It is a known fact throughout Chicago that he and his cronies make raucous jests about you at their "stag" parties. He speaks of you as a crazy old Witch, a feeble-minded Loon. Too many hours soaking your wrinkled, pachyderm skin in mineral baths have turned you into a *Sod*—a blithering *Hag*. And his blasphemies become the whispered gossip the next morning of the wives in the highest social circles. He actually *feeds* the papers with this filth. He says you were a terrible wife to your husband and a worse mother... Witness the fact that he is the only one who escaped your curse... As the Good Book commands, your son has Honored his Father, but with his Mother he has fallen quite short. I can assure you Robert does not *honor* you or love you.

MARY When Robert was born to us, we were not rich. It was in a cramped boardin' house—men playin' cards the night away—my husband doin' the circuit, rarely home. But I can tell you that on the day of his birth, his father and I were never happier. He was a source of great wonder to us. We were a circle—the three. Robert was my firstborn, and I have to this day held in him all the hopes a mother could have. Three of my sons were taken, but he *stayed*. I vowed to protect him as a *treasure*, which he is... was... to me. He's a hardheaded boy, but I always thought he'd come 'round—see the error of his ways. [*a beat*] Tell my son that I will expose his disastrous real estate schemes with *John Forsythe* to the papers, if he doesn't let me go.

MYRA *The* John Forsythe? The racketeer?

MARY Yes, Robert squandered a loan from me on Forsythe's shady buildin' contracts. Robert would do anythin' rather than have his name discredited in the press. I believe this information will serve you well.

MYRA [*in wonder*] You had so much hope for your firstborn. I had the same... [*goes to the window and looks out*] You are right about my daughter Myra. I never recovered from her death, and I have only myself to blame for it... I'd just had little Bessie... That day Myra had been out to rally the girls in the neighborhood, to circulate a petition against the Confederate Army—think of that! Her father had written the tract for her. It said anyone who betrayed the Union would be tarred and feathered. All day she and her girls were gathering signatures from neighbors. That night she caught a terrible chill. You know, it took her fifty-two days to die. I sat with her through all of them... I never came back... from that day...

MARY [*gently*] Oh, so now you are such an all-powerful lady, you control the weather and the atmosphere? You alone caused the wind and the rain to go in and chill her little body? I'm sure you must have dressed her exceedin'ly well. I know you, and I know you would've seen to that.

MYRA [*a beat*] She was so strong, I took her for granted. I was preoccupied with the baby...

MARY You are not responsible for the weather. In the same way I'm not responsible for the bodyguard drinkin' on the night my husband was killed...

MYRA [*a beat*] It was tempting fate to name her after me...Vanity.

MARY Love. You have a husband who loves you so much, he will do anythin' for you. Let you name your daughter after yourself...

MYRA A husband who won't forgive me. [*a beat*] I think of her...running across the snow...The sky is blue, from the cold...[*a beat*] I'd like my husband back...He always watches me with Bessie. She wants to please me so much. I try...I can't be myself with her.

MARY She will always want to please you. She will spend her life doin' so...You will have to go through Bessie to get to James. [*there is a knock on the door; Mary goes to answer it; she listens to someone outside the door*] My attendant says Robert asks for you in the Patriarch's office. It's urgent...You should go.

MYRA It's Dr. McDill from Wisconsin.

MARY The closest I'm gonna get to that state...I believe—despite the disingenuousness you all practice in your field—that you have the true spirit of reform, Myra. Though I am an old-fashioned lady, I am not unintelligent. In a different life, perhaps I would have done somethin' altogether surprisin'...

MYRA You've been surprising in this one, Mrs. Lincoln. [*taking Mary's hands*] Thank you. [*exits*]

Mary pages through Dr. McFarland's report, then dumps it out the window. Pages fly. She opens a package on the desk and inspects her four widow's caps. She holds them up to the light, testing the seams and the ribbons. She tries a cap on, but then takes it off and throws it out the window. She gets into bed, singing a hymn softly.

MARY "There are Angels hoverin' around..." [*Myra enters the room; she stands in the doorway*] You must return the caps. They are not well sewn. [*Myra is frozen; Mary goes to her*] Are they sendin' McDill? It's not your fault if they're sendin' me up to the lightless attic...Myra, shall I get you a glass of ice water? You know, in Germany it was impossible to get one...

MYRA They want you to go!

MARY What?

MYRA Mr. Patterson tells Robert it would be well if you could go *at once*. I believe the signed-certificate strategy and the bad press have tipped the scales. He also adds he simply doesn't like you.

MARY [*goes to the window*] Out?

MYRA Yes.

MARY Into the world. To the shops? [*goes to Myra*] Oh, my little Myra... [*helps Myra to sit on the bed*] Rest a moment. Put your feet up. The strain has been too much for you, my girl—this is perhaps why the Creator said no to us bein' lawyers—I will stop. I am incorrigible. My Husband said that. No more about my Husband. The Great One. [*hitting herself*] I will try to be less selfish, more rational. Like you. [*hurries to a trunk*]

MYRA [*speaking more slowly*] I said I would ask if you would see Robert.

MARY [*a beat*] Is he angry?

MYRA Well, I took him aside and said we would be obliged to expose his dealings with Forsythe in the press. Let us simply say extreme caution is necessary when speaking to him.

MARY [*finds cigarettes in her trunk*] These are almost sufficiently temptin' to induce strong-minded women to resort to them in a case of emergency. [*offers Myra a cigarette and takes one for herself; lights them both, and the two women smoke on the bed*] I'm always amazed how everythin' in these trunks has a divine purpose.

MYRA It is impressive... Your official release will be in three days. You'll take the nine o'clock train to Chicago, then Robert and you will board the fifteen-forty for your sister's in Springfield.

MARY Oh, what a ride.

MYRA [*slowly*] Robert says to take only *one* trunk. Since he knows you'll be back. I told him you'll take as many trunks as you want. And I have copies of all your keys.

MARY You seem to be windin' down like a clock...

MYRA I'm very tired...

MARY Of course, my girl, rest. When Robert returns my money, I'll appoint my own conservator and go to Pau in France. I find it necessary to place the ocean between him and me. Any country without waffles, batter cakes, egg corn bread, biscuits, light rolls, buckwheat cakes is a gastronomic desert. It's a curiosity to see how angry these French people can become. The most unprincipled, heartless, avaricious people on the face of the earth. With the exception of a few, I detest them all. Yet the *barometric pressure* there is constant and I speak French. [*looking at Myra*] I have never seen you like that.

MYRA Like what?

MARY Leanin' back, your feet raised. It becomes you. Your face is at rest, your eyes shown off, you have a nice mouth when you aren't pursin' it... You are an extremely handsome woman. A paragon of your sex.

MYRA I am breathing...

MARY You are smokin'. [*they laugh*]

MYRA I shall stay with you for dinner.

MARY No. Never stay at Bellevue one minute longer than you need. Go home... To James and Bessie...

MYRA [*a beat*] You know, she is so tall now, she towers above me...

MARY Impossible. You are a *mastodon*. Almost *masculine* in stature.

MYRA Bessie is a painter, of oils. She speaks French and German... What will I do? [*puts out her cigarette and goes to the window*]

MARY Try to avoid what I have done... [*joining Myra at the window*] I pushed him away, Myra... In many ways I found Robert a *stranger*... I did not bend to him, try... I was the woman I am, and refused. [*a beat*] There is still time... The cost is great, I can assure you.

MYRA I came to you because you were a case that would make me noticed.

MARY Hush...

MYRA [*a beat*] The bracelet you offered me. From your husband. I would be honored to have it, Mary. I was a fool.

MARY The bracelet is gone... It no longer exists. [*goes to her desk drawer and takes out objects*] There is the Pen that signed the Emancipation Proclamation, and this is a bloodstone seal presented to the Great One by the Sultan of Turkey... James should have it, it's brawny. He is a man of great distinction. Admit to him you never should've asked Bessie to run into the fire—even though you knew she would only do it if she could... Men like to think they are right... The Pen is for you... for your emancipations...

MYRA I will place it on my desk at the paper and sign with it every document that passes over. [*moves to the desk and gets her suitcase*]

MARY Give me your hand, Myra... I have learned the Hard Way that this... [*squeezes Myra's hand*] is the only "Great History" we have. You're right here—in the middle of it.

MYRA When you visit Chicago, you will come to us and dine. We will write to each other...

MARY In the night of my life, as I wander the earth lookin' at horizons that *level me*, takin' drinks that leave my throat *scorched*, list'nin' to music that only *blunts* my mind, I will think of you as a *light*... I adore you. You have saved my life. [*kisses Myra goodbye*] Find the key to unlock her, search for it, and I assure you it will unearth a gift you did not expect. I can say this because I did not.

Myra waits a moment, then exits, leaving the door open behind her. Mary stands waiting, then slowly starts to walk backwards out the door. A shaft of red light appears as the sound of a train gets louder and louder. The door shuts. The red light deepens as we see Mary's eyes looking out through the slot. Sound of her hyperventilating. Blackout.

Kidnap Road

TO MY FATHER AND MOTHER, JEAN AND ODETTE FILLOUX

Ingrid Betancourt's story can be found in the public record. Kidnap Road *is imagined as a two-person play based in part on those events. The play's design includes a detailed soundscape. Translation of the English text into Spanish is by Juan Posada, John Araoz, and Marco Antonio Rodriguez.*

Cast of Characters
Woman
Leader / Commander / God / Male Hostage / Father / Young Guerrilla / Guard / Colombian Prisoner, played by one actor.

Woman is in a wooden cage.

Lights shift. At her presidential campaign, sounds of a crowd and applause. Announcer voice-over: "Y ahora vamos a escuchar a la candidata del partido oxígeno verde."*

WOMAN Here is a condom. If you vote for me, you are wearing a condom against corruption. On Election Day let your vote be like Viagra for Colombia.

[*turns to address a different audience*] When you decided to become a guerrilla, when each of you decided, "I'm going to the mountains to fight," what was your intention? Was your intention to take away water and electricity from the poor people you wanted to defend? I don't think so. I believe you joined to say, "We're going to fight for a better society, for social justice." The war makes us all suffer. Together we can make our country a better place. For our children. A consensus for peace will strengthen your movement. A consensus for war will destroy Colombia. I propose that we make unilateral gestures that will allow Colombians to embrace the peace process. There is a gesture for the FARC: "No más secuestros, no más secuestros, no más secuestros."†

Faint sounds of a helicopter approaching.

The night when the game is played. The sky. Blue with a few clouds. Wide open. The beautiful sky, silent sky.

*And now we're going to hear from the candidate of the Oxygen Green Party.

†No more kidnappings.

Sound of chimes.

Quand je parle, je parle en français. O en español? But I am in England, Oxford, so, the language for now will be... English...

[*picks up a book*] And this is the book they gave me. The Bible. A bestseller.

Helicopter sounds get louder.

MEN [*voice-over; loudly*] *Todos, vamos! Vamos! Vamos!**

LEADER [*loudly; dashing by her*] *Vamos! Vamos!*

WOMAN We are in the middle of a coca field. A helicopter is waiting.

LEADER [*loudly*] *Vamos! Vamos!*

WOMAN The men from the helicopter are dressed in Che Guevara T-shirts, and one man—the leader—is holding a clipboard. The Absurd.

LEADER [*loudly*] *Entren en el helicóptero! Entren en el helicóptero! La tenemos que esposar!*†

WOMAN The leader wraps plastic around my wrists. A Venezuelan news station films me. What made me get in the helicopter? With the people dressed in Che Guevara T-shirts?

Helicopter sound fades and turns into the ticking of a clock. Commander forces her to march.

COMMANDER *Muévete! Camina! Muévete!*‡

WOMAN [*marching with Commander*] There are sixty seconds in a minute.

Sixty minutes in an hour.

Twenty-four hours in a day.

If I see the hands moving, then I know that you are here.

That you are in the same time as me.

But time is not chronological, nor logical, and what does it even mean here: time?

Commander orders them to stop marching, takes off his gun, and lies down. Assortment of jungle sounds.

WOMAN Just before dawn, the jungle is at its most still. But there is never silence. Ever. The flies buzz, the birds make their very *special* sounds...

Sounds of jungle birds shrieking and croaking.

Sometimes you have to laugh. A praying mantis crawls up the side of my cage. Then a scorpion. The light slowly turns the color black to green. God, if you give me a little bit of sky today, I'll give you...

God appears.

---

*Let's go, everyone! Let's go! Let's go!

†Get into the helicopter! We need to handcuff you!

‡Move! Let's get walking!

GOD What will you give me?

WOMAN Why do we bargain, God? Why do we have to bargain all the time?

GOD Well?

WOMAN I don't have anything left to give, God.

GOD [*laughing*] What about humility?

A beat.

WOMAN Those words, God? The ones I kept repeating in front of the guerrillas…?

GOD [*laughing*] Yes?

WOMAN "No más sequestros, no más sequestros, no más sequestros." They were laughing at me.

God laughs as he exits.

Okay, okay, okay. I am pretty. I am privileged. I come from a well-known Colombian family. I have strong ties to France. This is particularly offensive to those who hate me. But a woman shouldn't fight. Right, God?

GUARD [*voice-over; loudly*] Pónganse en fila! Preséntese!*

MALE HOSTAGE 1 [*voice-over*] Number one.

MALE HOSTAGE 2 [*voice-over*] Number two.

MALE HOSTAGE 3 [*presenting himself*] Number three.

WOMAN [*presenting herself*] Use my name!

OTHER HOSTAGES [*voice-over*] Number five. Number six. Number seven.

MALE HOSTAGE 3 Hey, can't you just give them a number?

WOMAN Why?

MALE HOSTAGE 3 You always have to act special. You know, everyone says you're a diva. You deserve a birthday cake for your daughter? You need special books of your own. You always have to make everything harder for us.

WOMAN Why do you want to be a number?

MALE HOSTAGE 3 Be quiet!

WOMAN It all begins with that "Why?"

Sounds of a plane overhead.

COMMANDER [*ordering*] Todos al suelo!† [*drops to the ground*]

Sound of a plane passing over. Woman continues to stand, listening as the sound of the plane fades.

*Line up! Present yourselves!

†Get down!

WOMAN *Why* don't you stop the kidnappings?

COMMANDER [*making fun of her*] *No más sequestros, ay Doctora. Somos las FARC.** We are the *people's* army, working to fight for the rights of peasants, fighting against imperialism. You're running for president, but you're no better than one of our own hundreds of guerrilla prisoners rotting in your government's jail cells. When you were a senator, why didn't you arrange for a prisoner exchange with us?

*We are the FARC.

WOMAN I came to your village—I tried to work with you...

COMMANDER You aren't in touch with the real people, *Doctora*—your presidential campaign is going nowhere. No one remembers you.

WOMAN I gave you a chance, I talked with you—we shared a meal together.

COMMANDER Kidnapping is a trade in Colombia.

WOMAN I listened to you.

COMMANDER Wasn't it you who just appeared on TV, so earnest with your makeup and your fancy sunglasses, your jewelry, repeating: *"No más secuestros, no más secuestros, no más secuestros..."*

WOMAN [*overlapping*] When everyone said peace is impossible, I said it is possible. And this is what you do to me—while I'm running for president, you take me hostage?

COMMANDER [*overlapping*] This is a good lesson for you, *Doctora*. How long will it take you to understand the lesson of what it really means to be poor and a peasant, fighting for your basic rights, with no privileges, no mansions, chandeliers, high-fashion suits, five-star restaurants? And with that air of false humility you've learned so well from your politician mother and your diplomat father.

WOMAN [*repeating to herself, like a mantra*] *Has tenido tantas oportunidades en la vida... Yo te veo... Has tenido tantas oportunidades en la vida... Yo te veo...*

FATHER [*enters echoing her words; sound of a piano*] The naïve romantic, *mija*, you never learn. You want to risk your life and the lives of your children?

WOMAN I have no choice. You never wanted my mother to do this kind of work, and you feel the same about me.

FATHER You are my daughter, and I want you to be safe.

WOMAN I have to fight. Look, I don't want to fight with you...

FATHER You're full of contradictions. You are right—I had opinions about your mother.

WOMAN I wish you could see her, I wish you could see me. You are not treating me for who I am. You want to see someone else.

FATHER You don't actually know what you want. *Mija*, listen, there is nothing more dangerous than a feminine feminist.

WOMAN Was it the condom, Father? Did that shock you? And the Viagra?

FATHER It is beneath you. Beneath us!

WOMAN Corruption is beneath us all. It worked. I won in the Senate. This is my country.

FATHER You shame me…

Sounds of rain and boards cracking.

WOMAN My wooden cage has a flimsy board. I begin to press my foot on it. It makes a cracking sound.

Guard looks over at her.

Does he hear what I did?

Guard looks away.

I check my pocket: the vitamins, save them. At night, in the dark, the best time to think. The flashlight I stole, that I hid in the *chontos*. Crumple the paper into a mound, a fake body so it looks like someone is still sleeping there. A sleeping body.

Sounds of a storm.

The wind. Finally. There's no choice. Who knows when there will be another storm like this? Crack open the board wider. Match the cracking with the thunder.

Sounds of cracking.

Squeeze through the hole in the wood, out of the cage.

Sounds of rain.

The pouring rain.
Feel only the leaves, the roots, tripping, running, one foot in front of the other, slipping downward, towards the river.
Never turn on the light—it's too dangerous if I am seen. The dark is safer than the flashlight.

Sounds of jungle intensify.

The dark is safer.
Pitch dark.

Lights go out completely.

I put my hands out in front of me. To feel my way.
What is there? A pit in the ground? A landmine? The sharp teeth of an animal?
I turn on the flashlight.

Explosion of light.

A gigantic banyan tree, vines strangling upward to the invisible sky.
I turn it off.

I'm free. I'm free. Running.
Get far away while it's still dark.
The river should be soon.

Dawn, alone in the jungle.
Bury myself under leaves.
Body under leaves.
To return.
Small orchids that look like little red birds...

The space of being out of the cage.

[*looks up at the sky*] The space to move. The sky.

YOUNG GUERRILLA [*finding her, points his rifle*] *Señora*, please, listen to me. You have to think clearly. To understand us better. My father was a coca farmer—he got killed in a raid—

WOMAN Listen, we'll go together—you can do it. We can run away together.

YOUNG GUERRILLA I grew up with the FARC—they gave me food, clothes, when I had nothing. They taught me to read and write—

WOMAN You know the jungle—you know the way. We can do it, don't use the handcuffs—

YOUNG GUERRILLA No one believed in my dignity that way, *Señora*. I'm a Communist, I believe in the revolution. Now come, come with me. [*handcuffs her*] They are going to punish you. That is what is going to happen. It will be very bad. Try to say nothing to them, *Señora*.

WOMAN I will say something! You are pigs!

YOUNG GUERRILLA Then you will only suffer more.

WOMAN During my rape, he...they...

Nothing.

The love of my mother and father, their strength like a mountain, their voices, their world. My children—her joy—his trust—their sweetness. The way their hands lace themselves in mine. In the fire of my center, their spirit is like a flame that never goes out. It simply burns steady. It cannot ever go out because of this love. It will never go out.

After
In cold muddy river water
Skin broken
Bathing
Washing my dirty hair
My body
Salt water falling in
Shock

For as long as they let me
Stay
In the green water, before they chain me.

COMMANDER Okay, *Doctora*, we're filming the Proof of Life. Come on!

Sound of whirring video camera. Commander provides her with a stool, motioning for the filming to begin. She sits and bows her head, sick, completely silent. He motions to someone to turn off the camera.

This silence is only going to make things worse for you, *Doctora*. You need to show the world a Proof of Life. That's your only chance for survival, *Doctora*. Laugh on camera a little for them, sing a little, tap your foot. Say something! [*motions for the camera to roll again*]

WOMAN [*speaking to herself*] Here, now, God, in front of the commander's camera, I give up on you.
Skin yellow. The waving of the white flag.
These are the bargains I make.
Don't come up for air
Don't look out the hole
Don't look for creatures who light up in the dark
Stay in this cocoon of the sleeping criminal
Limbo between life and death.
—I promise to let you know when you can come and take me for good.
Heart beating
Mouth breathing
Skin pores open
Shitting
Pissing
Tear ducts
Soul a crater with *stagnant poison*.
It's over. No Proof of Life for anyone—especially not you, God!
I've finally lost the "Why?" I surrender.

COMMANDER [*motioning for the camera to stop*] You better talk soon. Those special blue jeans you've tried to hide for so long—they wouldn't fit you anymore anyway. Put some fat on that ass!
And your hair and your moustache. [*takes away her stool*]

MOTHER [*voice on radio*] *Te amamos, ma chérie.**

WOMAN *Maman*, I wait every day for your voice on the radio.

MOTHER [*voice on radio*] *Estamos pensando en ti. Nos vas a ver muy pronto, te lo prometemos.*†

WOMAN I promise, too, I'll see you soon.

MOTHER [*voice on radio*] *No podemos comer tu plato favorito, coq au vin, hasta que te volvamos a ver.*‡

---

*We love you, my dear.

†We are thinking of you. You will see us again very soon, we promise.

‡We can't eat your favorite dish until we see you again.

WOMAN You're so funny—you stopped cooking coq au vin?

MOTHER [*voice on radio*] *Vamos a hacer coq au vin para tí cuando regreses. Estamos trabajando duro...**

WOMAN You hear that, God? She's working with the government on my rescue. She is always there because she knows. The stakes are in our bones.

GOD She left her children for politics, too. That's why you're being punished. Because you left your children. The legacy of leaving.

WOMAN [*overlapping*] Oh, shut up. Then why did the bullet hit him and not her?

GOD You're asking that again?

WOMAN Why did you take Galán? The best president we could've had? And my mother escaped his bullet by *a fraction*.

GOD Fate?

WOMAN What?

GOD That's why you came back to fight like your mother. It would be good for you to think about fate.

WOMAN When she speaks to me on the radio, does she think I'm dead?

GOD She has the same audacity as you. The entitlement of the wealthy, of those who have been handed everything on a silver platter!

WOMAN I need them to know I'm trying to get back to them, God.

MOTHER [*imagined voice on radio*] *Lo sabemos, amor.*†

WOMAN *Maman?*

MOTHER [*imagined voice on radio*] *Sabemos que estás haciendo el intento.*‡

WOMAN You can hear me?

MOTHER [*imagined voice on radio*] *Yo sé que estás viva, mija. Eres valiente, cariño. Entonces pues... Vamos a tomarnos una tacita de té.*§

WOMAN I can't have a cup of tea, *Mamita*. I'm imagining things.

GUARD [*voice-over; loudly*] *¡Pónganse en fila!*

MALE HOSTAGE 1 [*voice-over*] Number one.

MALE HOSTAGE 2 [*voice-over*] Number two.

MALE HOSTAGE 3 Number three.

WOMAN Use my name!

OTHER HOSTAGES [*voice-over*] Number five. Number six. Number seven.

MALE HOSTAGE 3 Hey, hey, hey, I'm really, really sorry you lost your election.

---

*We will make coq au vin for you again when you return. We are working hard...

†We know, my dear.

‡We know you're trying.

§Yes, I know you're alive, *mija*. You're brave, *ma chérie*. Now, let's go out for a nice cup of tea.

WOMAN I never think about my election anymore.

MALE HOSTAGE 3 Oh, hey, wow, forgive me—I never should have brought it up. *Sor-ry.*

WOMAN There's a word I've heard about in English. It's "passive-aggressive"?

MALE HOSTAGE 3 That's two words.

WOMAN I'm no longer a politician!

[*speaking in her role as a politician; sound of a crowd and applause*] Because of you, President Samper—you are aware—Colombians cannot travel abroad without being instantly suspected as drug traffickers. You have ruined our international image and plunged the country into terror and uncertainty. I am demanding an independent investigation of your corruption, one that is not infiltrated by the drug cartel. I call a hunger strike until our country is given an honest investigation.

God appears.

Okay, I lied to the "passive-aggressive" American hostage—I obviously *do* still think about my presidential election. It makes me angry that I lost, God.

GOD You didn't have a chance in *hell* of winning.

WOMAN Hell?

GOD Yes, I use that word. When it applies.

WOMAN Why?

GOD You're asking that again?

WOMAN I should have won. That's a secret! Please don't repeat it.

God laughs.

The problem is, there are no secrets from God. And God says different things on different days.

Male Hostage 3 pulls out the strands of steel wool from Brillo pads and throws them up in the trees.

WOMAN [*making fun of the way he speaks*] Hey, hey, hey, hey. What are you doing?

MALE HOSTAGE 3 Stole a box of Brillo pads from the kitchen—to get better radio reception. Why are they buildin' a fence around the camp?

WOMAN To make it harder for us to escape.

MALE HOSTAGE 3 Right, you are the celebrity.

WOMAN I'm not a celebrity.

MALE HOSTAGE 3 You're a star in France. Joan of Arc.

WOMAN Not exactly Jeanne d'Arc.

MALE HOSTAGE 3 The guerrillas' biggest trophy. As long as they have you alive they have negotiating power.

WOMAN They have no negotiating power—the government won't agree to exchange their prisoners for us hostages.

MALE HOSTAGE 3 Having you alive brings them fame. You keep the light on them.

WOMAN How did you think of that with the Brillo pads?

MALE HOSTAGE 3 That's all I have: *time to think*.

WOMAN Thank you.

GUARD [*voice-over; loudly*] *Pónganse en fila! Preséntese!*

MALE HOSTAGE 1 [*voice-over*] *Número uno.*

MALE HOSTAGE 2 [*voice-over*] *Número dos.*

WOMAN *Número tres.*

COLOMBIAN PRISONER *Número cuatro.*

WOMAN *Querido.*

COLOMBIAN PRISONER *Querida.*

OTHER HOSTAGES [*voice-over*] *Número cinco. Número seis. Número siete.*

She smiles at Colombian Prisoner optimistically.

COLOMBIAN PRISONER Someday we'll find each other, *querida,* on a street corner, and we'll say, Let's go in the middle of the day for a paella.

WOMAN We have an imagined language. I can read my friend's face like a book. He actually says *nothing*.
I say to him:

Don't.

Leave.

Me.

No me dejes.

A guard takes him away.
I knew him in the Senate, before we were hostages. Water is punching behind my lids.

Ne me quitte pas.

COLOMBIAN PRISONER [*voice on radio*] *Estoy vivo, querida. Los venezolanos me ayudaron a escapar y ahora Francia te va a ayudar a tí. Los gobiernos de Francia y de Colombia están luchando por tí!**

---

*I am alive, dear. The Venezuelans helped me to escape, and now France is going to help you. The French and Colombian governments are fighting for you!

106   *Mānoa* . *Eyes of the Heart*

WOMAN *Querido,* you've been rescued! Venezuela, France, Colombia—they're fighting for me.

COLOMBIAN PRISONER [*voice on radio*] *No te preocupes, todos te están esperando, tu volverás!**

WOMAN Yes, I will come home.

MOTHER [*voice on radio*] *Mi querida hija, todos los niños en nuestro orfanato están cantando y rezando por ti!*†

WOMAN The orphanage is praying for me.

MOTHER [*voice on radio*] *Ellos están muy agradecidos contigo por el trabajo que has hecho y agradecidos con nuestra familia.*‡

WOMAN No, I'm so grateful for the work you've done, *Maman.*

MALE SPOKESMAN [*voice on radio*] The American government refuses to negotiate with these terrorists. We simply have to sacrifice the hostages. They are like terminally ill patients.

WOMAN We are terminally ill. Actually we *are* ill. The guerrillas put us into a boat, and we take a long boat ride down the river.

Sounds of splashing water.

The same river where you and I tried to escape, *querido*. Why, God?

GOD "Why?" is your torturer.

WOMAN "Why?" is not my torturer, God. "Why?" is my salvation! You *see* the children—they know everything about peace. *Why* do the adults act like roosters at a cockfight? You know, the roosters are given muscle-building hormones and antibiotics so they can fight longer.

GOD You are getting off track with these roosters.

WOMAN You're right. But the children, God. My children.

Bright sunlight.

WOMAN [*to herself*] The sun. Oh, my God, he's so happy. The water...

BOY [*voice-over*] Try to catch me! Come in further, *Maman.*

WOMAN Don't go too far, *mon chéri.*

BOY [*voice-over*] You can see me, look!

GIRL [*voice-over*] You can see me, too, *Maman,* look!

WOMAN Yes, *ma chérie,* you're doing so well.

GIRL [*voice-over*] Can I go further?

WOMAN Not past your belly button. [*to herself*] Frothy all around. I can taste it. Salt on my tongue.

---

*Don't worry, everyone is waiting for you, you are coming home!

†My dear daughter, all the children at our orphanage are singing and praying for you!

‡They are so grateful to you for the work you have done, and to our family.

BOY [*voice-over*] I can swim!

WOMAN I see you.

BOY [*voice-over*] Come and get me. *Maman*!

WOMAN Sun on my skin, hot, bright...

GIRL [*voice-over*] Why does he get to go further, *Maman*? That's not fair.

WOMAN Because he can swim, *chérie*. Just make sure your feet can touch the bottom.

GIRL [*voice-over*] I want to swim! Your hand under my stomach, *Maman*.

WOMAN Yes, here. [*placing her hand*] Now, move your arms and your feet... Good... At the same time.

GIRL [*voice-over*] I'm swimming!

WOMAN You are, darling.

BOY [*voice-over*] I can swim, *Maman*!

WOMAN They're both so happy. We all are.

BOY [*voice on radio*] Eres buena gente, madre—eres dulce.*

WOMAN You're my sweet.

GIRL [*voice on radio*] Todavía estás viva! Sé fuerte. Como siempre nos enseñaste, mami.†

GIRL / BOY [*voices on radio*] Te adoramos.‡

WOMAN [*overlapping*] When you say I'm still alive, do you believe it?

There is only what we are.
Our *love* sewn together:
a trip we took...

Wave goodbye to your father.

BOY [*voice-over*] Goodbye, Papa!

GIRL [*voice-over*] Goodbye, Papa!

WOMAN Come—do you want to walk or take the bus?

GIRL [*voice-over*] The bus!

BOY [*voice-over*] I can't see his car anymore, *Maman*.

WOMAN He'll come back to get you, and I am with you now.

BOY [*voice-over*] Why don't you live with us?

WOMAN It's too dangerous for you in Colombia.

---

*You are good, Mother—you are sweet.

†You are still alive! Be strong. Like you always taught us, Mommy.

‡We adore you.

BOY [*voice-over*] Why don't you like Papa?

WOMAN I like him. I need to work for our country, like your grandmother. Do you want to put the money into the coin box?

BOY [*voice-over*] Yes! I paid for the bus by myself!

WOMAN You did, sweetie.

GIRL [*voice-over*] *Maman*, look at the flames burning in the lamps outside.

WOMAN They are coach lights. It's the Dakota. A famous lady lives there.

GIRL [*voice-over*] Who?

WOMAN Yoko Ono.

GIRL [*voice-over*] *You're* famous.

WOMAN No.

GIRL [*voice-over*] You're on the cover of magazines in France.

WOMAN I'm your mother.

GIRL [*voice-over*] The flames look like a campfire.

WOMAN They will never go out. What do you want to see today?

BOY [*voice-over*] The dinosaurs. Dinosaurs!

GIRL [*voice-over*] The whales, with sprouts . . . spouts!

WOMAN They run ahead
up the stairs.
Her white stockings—my son's blue coat.
His beautiful smile, her hair cut to her jawbone.

YOUNG GUERRILLA *Señora—despiértate!*

WOMAN I wake up with a start.

Always

With a start.

It is the sameness.
How has this happened?
Stasis, based on illness, hepatitis, complete and utter capitulation of the body.

I move my neck.
Can you take off the chain?
No, I won't ask.
Not asking is a victory.

Sounds of a plane overhead. Guard whistles.

YOUNG GUERRILLA *Todos al suelo!* [*drops to the ground*]

Sound of a plane passing overhead. Woman listens to the fading sound of the plane.

WOMAN Today is my daughter's birthday.

YOUNG GUERRILLA Pack up your things, we're moving to a new compound.

WOMAN I need to make her a cake. I need a birthday cake.

YOUNG GUERRILLA We're late—I'll talk to the commander in a minute!

WOMAN What is a minute right now?
It is sixty ticks of a clock.
Tocks.
Are all clocks the same?
Every day I do twenty pushups. *Real* ones.
For two years I do twenty-five.
Increase until I reach twenty-seven.
More years I stay at twenty-seven.
Then for a while I can only reach thirty.

I watch some of the guys doing...a lot more.

Ugggh. That makes me so mad.
Now, I start to do one more for me and one for my *querido,* my fellow Colombian. Right now, he's ill.

Jungle sounds.

COLOMBIAN PRISONER *Querida,* I found three more *tagua* seeds.

WOMAN Good! And I know you're making a calendar to remember your wife's birthday. *I'm* making a backpack.

Time *used* to feel like claustrophobia. The same claustrophobia as not seeing the sky. No light. I felt as if I was going crazy.

COLOMBIAN PRISONER And now?

WOMAN My bones feel like the soft bones of birds and at the same time like sharp needles.

COLOMBIAN PRISONER Don't be so dramatic!

WOMAN Everything is in contradiction. I hold only contradictions now. I want to drink something cool and refreshing like orange juice. I want to fall asleep, parched, as if the sweet liquid itself will kill me.

COLOMBIAN PRISONER Drink some water!

WOMAN What is the French word for fly?

COLOMBIAN PRISONER [*mispronouncing it terribly*] Mouche.

WOMAN [*a beat*] You are a brilliant student. And *se moucher* also means to blow your nose. I *mouche le nez de la mouche.*

COLOMBIAN PRISONER [*laughing*] I like that. *Mouche le nez de la mouche.*

WOMAN See, you just needed encouragement.

Don't show repugnance for the flies, or the sand where they burrow. It's the disease you get from sandflies. They feast on his flesh.

Sounds of buzzing.

Who wrote *Les Mouches*?

COLOMBIAN PRISONER Charles Darwin?

WOMAN Try...again. Charles Darwin? You have no idea. Jean-Paul Sartre wrote *The Flies*, based on the Electra myth. Existential. You never would have imagined you'd get to spend so much "quality time" in the jungle with me!

COLOMBIAN PRISONER "Quality time" is a *gringo* concept—in Colombia, there is no time that isn't "quality."

WOMAN I never was that good at English.

COLOMBIAN PRISONER You speak perfect English.

WOMAN You're always biased. Maybe you're in love with me? I am in love with you. You're my only reason for being and I have no reason for being at all, another contradiction. But we can talk of everything—that's why it's "quality time," right? Remember Rilke? *Letters to a Young Poet*? My boy would listen to a tape from school of Catherine Deneuve reading it. Could anything be more beautiful than his face, listening to her calm, serene voice? This is what I remember of Rilke now: "Even if you were in jail and robbed of all your senses, you would still have your childhood, that precious house of memories. Turn to that. Look for the hidden sensations in your plentiful past and you will grow stronger, your solitude will blossom and the noise of others will go away." [*joking*] Well, Rilke is a liar, an asshole, a charlatan, and a blowhard. Who wants solitude? I want my family. My "precious house of memories" is nothing! I despise Rilke! If I had his book right now, I would burn it!

COLOMBIAN PRISONER [*laughing*] You are a terrible liar. If you had his book, you would devour it. If only we had more books besides *Harry Potter*.

WOMAN I finished the backpack, but our food is rotting. We must make it to the river. With you I will succeed.

COLOMBIAN PRISONER What's a river full of piranhas after the corrupt politicians you've been fighting? *Querida*, I can't go—the booster shots are making me sick.

WOMAN You need to eat more. You'll get better. Soon we'll go.

COLOMBIAN PRISONER *Querida*, you're mad at Rilke—you want to make *new* memories, is that it? [*a beat*] No one is looking. You have a beautiful body. I noticed that long ago.

WOMAN Really? You never said. We'd pass each other in the halls—you barely looked.

COLOMBIAN PRISONER You're the most beautiful woman I've ever known.

WOMAN You are a terrible liar.

COLOMBIAN PRISONER "Quality time." [*takes a gentle step toward her*]

WOMAN For Camus it's all *Absurd*. Time moves fluidly, there is no past, present, future in the jungle. The Existentialists, the Absurdists, it's the perfect time to talk about the Absurd. Camus was happy in the theater. He called the theater "the night when the game is played." *Le soir où la partie se joue.* I was a philosophy student in France before I became a politician.

COLOMBIAN PRISONER Really?

WOMAN I directed Camus's play *The Misunderstanding* in college.

COLOMBIAN PRISONER Woah.

WOMAN I used a film noir style. Here is the play performed for you in the jungle.

COLOMBIAN PRISONER Theater, for me? Now?

WOMAN [*as Martha, in film noir style*] On dit que, dans ces régions, il y a des plages tout à fait désertes?

COLOMBIAN PRISONER [*joining in as Jan*] It's true. Nothing recalls man. At dawn one finds on the sand the traces left by the feet of the sea birds. These are the only signs of life. As for the evenings...

WOMAN [*as Martha*] Quant aux soirs, Monsieur...?

COLOMBIAN PRISONER [*as Jan*] The evenings are shattering. Yes, it's a beautiful country.

WOMAN [*as Martha*] J'y ai souvent pensé. Des voyageurs m'en on parlé, j'ai lu ce que j'ai pu.

COLOMBIAN PRISONER I don't get it.

WOMAN [*as Martha*] Je pense à la mer et aux fleurs de là-bas. Et ce que j'imagine me rend aveugle à tout ce qui m'entoure.

COLOMBIAN PRISONER I still don't understand.

Sounds of a helicopter.

WOMAN Camus says: Certainty is impossible. You don't know how long you're staying, or if you Exist. It's about you—all of us. How did we lose our country? No one can understand that.

Sounds of a helicopter.

LEADER [*loudly; dashing by her*] *Entren en el helicóptero! Entren en el helicóptero!* [*begins to handcuff her with a plastic cable tie*] *La tenemos que esposar!*

WOMAN The leader wraps plastic around my wrists. A Venezuelan news station films me to show we're alive. The news station wants to interview our guerrilla commander.

COMMANDER *Somos las FARC. Hablamos en el helicóptero!** *

*We are the FARC. We'll talk in the helicopter!

WOMAN Who are these people in the Che Guevara T-shirts?

There is a divide between the stagnant air of the jungle and the fluid air where the birds fly to get away.

God, why not let me fly away to them, my boy and girl?

GOD Because you're not a bird. You can't fly.

WOMAN Why do you have to be so damn literal, God?

GOD Why do you have to be such a dreamer?

WOMAN I'm not.

GOD The naïve romantic.

A beat.

WOMAN The terrible guilt of leaving them.

GOD The legacy of leaving your children.

WOMAN For a higher cause, God.

GOD What cause can be higher?

WOMAN That's easy for you to say. All the children are supposed to be *your* children, but I don't understand what you are doing to them!

GOD The misunderstanding.

Loud sounds of rain.

COLOMBIAN PRISONER *Querida,* hurry, it's coming down!

WOMAN Get the backpack.

Banging sounds of empty oil drums.

COLOMBIAN PRISONER The drums make too much noise.

WOMAN We'll need them to float—keep going—don't stop.

COLOMBIAN PRISONER Pitch dark.

WOMAN Hold on—hold on.

Sounds of guards talking, laughing.

WOMAN Run, the guards aren't paying attention.

COLOMBIAN PRISONER The mud.

WOMAN Crawl.

COLOMBIAN PRISONER I can't.

WOMAN Yes, one foot in front of the other.

COLOMBIAN PRISONER I'm *crawling*.

WOMAN One knee then.

COLOMBIAN PRISONER Okay, one knee.

WOMAN Jump in—float.

COLOMBIAN PRISONER Black—

WOMAN Like obsidian.

COLOMBIAN PRISONER *Querida*, the oil drums, you're a genius.

WOMAN Jeanne d'Arc.

COLOMBIAN PRISONER Jeanne d'Arc never got kissed like that.

WOMAN No.

COLOMBIAN PRISONER Piranha water.

The current carries them.

Look, the egrets, the birds.

WOMAN The clouds are so dark—the sky seems to go on forever.
I'm soaked, you can't see my tears.
The special jeans are wet in my backpack.

COLOMBIAN PRISONER You're still carrying those?

WOMAN There is never any sun. We can't transform into water animals. As the days go by, we are still human.

COLOMBIAN PRISONER So cold.

WOMAN We'll catch fish.

COLOMBIAN PRISONER We have too many fishhooks, and zero matches.

WOMAN Didn't someone teach you how to make a fire?

COLOMBIAN PRISONER Didn't someone teach you?

WOMAN Raw fish—sushi. Delicious. Really, delicious.

COLOMBIAN PRISONER [*laughing*] Okay. This is a great delicacy, created by you, on a leaf.

WOMAN Please, I insist, eat more.

A beat.

COLOMBIAN PRISONER You need to go on without me, *querida*. I'm holding you back. Please. I just need to go to sleep.

WOMAN If you fall asleep, you might not wake up.

COLOMBIAN PRISONER Go! This is your only chance—you'll make it.

A beat.

WOMAN Don't.

Leave.

Me.

I heard him say, in our imagined language. *No me dejes.*

COLOMBIAN PRISONER You can do anything, go! You almost ousted the president from office.

WOMAN But I didn't succeed. A good portion of the Senate was paid off by the cartel.

COLOMBIAN PRISONER [*laughing*] I wasn't.

WOMAN Would you tell me if you were?

COLOMBIAN PRISONER [*a beat*] Of course.

WOMAN Really?

COLOMBIAN PRISONER You were on fire. No one dared do what you did.

WOMAN The President was found innocent.

COLOMBIAN PRISONER So you'll try again!

WOMAN We'll wait for someone to come by in a boat. A fisherman. *Querido,* I won't leave you.

Sound of chimes.

[*picks up the Bible*] It's been years—my watch is still on jungle time, it's strange. But now the feelings I have for it are completely different.

I'm a student again. In England. Oxford, PhD, theology.
I was trying to negotiate with the guerrillas before I got kidnapped.
For the peace talks to work, the guerrillas have to be given the chance to participate in the government. We must suspend their jail sentences. It is essential that we make that move now! Land reform, disarmament—the high commander, who gave me this Bible, died. He is with God now.
And forgiveness...?

Sound of gunshot.

I wake up with a gashed face?
The machete goes through my forehead like an egg, it cracks so fast.
They are trying to stitch me up, and the blood is pouring out.
The guerrilla is barely a teenager. In camouflage. His skin so smooth. Sleek.

YOUNG GUERRILLA *Señora, no se preocupe,* we have our own hospital out here in the jungle.

WOMAN It would be okay for me to live without a face. I would depend, instead, on my soul...?

YOUNG GUERRILLA *No se preocupe,* we have very good surgical care here in the jungle, but you'll just have to wait your turn!

WOMAN Eyes, eyeballs are swimming in front of me into nostrils that dissolve into aquiline cheekbones that sag under the weight of a knife that went in too deep, with the neck shot in by an assault rifle. Look, mercenaries are training here in the jungle. Flesh splatters everywhere so that we are running across the forest to try to collect... fingers, ears? Yes, ears. If you can just retrieve the appendages for your face to be whole again...

Sound of gunshot.

I was dreaming. Dreams within dreams.

COMMANDER That look on your face, *Doctora.*

WOMAN Why are you forcing a sick man to walk barefoot? The jungle is filled with snakes.

COMMANDER Your *lover* is being punished for your escape down the river! You know you should never speak back to the guards. That just makes it worse.

WOMAN Why are you torturing him? Give him back his shoes!

COMMANDER You better stop!

WOMAN Give them back!

COMMANDER Now you will live in chains forever.

Jungle sounds get louder.

WOMAN [*marching*] I'll carry my chains. The Amazon is Existential; it goes on forever.

COMMANDER [*laughing*] *La ingenua romántica, Doctora. Ustéd nunca aprende!**

WOMAN You guerrillas aren't Communists with a plan to help your countrymen—I grew up on Che Guevara, too, on the romantic idea of revolution.

Commander laughs.

---

*The naïve romantic, Doctora. You never learn!

I thought you were rebelling against what I also hated. But you're drug lords—the army of the drug cartels. All you care about is *power*: the biggest trucks, rifles, the most beautiful girls to seduce with your toys. You're just as corrupt as the system you say you hate!

COMMANDER [*laughing*] *Ay, Doctora*, the truth is like this jungle. Look at this jungle. Is it predictable? You have to be ready for *anything*, like me and my woman. [*whistling*] Come to Daddy, baby, I know what my girl can do, but that's because *love* is unpredictable. Isn't that right? [*sound of a plane overhead; he whistles*] *Todos al suelo!* [*drops to the ground*]

Sound of plane passing overhead. Woman continues to stand, listening to the fading sound of the motor as the plane flies away. Sounds of rain.

[*laughing*] You're already the weakest of the group. Your books are too heavy, they're slowing you down, *Doctora*.

WOMAN I won't give up the books.

They march.

It's raining—can I take shelter in the tent?

COMMANDER Shut up, you know the answer!

They march.

WOMAN Can I use the *chontos*?

COMMANDER From now on, no *chontos*—you'll have to do it out here, in front of everyone. You don't get any special treatment. You're just an animal.

WOMAN You are the animal! *Don't you dare do this to me!*

COMMANDER Get down on the ground and shit.

She stumbles.

YOUNG GUERRILLA *Señora.* [*catches her*]

They are back on a forced march. She is sick with hepatitis and weak.

Some of the guerrillas spread rumors that you're a snake. I know you're not.

WOMAN I'm sorry you have to carry me.

YOUNG GUERRILLA We are always pushed aside by the government, *Señora*, so *we* know the true heart of the poor.

WOMAN What do you think it is?

YOUNG GUERRILLA I tell people: here, we have a place to start over, we protect our own—this land belongs to us all.

WOMAN Your smile reminds me of my son's.

YOUNG GUERRILLA We are talking about new kinds of crops for the locals...

WOMAN Which ones?

YOUNG GUERRILLA Yucca, corn, peas. Our roots grow deep with the locals. We are their government. You see, we understand that they have no jobs...

WOMAN You're right, they need to be given better chances.

YOUNG GUERRILLA So many have been killed by the military, *Señora*.

WOMAN Yes, and by the paramilitaries.

YOUNG GUERRILLA The fight is to give us back lives that matter. Why is your backpack so light?

WOMAN I got rid of everything. Except the Bible. Even the jeans. A present from my daughter. I was wearing them the day I was kidnapped... gives me such sweet presents...

YOUNG GUERRILLA You really need to eat! We're stopping for the day by this stream.

She starts to croak like a frog.

What are you doing?

WOMAN They're so happy. The frogs, watching them land, on lily pads. *Croak, croak, croak.* With the pink flowers.

Sound of whirring video camera. Commander is filming. She is silent.

COMMANDER We're filming the Proof of Life. *Doctora*, you're getting lazy, sleeping all the time. Your mother said something *very* important on the radio this morning. Don't you want to know? How do you think the other hostages feel when *you* get all the attention on the radio? You wonder why everyone hates you? We'll have to hand out this *silent, sick* Proof of Life, and what will it do to help us negotiate your release? [*motions for the camera to roll*] Say something. [*motions for the camera to stop; starts to leave*] Perra.*

*Bitch.

WOMAN Lying in my hammock, falling into the place of succumbing, I count five times trying to escape, the same excitement of getting away and the terrible crash of recapture. But all the escapes have Absurdly run into each other—I can't try again. Instead I will see the breezy white church with the blue mosaic of the Virgin...

YOUNG GUERRILLA What, *Señora*?

WOMAN I sit quietly with my mother as she prays. God is in the gold stars of the mosaic sky above the altar. He demands peace and serenity. She looks down at me and squeezes my hand, smiling. She has a smile that makes all my uncertainties disappear. I look down at my hand in her hand.

YOUNG GUERRILLA Whose hand, *Señora*?

WOMAN I wear little white gloves and even sometimes lace for the head. It is white and quiet and holy. My mother has the courage of the carelessly faithful, a faith equal to the gold stars of the mosaic sky, the courage of the Virgin Mary. Where is my mother?

Father!

Sound of an oxygen machine, breathing, and distorted piano music, as Father appears.

Father, they put me on oxygen.

FATHER *Mija, has tenido tantas oportunidades en la vida.**

**My daughter, you have had so many opportunities in life.*

WOMAN The president is corrupt. I told him I won't eat until he returns all the money to the people.

FATHER You have had so many opportunities in life. You're right, you have to give back. You have a debt to Colombia: to serve your countrymen. Even if you have to die. *Yo te veo.* I see you, *mija. Yo te veo.*

WOMAN You've been converted to my cause and to my mother's. Goodness, and kindness, and dedication. A man who opens his heart and *changes;* now that is true love—when someone can transform his heart. How can there be sadness when you, Father, are here?

The news of my father's funeral is printed in a newspaper that is wrapped around a squash. They don't want me to know my father has died. That's why they took away the radios. I don't say anything. I try to show no expression. My father was sick when I was kidnapped. On the last day I saw him, there was beautiful piano music playing in the house.

FATHER I'll be here, *mija,* waiting for you. [*crosses himself as he prays*] Jesus, take care of my child.

WOMAN Why am I not with you when you die, Father? Why can't I hold your hand, comfort you?

YOUNG GUERRILLA [*approaching with a book*] Señora, I know with the chain you can do nothing. If you vomit again tonight, I'll help you clean it up. Here, take this, hold on to it.

WOMAN Yes, my son.

God is in the love of my mother and father, my children, their strength like a mountain, their voices, their world.

YOUNG GUERRILLA From the high commander.

WOMAN A Bible?

YOUNG GUERRILLA You've been asking for it for years.

WOMAN Suspicion is no longer worthy of my time. [*takes it and reads*]

U.S. AMBASSADOR [*voice on radio*] Our government is looking for the hostages in an area the size of Texas.
Triple
Canopy
Jungle.
The pilots can't see down from the sky.

WOMAN God is an Existentialist.
He comes in the uncertainty.
How many years?

PILOT [*voice-over*] Darkness, green.
An' we're told they keep moving.
But we can't see. We really don't see distinguishing bodies.
Don't know what they're doing down there...

GUARD [*voice-over; loudly*] Pónganse en fila! Preséntese!

MALE HOSTAGE 1 [*voice-over*] Number one.

MALE HOSTAGE 2 [*voice-over*] Number two.

MALE HOSTAGE 3 [*presenting himself next to Woman*] Number three. Hey, hey, they arrested the commander's girlfriend and sent her to the U.S. The commander has two U.S. indictments: for our kidnapping, and one for the narco-trafficking.

OTHER HOSTAGES [*voice-over; in the background of Male Hostage 3*] Number five. Number six. Number seven.

WOMAN They're making deals.

Sounds of a helicopter.

COMMANDER Somos las FARC. Hablamos en el helicóptero!

WOMAN Who are these people? What is happening?

COMMANDER You will be taken in a helicopter to meet the top guerrilla leader. Vamos!

WOMAN [*crosses herself as she begins to pray*] "Our Father, Who art in Heaven, hallowed be Thy Name..."

[*scratching her bug bites*] I'm sorry, but I have to scratch myself. I'm burning up with bites.

I hear the distant voices of the families on the radio—there are entire radio stations dedicated to those who have been kidnapped in Colombia.
I have been here
two thousand
three hundred
and twenty-one days.

Sounds of a helicopter.

The leader wraps plastic around my wrists.

LEADER [*handcuffs her*] It's just precautionary. Hurry and get in, don't waste time! [*calling out*] Get into the helicopter!

Suelten las armas! Rápido, tírala!*

*Put down your guns! Hurry, throw it down!

WOMAN In the last minute, the leader tosses down some cases of beer for the guerrillas.

The Absurd. Camus says: Certainty is impossible.

Helicopter sounds get louder.

The helicopter ascends. When we are in the air, the leader beats up the two commanders and injects them with a needle.

LEADER Are they down?

WOMAN The commanders pass out. The leader calls out to us.

LEADER We are the Colombian Army!

WOMAN I am happy in the theater, Camus says. Why?

LEADER You are free!

Helicopter sounds fade.

WOMAN [*holding the Bible, as in the beginning*] The beautiful sky, silent sky.

Sounds of chimes.

Quand je parle, je parle en français.
O en español? But I am in England, Oxford, a student, theology, so, the language for now will be... English...
And this is the book they gave me.
The rescue?
A helicopter
Out of nowhere.
I am here.
It is not for the faint of heart.
To allow *life* to touch you completely,
To allow yourself to touch it
There is a profound loneliness
So that I say every day, may I see you all one more time again?

She exits from the cage. Her children appear in the distance.

Is that you...?
You're both so much taller.

J.P. HUTU TRAINER, TUTSI INFORMANT

Lemkin's House

TO MY PARENTS

Cast of Characters
Lemkin, Polish-American lawyer; eyeglasses, balding, pale; fifties.
Proxmire / Jack / Antoine / Hasan, a Western white man, forties to fifties; plays multiple roles.
Mother / Caitlin / Tatjana, a white woman, thirties to forties; plays multiple roles.
JP / Militaman / Victor / Palmer, a black man, thirties to forties; plays multiple roles.
Nausicaa / Agathe / Rose / Guard / Voice of Female Aide, black woman, thirties to forties; plays multiple roles.

Notes on the Play
Setting is a dilapidated house. The play is performed without an intermission.

Act One

Lemkin, in a rumpled 1950s gray suit, holds a battered briefcase as he stands outside an office door.

LEMKIN Hello. Is the senator here? I'd like to speak to him.

AIDE'S VOICE I'm sorry, he's in a meeting right now.

LEMKIN Could I wait?

AIDE'S VOICE Look, you don't have an appointment.

LEMKIN [*ironic*] Right. Tell him it's that "pest" Raphael Lemkin.

AIDE'S VOICE He's booked solid—he has other priorities, Lemkin.

LEMKIN We need to reopen hearings. Can you give him these papers?

AIDE'S VOICE He already has them. The senator has all of your materials, Mr. Lemkin. Every single sheet of paper. I'm closing the door...

LEMKIN [*trying to hand her a manila envelope*] First they burn books, then they burn bodies! Read the evidence.

AIDE'S VOICE [*trying to close door*] Mr. Lemkin, move your foot away...

LEMKIN Did fifty of my family members die in vain? I have to leave them some epitaph. [*stuffing the envelope through the closing door*]

AIDE'S VOICE Remove the envelope. You're ripping your own materials.

LEMKIN [*clutches his chest, starting to have a heart attack*] Oh, my God...I can't breathe. A glass of water, please. [*collapses*]

Lights shift, revealing Lemkin inside a dilapidated house. The windows are covered. Lemkin wakes and opens a door inside the house. Behind it is a brick wall.

They think I'm so "annoying" they buried me alive? [*sees a newspaper on a chair and picks it up, reading*] "Philip Noel-Baker nominated for Nobel Peace Prize." Damn. [*reading*] "Raphael Lemkin: heart attack"? [*looking at newspaper's date*] August twenty-ninth, 1959? Tomorrow's *Times*? [*reading*] "Death in action was his final argument. Senators used to feel a certain concern when they saw the slightly stooped figure of Raphael Lemkin stalking the halls of Congress." Oh, my God, it's my obit. [*reading on*] "They will no longer have to think up explanations for a failure to pass the genocide law for which Mr. Lemkin worked so patiently." I'm wormwood. Well, if they think I'm going to stop now, they've got something else coming. There's no reason why you can't continue lobbying Congress when you're dead!

He goes to a desk with a typewriter, sits, and begins to type a letter.

Senator, let me reiterate: as my parents were being gassed to death, or slaughtered in the woods outside their home, I invented a word. [*typing carefully*] *Genos*, from the Greek, meaning race, tribe. [*typing tenderly*] *Cide*. Latin: to kill. Race-murder. *Genocide*. The word stops you in mid-sentence, doesn't it? Senator, it went straight into *Webster's* in '44—in '48 my genocide treaty was approved. It's more than a decade later, and the U.S. has still not ratified my law. Only man has law. Law must be built. I demand an immediate response. I am, Lemkin.

He puts the letter in a mail slot on the wall. A door opens and Proxmire, in a suit, enters, raising a champagne glass.

PROXMIRE "Fellow colleagues, Lemkin died twenty-nine years ago. He was a great man." I just told the Senate that.

LEMKIN Twenty-nine years? Time flies when you're lost in paperwork!

PROXMIRE [*giving Lemkin a document*] Raphael Lemkin, I would like to present you with your law.

Flashbulbs pop as the two men pose for a photo opportunity.

LEMKIN You got my letter?!

PROXMIRE The U.S. finally ratified it today—November 4th, 1988—the ninety-eighth country to do so, I might add.

LEMKIN [*dusting off his glasses*] Ashes. [*reading*] "The Genocide Convention Implementation Act." Oh, my God! It passed! It passed!

WILLIAM PROXMIRE

PROXMIRE [*pouring champagne*] Have some champagne. It's from Poland.

LEMKIN [*looking at the champagne label*] Nigdy Więcej. "Never Again." What absolutely amazing champagne!

PROXMIRE I had an aide scour the wine shops for it.

LEMKIN We did it! Today is the most beautiful day of my life. Genocide is now an international crime. [*clinking glasses with Proxmire*] It's going to be a better world! [*shaking Proxmire's hand*] What did you say your name was?

PROXMIRE William Proxmire. Senator from Wisconsin. [*giving him a hug*] Congratulations. People hug: it's the eighties. Men, too.

LEMKIN Really? Hugging... William from Wisconsin, the American people are finally on our side!

PROXMIRE Not necessarily. [*showing him a newspaper*] I wasn't invited to the signing. Too "annoying."

LEMKIN Ah yes, Washington's classic "he's too annoying" response—tell me about it. [*giving him a big fatherly hug*] We're soul mates. Guess that's the way you get things done, huh: become too annoying?

PROXMIRE I made three thousand speeches on the Senate floor. I'm an old man.

LEMKIN And I'm dead. [*they laugh together*] Even as a boy in Poland, I was obsessed with the slaughtered races—it was in my bones. Thank you, Proxmire. It paid off! An epitaph for my mother's grave.

PROXMIRE Frame it.

LEMKIN [*reading from newspaper*] "With this law we finally close the circle today." Who said that? [*reading*] "Ronald Reagan"? The B actor? President?

PROXMIRE Yeah. 'Fraid so. [*looking around*] So you moved upstate! Time to retire, do some crossword puzzles!

LEMKIN Always hated 'em. [*drinks champagne*] Please, have some more champagne.

PROXMIRE There were extenuating circumstances surrounding the passage of your law.

LEMKIN [*enjoying champagne*] Delicious.

PROXMIRE [*looking around*] Sure this is the optimal place to retire? It's going to need a lot of work.

Sounds of a thump and crumbling.

LEMKIN What in heaven is that? [*building sediment falls from the rafters as he looks up*] That's quite a leak.

PROXMIRE [*firmly*] Now promise me you won't do anything with the house till you get some rest.

LEMKIN Well, the house does have some nice Victorian touches. I may putter around.

PROXMIRE One chore a day. [*picking up newspaper*] The *Times* has a great crossword. [*reading from puzzle*] One down, six letters: "Restore what is torn or broken."

LEMKIN [*takes the newspaper and sits at the desk*] Yes, I need a more comfortable chair. I'm not in an office anymore. It's time to relax! [*starts working on puzzle*]

PROXMIRE Would you mind if I got some rest before I head back?

LEMKIN Where?

PROXMIRE [*starting to go*] I'll just take a look around upstairs. Don't let me disturb you. [*exits*]

LEMKIN [*looking at champagne bottle doubtfully*] Poland? [*relaxing with newspaper*] Crossword puzzle... Ahhh, last time I kicked back? France, '48. A small casino. The one time I danced the tango. [*mimes the tango with his arms, happily; then starts doing puzzle, relaxing*] "Infant," four letters: *baby*. "Little goat," three letters: *kid*. [*trying a new clue*] "Where Orwell's animals live"...

Mother steps out from the large fireplace, carrying dough on a wooden board and moving to somewhere else in the house.

MOTHER Just passing through, Raphael. I'm sorry to disturb you.

LEMKIN Mother, it's not possible. [*showing her the document*] My law! My law! Look, it passed!

MOTHER [*looks at the document*] What's this? A letter? A marriage proposal to a young lady?

LEMKIN No, it's my genocide law.

MOTHER [*stopping to think*] Please don't remind me; I can remember myself. Ah yes, I was on my way to get... some flour! [*starting to go*] I'll be out of your hair in no time. [*takes him in for the first time*] Raphael, my dear son. [*stroking his bald head*] What happened?

LEMKIN [*pouring champagne for her*] Yes, there were three things I wanted to avoid in my life: wearing eyeglasses, losing my hair, and becoming a refugee. All three have happened in implacable succession. Have some champagne, it's from Poland.

MOTHER [*starting to go*] There isn't any champagne in Poland.

LEMKIN From the sunnier part.

MOTHER Shhhshhh. You didn't see me, all right? [*opens the door with the brick wall behind it*]

LEMKIN What are you doing?

MOTHER Baking the bread. [*looking around*] You're not going to stay cooped up in this dark hole, I home. I mean house, I *hope*. Hope, home, a hole.

LEMKIN What are you talking about?

MOTHER Your life.

LEMKIN The U.S. ratified my law!

MOTHER If you wouldn't interrupt me, I was on my way to... [*starts to go*]

LEMKIN [*helpfully*] Get some flour?

MOTHER [*begins to knead and braid dough on the wooden board, making challah*] Flowers don't go so good with bread, son. Cheese does. And strawberry jam, tea, pickled herring sprinkled with salt. Hold the *chleb** to your heart. You must always slice down. If you break bread, you are vowed to wed. This house smells.

*bread

LEMKIN [*showing her the document*] This is a great victory!

MOTHER The life of the *heart*, my boy, that's the victory!

LEMKIN [*pointing at the document*] Ronald Reagan.

MOTHER My son who invented a word.

LEMKIN Like Eastman inventing *Kodak*. How did you get in here?

MOTHER I came down the chimney. When I think it all started with the Armenians!

LEMKIN Don't forget the Albigensians.

MOTHER Oh, think of how your father and I felt having a little boy who places the slaughtered races in alphabetical order! The Albigensians, the Alva, the Armenians, the Assyrians... And that's just one letter. Worrisome. What's that smell?

LEMKIN Mother, I'm going into retirement today!

MOTHER In the dark with the dripping and the thumping? Now what would Father say?

LEMKIN Father?

MOTHER We got separated. I have to find him. And your brother in the forest.

LEMKIN Samuel died.

MOTHER And you left.

LEMKIN I came home for you.

MOTHER [*gets down on her knees as fireplace starts to glow*] Yes, you were on your knees. "To Sweden, please!"

LEMKIN Not that again.

MOTHER "He'll kill us all... Read the words of *Mein Kampf*." That's what you said.

LEMKIN I'm giving up books and laws today, especially *Mein Kampf*. I'm retired, Mother. Let's celebrate!

MOTHER [*touches his head as if anointing him, then speaks in Yiddish*] Voos iz áynin iz buhléept.*

LEMKIN Voos iz áynin iz buhléept.

MOTHER Now what was I looking for? [*starting to go*] To try to remember. It's a mind exercise for those who grow old.

LEMKIN [*to himself*] To try to forget. A mind exercise for those who grow up.

MOTHER I was looking for... yeast? for jam? [*turning to look at him*] I was looking for you.

LEMKIN Me?

MOTHER I wanted to tell you—don't remind me—that the stars in the sky are blue.

LEMKIN Blue?

MOTHER The smell of the air is fresher from a rooftop. [*looking around*] Where are the windows?

LEMKIN They're all covered.

MOTHER I wanted to tell you that when you fly into the air—the ashes—well, Raphael, it's *awful*. [*looking at the document*] The Law. Let's celebrate! Pour me some champagne.

LEMKIN [*pouring champagne, showing her the label*] Nigdy więcej. [*toasting*] Na zdrowie!†

MOTHER L'chaim!‡ [*holding out arms*] Come here. How proud a mother can be on her son's wedding day.

LEMKIN It's not my wedding day.

MOTHER Don't tell me: your graduation?

LEMKIN My retirement.

MOTHER The Nobel Peace Prize! They finally decided to give it to you. Congratulations!

LEMKIN I fell in love, Mother—she was intelligent, beautiful. We danced the tango, she told me she was from Chilé...

MOTHER Ah, a dark-eyed beauty, Raffy?!

LEMKIN I told her about the extermination of the Aztecs and Incas; this was not seductive.

---

*One's own is beloved. (Stresses on *áynin* and *buhléept* are similar to those in the phrase "What's mine is yours.")

†Cheers!

‡To life!

MOTHER Oh no, it wasn't. What's wrong with you? With your nerves, shouldn't you have been thinking of ways to calm down? [*rain falls on the roof*] Showers?

LEMKIN Yes, it's starting to rain.

MOTHER Like the day you left us. Don't mind me, just point me in the right direction. [*exits back into the fireplace as the glow fades*]

LEMKIN [*takes a look around the house*] High ceilings... A crack along the wall. Ugh, the fireplace is a mess—the last owners really did a number on it! [*tries to fill his glass with water at a faucet, but the faucet doesn't work*] It's a fixer-upper. "One chore a day." [*looks in a large pitcher, which is set in a basin*] The water has small bugs in it. I'll change the filter; that will solve the problem. [*sound on the roof*] Hmm, what's that thumping? Retirement? Finally. [*picking up his crossword puzzle*] "Dead, according to Nietzsche." [*easily writes in the word*] "Lily of Utah": sego. [*trying a new clue*] "Land of a thousand hills"...? [*staring at a crack in the wall*] Woah, that crack is expanding! What's happening?

JP, a Rwandan man in military uniform, squeezes in through the crack, turns off the lights, and uses his cigarette lighter to illuminate the darkened room.

JP Recorders? Surveillance? Are there any?

LEMKIN Are there any what?

JP Bugs?

LEMKIN No, just the ones in the water.

JP General, this is no time for jokes!

LEMKIN General?

JP Are we being watched?

LEMKIN Where did you come from?

JP I've got a deal for you, but I only have five minutes.

LEMKIN I don't know who you are.

JP JP, a trainer for Hutu Power.

LEMKIN Hutu Power? Is this some kind of tribal dispute?

JP Don't play dumb! [*notices the champagne bottle*] Champagne at a time like this? Lay your gun down on the table.

LEMKIN I carry a pencil. Now would be an absurd time to start carrying a gun.

JP Ha-ha. General, thousands of machetes just came in from China...

LEMKIN [*blows out the flame of JP's lighter and turns the lights back on*] No open flames in here.

JP I'm training Hutus to kill in Rwanda!

LEMKIN [*referring to crossword puzzle*] "The land of a thousand hills."

JP They've got caches of weapons for the militias. *They will kill every Tutsi child.*

LEMKIN "Tutsi"? That would be down near Teutonic Knights and Prussian Pagans.

JP They've made the lists of people to assassinate.

LEMKIN [*starting to go*] All right, take me to these weapon caches, and we'll go from there.

JP I show you the caches when *you* get me... passports, protection for my wife, kids, transport, General.

LEMKIN It's kind of you to give me such rank...

JP [*hands Lemkin a list*] These are my family's names.

LEMKIN [*passes his hand over the names on JP's list*] All neatly written in a row. I carried a list like this at Nuremberg. Is that what *you* are? Tutsi?

JP Worse—I'm an informant. One thousand can be killed in the time we've been talking. How long has it been?

LEMKIN Two minutes. [*picking up his law*] Let's go.

JP First, you make me a promise of protection.

LEMKIN [*referring to law*] *This* is your protection. Genocide is condemned by the civilized world.

JP [*laughing*] Civilized?! I'm going to get hacked to pieces! *What about my family?* If I can't get them out of here, their deaths will be on your head.

LEMKIN [*starting to go*] Listen, I know people—I can help. Take me to the weapons.

JP Not without a guaranty.

LEMKIN [*showing law*] Here it is.

JP [*throwing law on floor*] That's just a worthless piece of paper to clean your ass. [*exits through crack in wall*]

LEMKIN [*picking up law*] I need to patch that crack.

PROXMIRE [*reenters from where he exited*] Thanks for your hospitality, Lemkin. Did I mention the incident at Kolmeshoehe?

LEMKIN The cemetery in Bitburg? No.

PROXMIRE The fluke that made your law pass.

LEMKIN Fluke?

PROXMIRE Reagan laid a wreath at Bitburg for the anniversary of World War Two...

LEMKIN He did? At the graves of the SS?

PROXMIRE He enraged the left and the right. Reagan couldn't look soft on Nazis. Your law made good press. I'm sorry.

LEMKIN I just had a frightening visit from a Rwandan trainer. The crime of barbarity repeats itself with near biological regularity.

PROXMIRE Hey, what about those crossword puzzles? I don't see you resting! [*exits*]

LEMKIN I'm not.

He turns on another light and starts to sit. An old shoe falls from the rafters. Mother comes out from the fireplace, holding spoons and a knife and moving toward a door.

MOTHER That was a shoe, Raffy. A strange one. [*trying to remember*] What birds fly south away from danger?

LEMKIN Is this one of your tests, Mother?

MOTHER Ah yes, your lessons. The Cro-Magnons making love!

LEMKIN You'd paint scenes of anthropology for my exams. Why not take it up again?

MOTHER Painting? The part of the brain that knew colors died in a snowstorm, Son.

LEMKIN There is a margin of error, Mother.

MOTHER [*playacting with a knife chasing spoons*] What could we tell our dinner guests when they saw our little boy under the dinner table playing "genocide" in the dark? Spoons running across the floor chased by evil dictators, *the knives?*

LEMKIN [*playacting with the spoons and knife*] Mom, when I grow up, I'm going to get us a big house where we'll be safe. [*playing Mother spoon*] With a garden? [*playing his younger self*] Yes, we'll never have to run away.

MOTHER [*taking back the spoons and knife*] We'd have to lure you back up with sugar!

LEMKIN I loved the desserts—strawberries from the farm, the cream.

Grains of rice spray from the ceiling.

MOTHER Oh, a wedding! Is your lady friend arriving soon?! *Rice!*

LEMKIN Mother, I'm afraid it's a bit late for marriage.

MOTHER [*picking up shoe*] Why do shoes fall from the sky?

LEMKIN [*studies the ceiling*] I haven't checked the entire house. I may have termites. I should get poison.

MOTHER [*looking at shoe*] Big ones.

LEMKIN I'm looking for a sliver of... [*searches through cabinets, finding a bottle of white poisonous powder*]

MOTHER Cake?

LEMKIN [*ignoring her*] Would it be so bad to ask for a modicum of peace?

MOTHER [*nodding*] Peace cake.

LEMKIN [*gets on his knees, laying the poison on the floor*] Peace isn't a cake, Mother.

MOTHER It *is* most certainly a cake, and a very delicious one.

LEMKIN Dessert just isn't everything.

MOTHER You left. [*going to typewriter on desk*] You could have been a novelist—written about something happy. Sunsets, cowboys?

LEMKIN [*as he lays the poison*] Cowboys? I'd like a house, a place to live in, some semblance of...

MOTHER [*brightly*] Sawdust?

LEMKIN That's not helpful, Mother. I'm trying to remember. [*looking around*] What was it? What we thought the world would be? Before the pogroms?

MOTHER A Renaissance festival!

Nausicaa, in a nurse's uniform, rushes through a door, dropping a machete at Lemkin's feet.

NAUSICAA Doctor!

MOTHER Perfect, you might as well stay on your knees for the proposal.

LEMKIN Mother...

NAUSICAA It's blades-gone-mad out there!

MOTHER Her face is cut.

NAUSICAA I saw... breasts and vaginas hanging from the trees...

LEMKIN [*taking the machete*] The Hutus are using these?

MOTHER You don't offer a bride something to eat?

NAUSICAA I *saw* them in the branches, I didn't make it up! Running from the murder site.

MOTHER How can a vagina hang from a tree?

LEMKIN Mother, you shouldn't be listening to this. [*to Nausicaa*] Didn't JP get someone to raid the caches?

NAUSICAA JP. He was hanged. [*picking up Lemkin's battered briefcase*] No time, your doctor's bag, hurry!

NAUSICAA - RWANDA.

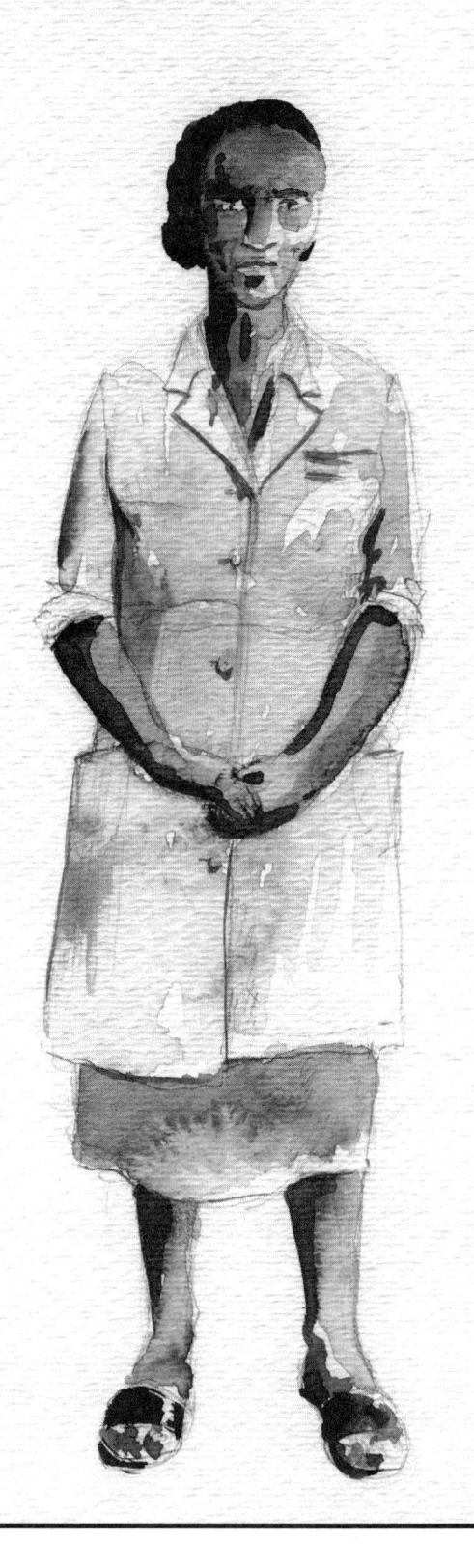

LEMKIN I'll help you carry people. [*looking at cut on her forehead*] First let me wash that. [*cleans the cut with a handkerchief*]

NAUSICAA Nothing compared to what I've seen, Doctor. At the church—south—there's about ten, chopped to pieces.

MOTHER Women are always the first to be marked, Raphael. [*exits into fireplace*]

NAUSICAA The West says, "Be patient."

LEMKIN Yes. When the Reich wrote the book of death in my family's blood, I was told to be patient. [*finishes cleaning the cut*]

NAUSICAA [*starts to exit, clutching Lemkin's briefcase*] Thank you. Now, come. [*Lemkin tries to follow*] Come on.

LEMKIN I can't.

NAUSICAA What do you mean you can't?

LEMKIN I can't move.

NAUSICAA What?!

LEMKIN My body won't go.

NAUSICAA What are you saying?

LEMKIN When I was alive, I was haunted by the dead. Now I'm dead, and I'm haunted by the living.

NAUSICAA [*slapping him*] You're crazy!

LEMKIN Please, listen, help your family escape.

NAUSICAA Fly away in a silver machine?

LEMKIN Don't go until they come with you.

NAUSICAA Leave the land of our ancestors?

LEMKIN *I* sailed away. What's your name?

NAUSICAA Nausicaa—I'm *Tutsi*—now I'll die—come! Come through the damn door, Doctor, and help.

LEMKIN [*going back to his desk*] I'm stuck here, but the U.N. will stop it.

NAUSICAA Just a crazy old man living life from his chair. [*exits*]

Lemkin picks up the lighter JP left on the desk and ignites it, troubled. He flicks it off, going back to the crossword puzzle.

LEMKIN "Traumatic stress." *Yes!* Acronym... four letters?... [*trying a new clue*] "Sommelier's concern": *wine cellar*. "Prefix denoting the opposite action": *U-N*. [*filling in letters*]

Jack, a natty U.N. official, enters with his female assistant, Caitlin, who holds folders and a box of baked goods. They begin to do paperwork.

JACK General, what are you doing here?

LEMKIN I live here.

CAITLIN At the United Nations? [*looking to Jack for help*] Jack?

JACK What are you talking about? No one lives at the U.N. And I must say, as the Assistant Secretary-General to Africa, shouldn't you be in Rwanda, General?

LEMKIN Rwanda. If I'm truly the general, Jack, then let's follow the rules of engagement and seize the caches now.

JACK That's outside your mandate. General, you're not going to be able to stay long. We need to write our weekly Department of Peacekeeping Operations memo.

CAITLIN It was due an hour ago.

LEMKIN Where is your boss? He must not be receiving the cables from Rwanda. They're stockpiling weapons. If we act now, we can stop this before it starts.

JACK There's no mandate to intervene, and Mr. Annan is not in the country.

CAITLIN He's in Paris and then he goes to Rome.

LEMKIN Does Annan know this is a *genocide*?

JACK We don't use "the G word."

LEMKIN "The G word?"

JACK It hasn't escalated to that level. We aren't allowed to use that word.

LEMKIN Dismemberment of Tutsis, Tutsi women's sex organs hanging from trees is not sufficient escalation for you?

JACK The word makes certain Security Council members nervous.

LEMKIN [*getting dictionary on desk*] If you open the dictionary, Jack, you'll find *genocide* between *genius* and *genome*.

JACK "The G word," General—we don't even like to say … "ethnic cleansing."

LEMKIN There are actually leaders who think if they don't use a word, they don't have to do anything about it?

CAITLIN Yes.

JACK One who is very important to us.

JACK / CAITLIN U.S.?

LEMKIN But the U.S. leads the world.

JACK Any intervention the U.S. is going to veto. They don't want another Somalia.

LEMKIN Do these politicians have a *Webster's*? Would they prefer the word *holocaust*?

JACK No, no. General, your job is to chisel out a peace accord.

LEMKIN With what? Machetes?

JACK Look, your cables have been put in the black folder.

CAITLIN The top-priority folder for the Security Council.

LEMKIN Apparently your color-coding system isn't working. I don't care if "Mr. Annan" is in Paris or on his way to the ninth circle of hell. Get me the President of the Council.

JACK The Council isn't meeting today.

CAITLIN [*overlapping*] I'm so sorry, Mr. Keating's not available.

LEMKIN [*picks up the machete Nausicaa brought in and threatens them*] I need to see someone on the Council.

JACK That is an utter impossibility. Where are you staying?

CAITLIN What hotel?

LEMKIN I'm staying here. On this beautiful Turkish carpet.

JACK It's not Turkish.

CAITLIN It used to be in the Cambodia department, but when we stopped the *genocide* talks, we put in a request for it.

JACK Caitlin.

LEMKIN [*to Caitlin*] Cambodia?

JACK Call him a car.

CAITLIN One point seven million died. I think that's a genocide.

JACK There was nothing to do, borders were closed.

LEMKIN And no one broke down the borders?

JACK General, are you sure you're not going native on us? There are rumors you're turning into a cowboy over there.

LEMKIN [*to Caitlin*] Cowboy?

CAITLIN Off the record. You want to shoot off your guns.

LEMKIN Cambodia. Right before Ceylon on the genocide list...

JACK [*correcting him*] "G word" list.

LEMKIN Shut up.

JACK – UN. BUREAUCRAT

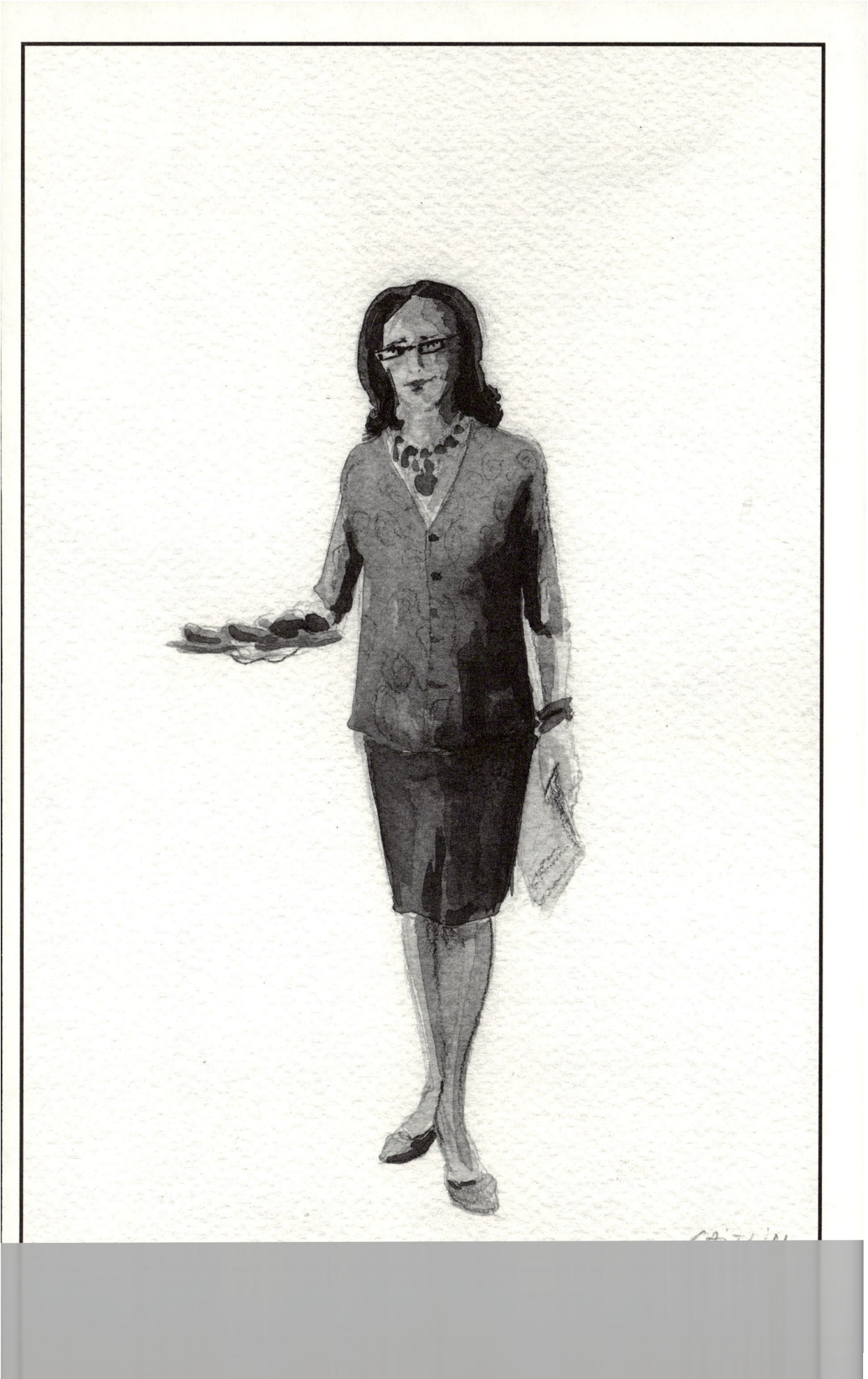

CAITLIN [*offering Lemkin the box of baked goods*] Why not have a donut? They're from Between the Bread.

JACK Actually a *beignet*.

CAITLIN We just call them donuts—makes it easier—but technically they're apple.

JACK Like turnovers. I'm not sure why we call them donuts. This is the U.N. We should call them what they really are.

CAITLIN Have one.

LEMKIN I find it difficult to understand why we are talking about *donuts?!* [*banging machete on desk*] Don't you care?

JACK Doesn't matter if I care. There's no political will, General.

LEMKIN But you're alive, Jack?

JACK Last time I checked.

CAITLIN [*muttering*] Barely.

LEMKIN Then you're the political will.

Jack motions furtively to Caitlin, and they quickly exit.

An old radio in the house begins to blare a Hate Radio broadcast. Loud gunshots surround the house, and a Hutu militiaman, high and drinking beer, bashes through a door.

MILITIAMAN [*treating Lemkin as a little boy*] Where is she?

LEMKIN This is a private home. Get out.

MILITIAMAN No home is private to the *Interahamwe*.

LEMKIN [*figuring it out*] "Hutu Power." [*reciting Psalm 122 to himself*] "Peace be within you. For the sake of the house."

Agathe, well dressed, enters through a door, throwing Lemkin a mobile phone and speaking as if to appease a small child.

AGATHE My little lad, press number six on the telephone and warn the general.

LEMKIN Little lad? I feel ninety-four.

AGATHE Don't play games. Mommy is interim prime minister. Press number six. [*to Militiaman*] Be calm.

MILITIAMAN [*taking out a gun*] Calm people are dead people.

LEMKIN Leave her alone! [*looking at phone*] No cord?

Militiaman grabs the phone from Lemkin.

AGATHE Stop playing, love, and run tell the peacekeepers to escort Mommy to the radio station.

AGATHE.

LEMKIN I can't go outside.

MILITIAMAN [*taunting Agathe with his beer bottle*] Drink from my bottle, Agathe!

AGATHE [*to Lemkin*] The militias are putting up roadblocks.

MILITIAMAN [*to Agathe*] Drink! What, my beer's not good enough for you?

A voice from the radio says, "Inyenzi! *Cockroaches! Kill the cockroaches!*"

LEMKIN [*urging Agathe*] Run, "Mommy," run out the door!

AGATHE [*opens the door with the bricks behind it; to Lemkin with forced calm*] Son, you must listen to me carefully...

MILITIAMAN Such a beautiful home to be full of cockroaches.

AGATHE I am Hutu, like you.

MILITIAMAN Those who live with cockroaches die like cockroaches.

AGATHE Peacekeepers are waiting outside to take me to the station.

MILITIAMAN Peacekeepers? Ha-ha-ha!

LEMKIN Yes, peacekeepers—they're right outside.

MILITIAMAN And I'm going to listen to a little boy? [*taunting Agathe with beer bottle*] What's wrong, Mommy? You prefer your fancy wine from your fancy wine cellar? Don't you want some of mine? *Drink, slut!*

LEMKIN [*grabbing beer bottle from him*] Get away from her!

MILITIAMAN [*pointing gun at Lemkin*] One more move and you're dead.

LEMKIN Again?

AGATHE [*urgently*] My little love, go hide.

MILITIAMAN Your peacekeepers are all dead, Agathe.

AGATHE [*to Lemkin*] Tell the general he promised to save *Agathe's little boy.*

MILITIAMAN My little love! [*in stylized movements, pins Lemkin and Agathe against the brick wall*] Cockroach! [*shoots Agathe in the face, then raises her skirt and forces Lemkin to stick the beer bottle in between her legs*] Drink from my bottle. [*exits with Agathe*]

Lemkin stares after Agathe. Mother appears. She is in a train car. Sound of trains.

MOTHER We can't come with you, Raphael.

LEMKIN Come with me?

MOTHER Our journey lies in another direction.

LEMKIN Which way?

MOTHER But there are some clothes you can take—they're hanging on the wash line... We follow the one ahead. A star. And come to a fork in the road.

LEMKIN A fork?

MOTHER A crossroad. Inside the woods. Left. Or right. Walking. I don't remember. A fork or perhaps a spoon, the kind you lap up cream with.

LEMKIN And... you go?

MOTHER Left. Into the chamber. The bark is white, paler than old telegrams I can be certain, and some others darker than an egg in a dove's nest. Firewood.

LEMKIN How long... did you last?

MOTHER Longer than the hair on a ribbon that got away, but shorter I think than the drip of ink drying on paper.

LEMKIN My law's a bad Polish joke, Mother. Meaningless words.

MOTHER Your syllables. [*tenderly*] Shaping in your mouth, that can help.

LEMKIN Genocide destroys a culture like fire destroys a house.

MOTHER [*smiling*] Ah, the intellectual.

LEMKIN Yes, the jewel of the family.

MOTHER Watch out for the bubbles. [*exits*]

LEMKIN [*takes a sip of the champagne; it has gone sour*] Baah.

He sits at his desk and inspects the mobile phone Agathe brought in. He closes it and goes back to the crossword puzzle.

Seventeen down: "Persistent rock pusher." Who writes these things? [*filling in the word*] "Elephant of children's tales": *Babar*.

Rose, a woman in labor, enters, screaming.

ROSE Help me! The baby, it's coming! It's coming! The baby!

LEMKIN Look, this is a disaster area. It's no place for a baby.

ROSE A towel, please. The birds are circling. That's where the killing is. I was running.

LEMKIN [*finds a towel in a cabinet*] Here, use this, please.

In stylized movements, Rose knocks away the towel; starts to deliver her baby.

ROSE Thank God, Doctor, you are here. Thank the Lord!

LEMKIN I'm not a doctor.

ROSE Don't leave! [*grabbing his arm*] Help me. I lived in a house right next door to him.

VICTOR

LEMKIN Who?

ROSE The man who raped me. Hutu. [*in pain*] He made me drink lighter fluid.

LEMKIN Just try to breathe. That's good. You are Tutsi?

ROSE Yes. *Aaahhh.*

LEMKIN [*looks under her skirt, trying to help her*] I see its head. It's coming. Oh, my God! I don't know how to deliver a baby.

ROSE *Owwwwwwwww!*

LEMKIN I see its brow, its chin. What's your name?

ROSE Rose.

LEMKIN Push, Rose, one good one for me!

ROSE *Aaahhh!*

LEMKIN Here comes your little boy!

ROSE This baby comes out in flames!

Sound of baby crying. Lemkin delivers the baby from under Rose's skirt. The baby is represented by fabric from her skirt.

LEMKIN [*looking at newborn baby*] Look, Rose. No smoke, no fire. You ran far enough, you kept him safe. See, no flames—just eyes, a nose, a perfect little human being. [*offers her the baby*]

ROSE [*refusing*] Take him. No food for orphans. He's yours.

LEMKIN I'm sorry, Rose, but I'm somewhat ill equipped for infants...

ROSE You take care of him. I'm tired.

LEMKIN [*holds the baby*] What's his name?

ROSE Cockroach. Give them what they hate. [*staggers off*]

Note: During the interlude of the New York City production, Lemkin holds the baby and his mother enters behind him. They share a moment looking at the baby, then she exits.

Act Two

Lemkin, withdrawn, holds the baby. Sounds of a helicopter; he watches its lights. Victor, carrying a briefcase and wearing a military cap, enters through a door.

VICTOR General, we're going to need to get those numbers before you go.

LEMKIN What numbers? [*to baby*] Shhshh, sleep.

VICTOR [*introducing himself*] Right. Victor here to debrief you. [*picking up the machete*] Now is this really an appropriate souvenir to take home, General? Wouldn't your wife prefer a bolt of pretty fabric?

LEMKIN An appropriate reminder for me to look at. Regularly.

VICTOR [*writing himself a note*] Uh-oh. [*finds files in a cabinet and puts them on the desk*] Very well organized. Now, I know the ends of missions are always hard, General.

LEMKIN Yes, they are. [*cradling baby and speaking urgently*] A woman was screaming for help...the baby...

VICTOR Time to go, huh? You'll have plenty of time to say your goodbyes and catch your chopper.

LEMKIN I'm not deserting him.

VICTOR [*referring to files*] Now, now, if you can just tally up the casualties by dates—the time from April sixth to August nineteenth—we at the reporting department want to figure out a unifying equation so the American people might better understand what happened here in Rwanda.

LEMKIN You count bodies after a genocide is over?

VICTOR You know the files. Do you have an assistant? Secretary? Intern?

LEMKIN [*moving to desk and holding baby*] No. Generals always tally the lists of the dead. Look, I know the numbers by heart. Starting from April sixth, I couldn't do anything for them. I see their eyes, Victor. [*sitting at desk and holding baby, starts to tally numbers with a pencil*]

VICTOR General, we're simply looking for the amount of dead that would be needed to justify one fallen American soldier.

LEMKIN [*tallying numbers and comforting baby*] It's all right...

VICTOR [*hands him a calculator*] Here, use this.

LEMKIN I can't get the bodies out of my mind...

VICTOR There's a lot of dust in here. Shall I open a window?

LEMKIN [*abruptly*] Please! Don't.

VICTOR Um, are you getting enough to eat? [*looking up as he hears thumping*] What *is* that sound?

LEMKIN Squatters.

VICTOR What?

LEMKIN Tutsis living in the ceiling. The rice? The shoe? They're still under our protection!

VICTOR You need to relax.

LEMKIN I'm accountable.

VICTOR [*referring to Lemkin's tally*] Look, I'll submit the final statistic in our report for future peacekeeping missions. It'll help, I promise.

LEMKIN I should have taken the law into my own hands, used force...

VICTOR You did well to play by the rules, General.

LEMKIN Thousands, hacked, slashed...?

VICTOR You didn't desert your troops—we respect you for that.

LEMKIN I don't. [*staring at tallied numbers*] Damn, I'm not seeing straight.

VICTOR [*taking Lemkin's tally*] Okay, definitely a pro. Woah, no wonder. These figures have post–traumatic stress disorder written all over them. [*taking out a tin*] General, I have some sardines. They're the ones soaked in tomato sauce. I'd feel better if you'd eat some sardines.

LEMKIN [*singing a Polish lullaby, "Raisins, Nor Almonds," and rocking baby*] Lulinke mayn zun, lulinke mayn zun.* My son.   *Go to sleep, my son.

VICTOR [*looking toward the windows*] A couple years ago, I was here in Rwanda. Streets were buzzing, humming with life.

LEMKIN Victor, there are notes in these files asking for help when the weapons started pouring in—an informant who switched sides warned me, and was executed. And you actually left a "general" no recourse but to *watch* a genocide?

VICTOR [*reviewing Lemkin's tally*] Ouch... The number's eighty-five thousand, General.

LEMKIN Eighty-five thousand what?

VICTOR Eighty-five thousand dead Rwandans are worth one dead American soldier.

LEMKIN [*protectively*] Well, *his* little life is worth more.

VICTOR Classic symptom: over-empathizing with the victims. [*opening a plastic container*] Take these. Pills for post–traumatic stress disorder.

LEMKIN Traumatic stress was in the crossword.

VICTOR Good idea, crossword puzzles. They occupy the mind, and your mind is going to need to heal. [*showing him the container*] One in the morning, one at night.

LEMKIN [*staring at pills*] There's actually a pill for genociditis?

VICTOR There is.

LEMKIN [*panicking*] I can't breathe.

VICTOR Sit in that chair, lower the lights... [*flips open a cassette player*] Relaxation tapes. And here's your subpoena. Now remember, at the war crimes tribunal, you're only being called to testify against the mayor of Taba.

LEMKIN Taba?

VICTOR Taba.

LEMKIN Taba?

VICTOR Taba! The rapes of the Tutsi women there. Everything else, the U.N. forbids you to talk about.

LEMKIN How can they forbid me to talk about it?

VICTOR You may want to write down what I said. You may forget.

LEMKIN No conscience, Victor?

VICTOR Who has time for guilt? [*starting to go*] I'm an Observer.

LEMKIN I won't forget. You know why?

VICTOR Why?

LEMKIN Because I blame you for everything. Someone with more skill would have been able to get them to stop the killing.

VICTOR [*sticking a tape into the cassette player*] Relax, you're just the fall guy. [*exits*]

Sounds of the ocean as Lemkin nestles the baby. He finds a vodka bottle underneath his chair and drinks deeply.

LEMKIN We've got to move, little lamb. How 'bout Baja California? A *palapa*—a grass hut by the sea? No genocide ever recorded in the history of Baja. People there are poor, but they're happy eating fish and crustaceans. This peninsula—neck of land as they call it—is too skinny to be of use to anyone, my boy. The sunsets, the Pacific! The waves with their generous dumping of salt water, incessantly lush.

This barrack is really starting to feel like less than a house, don't you think? [*remembering*] Of course, even in Baja, there was the genocide of the indigenous Indian tribes, fleeing as they were slaughtered by the colonists. *Lakota, Navajo, Sioux.* Such names. [*the baby cries*] Damn it. Kid, even on the smallest slice of land, it can't be avoided.

[*pours out a pill from the container and washes it down with vodka*] A pill to counter human hatred. An interesting idea. Wash it down with some vodka, useful for the most despairing moments. [*drinks, starts to offer some to baby, then decides not*]

A cockroach? Is there a gene that makes people see humans as bugs? I see eyes *everywhere*—thousands of ghosts in the ashes. What I wouldn't give for a *kanapka:** a pickle, and some good *chleb* to break. That's what they eat at funerals in Poland. [*looking at baby*] I may not be up to taking care of you, lad. Hey, little guy. Tiny little fists. Born from hate. Oh. [*kissing him*] Hello, "Little Cockroach."

Tatjana, coughing, with blood on her clothes, is pushed into the room by Guard with an AK-47, who then exits.

*an open-face sandwich

LEMKIN Oh, my God.

TATJANA [*looking at Lemkin with disgust*] What are you waiting for? Just do it.

LEMKIN Do what? [*looking at her*]

TATJANA [*seeing his stunned state*] What's wrong with you? Turn off the light, Chetnik.

LEMKIN Chetnik? I'm Polish.

TATJANA Yeah. *Do it!* Get it over with.

LEMKIN I don't know—

TATJANA Turn off the light so I won't have to see your face.

LEMKIN Why?

TATJANA I'm not up for your fucked-up, weird game. Just do it *fast* or give me something. Do you have any alcohol?

LEMKIN No!

TATJANA Pills?

LEMKIN No. [*showing her the baby*] I was unexpectedly left with a baby. He's a cute one, yes?

TATJANA Oh, God, a nutcase. Camp getting to you, buddy? [*sees Lemkin's vodka and pills and takes some*]

LEMKIN Camp? Why do you want pills?

TATJANA [*coughing*] Do you know how to get to the roof?

LEMKIN Actually I haven't checked that part yet. What's your name?

TATJANA Tatjana. Who are you?

LEMKIN Well, I was a lawyer. I made up a word which is causing a certain amount of turmoil.

TATJANA [*coughing*] What word?

LEMKIN *Genocide.*

TATJANA Right! You look homeless.

LEMKIN I toted a fine leather briefcase, wore this white suit. [*looking down at suit*] It was white.

TATJANA [*looking at baby*] Okay, okay! What's up with the baby?

LEMKIN A woman named Rose left me with "Little Cockroach." He misses her. Can you hold him?

TATJANA I can't stand it. [*coughing*] I'm sick. Just give me something.

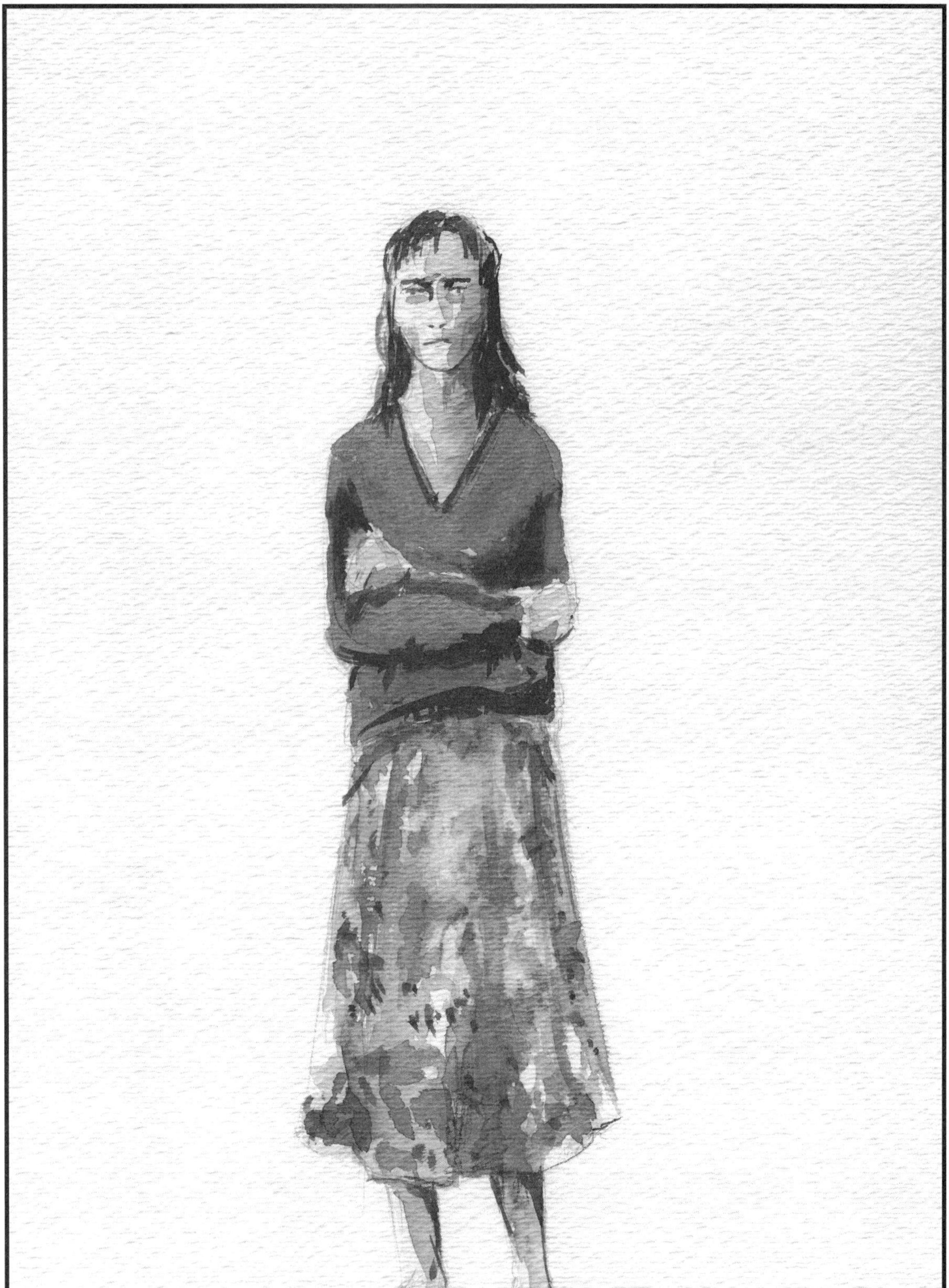
TATSANA.

LEMKIN You took my pills. They're for my stress disorder.

TATJANA PTSD?

LEMKIN [*looking at crossword*] An acronym, four letters. How did you know?

TATJANA I'm a physician. Was.

LEMKIN We could have used you a few minutes ago. To deliver this guy.

TATJANA Right. Can you take me to the roof?

LEMKIN Why?

TATJANA I can escape out a window upstairs if we can just tie some sheets together. Can you help me?

LEMKIN Escape from where?

TATJANA The camp.

LEMKIN What camp?

TATJANA Listen, men used to break their backs in this iron mine; now they're breaking ours. The Serbs say they want to bless us with their babies to populate the race. Can you get some sheets?

LEMKIN You hold Little Cockroach. I'll see what I can find. [*places baby in her arms*] His mother has quite a spirit, like you. [*exits*]

Guard with the AK-47 enters with Antoine, a male aid worker. Lemkin hides behind an open door as Tatjana puts the baby in a basket.

GUARD You can start in here.

ANTOINE I cannot begin my interviews of the prisoners until the Norwegian ambassador gets here.

GUARD No, you'll start now, with her. She has...another appointment. [*motions to him with his gun*]

ANTOINE The Ambassador will file a complaint. [*Guard shrugs as Antoine moves Tatjana away; she coughs*] Are you okay? Come, stand over here so I can look at you.

TATJANA How did you get in here?

ANTOINE Antoine, International Red Cross. [*handing her a bottle*] Here, drink some water. [*Guard grabs the bottle from her*] We have received approval from the head of the camp to check on the health of the prisoners.

TATJANA I need pills.

ANTOINE [*speaking softly*] Are they feeding you?

TATJANA Pills.

ANTOINE [*softly*] Are there human rights abuses?

LEMKIN [*stepping from behind door*] Yes!

GUARD [*looking at him*] Who are you?

LEMKIN The Ambassador. We have permission from your superior to make a list of the sick prisoners. [*goes to the desk and gets paper and pencil*]

GUARD Only the men.

ANTOINE [*catching on to Lemkin*] Yes, the Red Cross and the Norwegian embassy are working together to authorize their release.

LEMKIN And, Antoine, we'll need to make a list of the names of the women who are sick.

GUARD Don't be stupid.

LEMKIN International law.

GUARD There's no law.

ANTOINE Resolution 3318. United Nations Commission on Human Rights. Protection of Women and Children in Emergency and Armed Conflict.

LEMKIN You heard him—3318—it's the law.

Guard scowls at Antoine, motioning towards Tatjana with the gun. Antoine checks her pulse, eyes, and forehead for fever.

ANTOINE Can you tell me how many women are in your area?

TATJANA Eleven.

GUARD Just give her the medicine.

LEMKIN Do you know any of the women's names?

TATJANA All of them.

GUARD The medicine.

ANTOINE We have been sanctioned to make this list.

LEMKIN Please begin.

TATJANA Others have tried this before; it didn't work.

LEMKIN This is a list that will work. The names, please.

TATJANA Yes. Gordana, Amela, Emina.

Lemkin writes.

GUARD This is pointless.

TATJANA Alexandra, Mirza.

LEMKIN "Z" or "s"?

ANTOINE - RED CROSS AID WORKER

TATJANA "Z." And Fatima, Sonja, Mirjana, Selma, Tatjana...

ANTOINE [*softly*] Is this a rape camp?

TATJANA [*nodding*] There are two Tatjanas...

LEMKIN [*writing*] Two Tatjanas. With a "j," your name?

TATJANA [*to Antoine*] Yes.

Guard points the gun at Antoine.

LEMKIN [*handing the list to Antoine*] Present this to the head of the camp. We expect the international community to demand the release of all prisoners on this list. Is that clear?

GUARD [*laughing*] Not a chance in hell. See you...soon, Tatjana. [*ushers Antoine out*]

LEMKIN [*searches the room and finds pieces of cloth*] Here, we can tie these together.

TATJANA Sheets.

LEMKIN [*picks up the baby from the basket*] It'll be our plan B...The Norwegians are working on your release.

TATJANA Sure, but I'll feel better if we start tying these, just in case. [*tears the sheet into three strips and ties the ends together to make a rope*] My "godchild" was a baby girl, a Serb.

LEMKIN You're Muslim?

TATJANA Yes. I bought my friend's baby a gold bracelet. It said her name and the date she was born. The little chain looked so delicate on her arm. That there could be fingers so small, nails. Sometimes her mother would leave her with me, as if she was mine.

LEMKIN The Serbs are exterminating the Muslims.

TATJANA [*nodding*] We set our books on fire. One by one, watching the words we shared burn in front of us, rubbing our hands over charred words to stay warm.

LEMKIN The same nationalistic zeal—it's happening again.

TATJANA They say the Chetniks grind dead prisoners into animal feed.

LEMKIN [*hearing a noise*] The guard's coming back.

TATJANA Don't say anything. [*hides the rope she is making under the desk and goes to the door as Guard enters*]

GUARD The sick prisoners will be released. Including the women.

LEMKIN I knew it would work.

GUARD However, three women's names were not on the list.

TATJANA Mine?

GUARD [*throws her a package*] They left you some bread! [*laughs as he exits*]

LEMKIN They promised everyone on the list would go free.

TATJANA There were two Tatjanas. That's the problem with my name—everyone in Bosnia has it.

LEMKIN We need to speak to the Serbs.

TATJANA They know who gave out the names. I'll be dead by tonight. [*pulls out the rope from under the desk*] We need to finish this. Help me. Most of the women were released because of you—you're brave! I know another woman escaped from the roof. It's possible.

LEMKIN Let's talk to them.

TATJANA There's no time. I've been here for months, I know. [*Lemkin holds the ends of the three strips while Tatjana braids them; she looks at baby*] I used to dream of babies. I wanted a daughter. I even had a name—Alma... What's yours?

LEMKIN Raphael.

TATJANA Do you have children?

LEMKIN I never married. One of the great tragedies of my mother's life. And mine.

TATJANA It might still happen?

LEMKIN No.

TATJANA If you had a baby, would you want a boy or a girl?

LEMKIN I'd be very bad with babies.

TATJANA No. I know you'd be good.

LEMKIN During the First World War, my family had to hide in the forest. I kept Samuel, my baby brother, calm. I'd do birdcalls. [*does a birdcall*]

TATJANA How'd you do that?

LEMKIN Simple magic tricks. Anything to make him laugh. He didn't survive. I'd make up lullabies.

TATJANA Really?

LEMKIN [*singing to the tune of the Polish lullaby "Raisins, Nor Almonds"*]
> Sleep, my dear boy
> The moon is in the skies
> Dreams full of joy
> Soon will fill your eyes

TATJANA [*joining him*] And in the morn

LEMKIN *We'll face the rising sun*

TATJANA *And know, my dear boy*

LEMKIN *The new day has begun.* [*stops singing*] I'm no father. I read about death all night, never go to sleep.

TATJANA But with a nice wife?

LEMKIN She'd love a man who writes one hundred letters a day for a law about slaughter? My parents died in a camp. [*she pulls herself to him by the braided rope; he speaks in Yiddish*] Voos iz áynin iz buhléept.

TATJANA Buhléept?

LEMKIN One's own is beloved. [*she kisses him*] I was afraid I'd love a child too much. I'd stop working for the world.

He puts down the braided rope as Tatjana takes the fabric of the baby and puts it on her head as a scarf, transforming into his mother.

MOTHER My son, that thin coat? You're weak...

LEMKIN You and Father must come with me. Please.

MOTHER [*beckoning towards the fire*] Come, sit by the fire.

LEMKIN Hitler will kill us all.

MOTHER Let me give you some hot water. You're so tired, smell the warm bread, in the oven. The life of *the heart,* my son.

LEMKIN Sweden. We have to go now.

MOTHER Sweden? Have you lost your mind? We have a home. Our village will stick together.

LEMKIN I lost my job.

MOTHER You were fired?

LEMKIN Everyone Jewish has been fired.

MOTHER Drink.

LEMKIN He will celebrate our *deaths* even more than our exclusion.

MOTHER You're home!

LEMKIN Mother, I'm trying to tell you, we must—

MOTHER Tell your father to call them next door. They have a daughter just returned from Warsaw, too. A family—Raphael—children—Raphael...

LEMKIN [*kneeling in front of her*] There's no place safe. You know I never get down on my knees.

MOTHER [*smiling*] That's the problem.

LEMKIN In my pocket there's a draft of my law.

MOTHER *Shhshh,* enough.

LEMKIN We have to go. It's our only chance.

MOTHER [*touching his head as if anointing him with a wand*] *Voos iz áynin iz buhléept.* One's own is beloved. My home is here. *No one* can make me leave. You stay.

LEMKIN I can't. [*standing*] Goodbye, Mother.

Mother takes off the scarf and becomes Tatjana again as she cradles the baby. Lemkin picks up the braided rope.

TATJANA The rope is done.

LEMKIN Good.

TATJANA You know, it was always hard for me to look a man I love in the face.

LEMKIN I can imagine your child. Alma.

TATJANA [*cradling baby*] Such a teeny one. His fists are fighter fists. Little Cockroach. What a sweet face. [*admitting her grave situation*] The ugliness, Raphael.

LEMKIN [*retrieving piece of bread from the package*] Eat. [*eating a piece with her*] If you break bread, you are vowed to wed.

TATJANA [*putting the baby in Lemkin's arms*] Cover his head so he doesn't catch cold. [*the baby cries*] Oh, he's waking—lull him to sleep ... If you had a family, where would you live?

LEMKIN Right here, with you.

TATJANA I want you to sing with me. Don't look. Turn around.

LEMKIN [*turning away from her*] What shall I sing?

TATJANA Your lullaby for Alma. [*exits with the rope*]

LEMKIN [*singing to the tune of "Raisins, Nor Almonds"*]
    Little Alma, close your eyes.
    Tate* sings his lullaby.   *Father

TATJANA [*offstage*] Alma, almond-shaped eyes.

LEMKIN A daughter. [*singing*] Alma, don't you cry—

Upstage, the braided rope is thrown over a pipe. Sound of a stool being kicked away, and the rope goes taut, swinging. Lemkin goes to investigate, returns, and sits.

LEMKIN On a pipe, by a noose.

He pulls away the cloth the baby had been wrapped in, but the baby is gone. Simultaneously, Palmer briskly enters in a rumpled suit holding a newspaper and a battered briefcase, sipping coffee. He sits at the desk and starts to type a resignation letter.

PALMER

PALMER That's it—I quit. That picture of "Tatjana" hanging from the pipe? Everyone in Washington says, "Hey Palmer, she looks like your wife." [*Lemkin dry heaves*] You okay? [*reading as he types*] "The spy satellites snap thousands of photos a day and we pretend there's no genocide." I'm putting that in my resignation letter to the State Department.

LEMKIN Wait. Didn't you say it yourself—the photo looks like your wife?

PALMER Raphael Lemkin.

LEMKIN You can't quit! Our warning is like Paul Revere's: through fog and light, the fate of humanity is riding tonight!

PALMER Still the genocide man.

LEMKIN Thank you. I didn't have the good sense to prepare a disciple to continue my work. Here you are. *Tatjana's death must mean something.*

PALMER [*facing him*] Lemkin, I'm not your mirror image. Never had a bit of charm.

LEMKIN Now wait a minute.

PALMER I'm not diplomatic. And I get too emotional.

LEMKIN *I'm* emotional.

PALMER Too obsessed—don't eat, sleep.

LEMKIN I don't, either. Someone recommended crossword puzzles.

PALMER Hate 'em. In the seventies in Cambodia, I listened to the refugees. No one believed me.

LEMKIN Cambodia. *I* believe you.

PALMER In the eighties, Iraqi Kurds, gassed to death. No one cared.

LEMKIN The Kurds—that would be right after Iraq-ruled-under-Hulago in the thirteenth century.

PALMER Alphabetized? I do that, too.

LEMKIN That's wonderful.

PALMER I keep hearing the gassed birds thumping on the roof...

LEMKIN [*looking up*] Oh, that's what that is.

PALMER I called the gassing Iraq's Final Solution. Congress didn't like the Holocaust reference.

LEMKIN But it's essential.

PALMER I know. I proposed sanctions, but we were allies with Hussein. My real downfall: I don't iron my shirts or wear a clean tie.

LEMKIN I used to wear a crisp white suit when I lobbied Congress.

PALMER What happened?

LEMKIN The end of my life. But you can't keep a G-man down. [*picking up the newspaper*] The genocide's still happening in Bosnia. We are going to stop it!

PALMER Clinton administration turns a deaf ear.

LEMKIN There's got to be a survivor out there. Which organizations are on the ground?

PALMER [*stares at him, putting on his phone headset*] You are the real thing, man.

LEMKIN [*acting like a cowboy*] No, you are, partner.

They do a little buddy-type hand movement.

PALMER I'll give it one more shot, but at Srebrenica there may be no one left. [*clutching his chest*] Shit, my heart is beating too fast. This career isn't healthy.

LEMKIN Relax.

PALMER [*speaking on his phone headset*] Put me through to the Sarajevo aid workers. I need a refugee who can testify. [*presses buttons on his desk*]

Lights cross-fade to Hasan, a male refugee, taking off a bloody blindfold and giving testimony.

HASAN Instead of roots and insects, the earth is jammed with bodies. I push off blindfold. I only wearing underwear. I see gray hand above me in dirt. The blue finger has wedding ring. A man's thigh drips blood onto my chest.

LEMKIN Start at the beginning.

PALMER What's your name?

HASAN Hasan. They bring us into stadium at Srebrenica. Tell us to say our families goodbye. He promises us nothing will happen.

PALMER Who?

HASAN Mladic. Many of the men believe him. They tie our hands, load us into stolen U.N. trucks. "Remove clothes!" loudspeaker says. "Not Allah, not U.N., not anything can help you. I am your God."

LEMKIN Where did they take you?

PALMER Show us on the map.

HASAN Outside of town.

PALMER [*speaking on phone*] Have the Secretary of State check the satellite photos for mass graves.

HASAN In meadow, I see muddy trench. "Turn around," they say to us. A bullet grazes my skull. I wake up under bodies, buried. I take these clothes from a corpse and run into the forest! I raise up my head. I see sunlight! I hear birds sing!

HASAN

LEMKIN When I fled Warsaw, I came out of the forest above my village. My eyes were wet and it made my land shine.

HASAN But when I run near Žepa, I hear shooting. They kill all Muslim men in Žepa now. You can still save some.

Lights on Hasan go out.

LEMKIN We can't give up.

PALMER [*speaking on phone*] Tell the Secretary of State Žepa is next. We have the testimony from a survivor. [*listening*] I don't give a fuck about The Hague. This is *now*. People don't just disappear. Refugees don't lie.

LEMKIN After Žepa, there'll be more.

PALMER [*speaking on phone*] Tell him we need air strikes. [*listens, shocked; call ends; removes headset in disbelief*] Clinton is bombing.

LEMKIN [*ecstatic*] You did it! The U.S. is intervening. [*to himself*] Tatjana...This *is* the most beautiful day...

PALMER We're actually back at square one. Three ethnically divided states. And Serbia's ripe with nationalist neo-Nazis...

LEMKIN Progress is slow, it takes time.

PALMER [*puts his resignation letter in the mail slot on the wall*] Time to resign. I have a daughter. *She* keeps me up at night now.

LEMKIN That's exactly why you have to go on.

PALMER I want to relax, work on my house.

LEMKIN *No, trust me, that's a bad idea!* You and I, "we can change the world." My mantra. Repeat it over and over.

PALMER [*packing his things into his briefcase*] A ten-year-old girl raped to death in Liberia while her mother has to watch. And now Darfur.

LEMKIN Listen, we'll indict every country that breaks the law.

PALMER Sue the world? That's a dream.

LEMKIN It's not a dream, it's the *law*. But someone has to enforce it.

PALMER You're not of this world.

LEMKIN What's that supposed to mean?

PALMER [*with disdain*] A ghost lawyer?

LEMKIN Who better to speak for the victims?

PALMER I have to go.

LEMKIN [*grabs the manila envelope used at the beginning of the play*] Read the evidence. Did you know I wrote a book on rose cultivation?

PALMER I have to go!

LEMKIN [*offering the manila envelope*] I never once lived in a place with a garden. My flowers were *words* on scraps of paper—make them bloom!

PALMER The truth is people couldn't care less. One's own is beloved.

LEMKIN What?

PALMER They're just looking out for themselves. [*looking at him*] What is it you can't let go of?

LEMKIN The other G word.

PALMER Guilt.

LEMKIN Yes.

PALMER I'm through with that shit. I'm going to read my daughter bedtime stories. [*exits as lights shift*]

LEMKIN I always wanted a garden. *Róże, stokrotki*. Roses, daisies. All my life was a denial of what I liked... [*looks around the house*] The faucet, the pipes, the chimney? [*knocks all his papers and materials off desk*] I hate this place. [*puts the law on the table and gets the basin; his mother enters, carrying a suitcase*] You shouldn't be here.

MOTHER Why, because I'm dead?

He flicks the lighter and sets the law on fire; drops it into the basin.

LEMKIN Your body, eaten by
    Fire.
    Your skin. Splitting.
    Your hair, cut. Bodies, eaten by Fire.
    I couldn't save you or anybody else.
    I failed.

MOTHER [*referring to law*] It wasn't perfect. But what is?

LEMKIN You.

MOTHER [*laughing playfully*] I can barely remember what I'm doing one moment to the next. Where am I going? Where did I come from? What was I planning to cook?

LEMKIN My word became destructive, Mother.

MOTHER [*goes to the basin and sprinkles in some flour, kneading it into the ashes*] No word can capture it, Son, but it's in the pudding. *Nothing is ever wasted.* You bring us such joy—you honor us—that's what counts.

LEMKIN [*looking at basin*] When you fly into the air, it's awful.

MOTHER Listen, there are parts of our country,
   Where green grass grows.
   Cows look up at us,
   Clouds roll by, electric.

LEMKIN To be with you.

MOTHER You are. Breathe. There's a stillness in parts of our country.

LEMKIN That has never been touched.

MOTHER *You're my witness.*

LEMKIN I left.

MOTHER I stayed.

[*pulls out the law, now reconstituted, from the basin and gives it to him*] Paper burns, Raphael, but law makes us human.

LEMKIN Human?

MOTHER Come. [*leaves the suitcase for Lemkin and exits as the glow of the fire fades*]

Birds sing as light starts to stream through the windows. Lemkin goes to a window where sunlight streams in.

LEMKIN [*looking out*] It's ugly and inhospitable. But stocked full of joy. *Chleb*, with a hard-boiled egg. Held tight to your heart. You must always slice down. You scrape, and you gut, and polish, and destroy. And what will it become?

The walls of the house begin to disappear, and he is surrounded by blue sky and singing birds.

A house. A hearth... [*picks up the suitcase and begins to leave*] A home. [*exits*]

Playwright's Note
Since the early 1990s, I have written four plays about the aftermath of the Khmer Rouge genocide in Cambodia. In 2001 while researching my play about Pol Pot, *Silence of God*, I was fortunate to meet David Scheffer, the U.S. Ambassador for War Crimes during the Clinton Administration, and was struck by the tenacity of his cause. From this encounter I learned more about the U.S.'s involvement in genocides around the world. In 2003, with the luxury of time afforded by a James Thurber Playwriting Residency in Columbus, Ohio, I was able to carry on research and read in depth about the genocides that took place after the Cambodian one: in Rwanda and Bosnia. As a juror for the MES International Theater Festival in Sarajevo in 2004, I did further research. Due to my own sense that I was becoming a "pest" in terms of my obsession with the question of genocide and responsibility, I found Raphael Lemkin to be a historical soul mate on my journey: a journey in which knocking on closed doors had become a daily

occurrence. Lemkin spoke like no one else to my theatrical imagination, so that rather than write about him biographically, I developed his afterlife into the metaphor of a house: his house, which is our house. Special thanks to Samantha Power, Elizabeth Neuffer, Beverly Allen, Alison Des Forges, Philip Gourevitch, among many authors whose books I have read. And to Jerry Fowler for his generosity, James Fussell for his insights, and to Jean Randich.

Eyes of the Heart

TO JOHN DAGGETT

Cast of Characters
Thida San, a Cambodian woman, fifty.
Kim, Thida's brother, a Cambodian man, forties.
Dr. Lynn Simpson, an American eye doctor, thirties.
Serey/Oun, a Cambodian woman, Americanized, eighteen. Oun, Thida's daughter, is seen in flashbacks.
Savath Chin/K.R. Soldier/Sipha/Barber/Mugger, a Cambodian man, twenties.
Chhem, a Cambodian woman, traditional, fifties to sixties.

Notes on the Play
Scenes are set in Long Beach, California, in the late 1980s and in Cambodia in the 1970s. Scenes are played in different areas of the stage; locales are suggested. Because Thida is blind, the play has a soundscape, which helps suggest her world.

Thida uses a microphone when speaking aloud her thoughts. In the text, her thoughts are italicized. In one instance, Dr. Simpson also uses a microphone to speak her thoughts aloud. The dialogue of residents 1, 2, and 3 is heard as voice-overs.

Scene One

A flight announcement is mixed with airport sounds. A security alarm wails. Using a cane, Thida San* is escorted in by Savath.† Thida shrinks back from the assault of sounds. Kim rushes to her. He bows with palms together.

*pronounced
Tee-DAH Sahn

†pronounced
Suh-VAHT

KIM Thida! Sister, you are finally here! We've waited so long. I'm pleased to welcome you to my new home. [*embraces her*] Thida? It is me, your brother, Kim.

SAVATH She isn't speaking.

KIM [*confused*] Isn't speaking? Why?

SAVATH I'm not sure. They didn't mention it in the papers. She must be overwhelmed.

KIM [*maintaining cheerfulness*] Okay. [*speaking louder*] We are so happy to see you. It is a miracle you have finally arrived. How was your trip? Are you all right?

SAVATH She can hear you. She's probably just not talking.

THIDA *I asked to stay at the temple.*

KIM [*quickly motions to Serey**] This is Serey, your niece.

SEREY [*lightly touches Thida's shoulder*] Hello, Aunt.

THIDA *Like Oun...†*

*pronounced *Say-RAY* (with a rolled R); it means free

†pronounced *Own*

KIM You remember how she liked to visit you? In your house, where you had so many lovely things?

SEREY Dad.

THIDA [*patting something under her shirt, near her heart*] Like Oun, in the photograph.

KIM [*introduces Savath*] And you met Savath Chin—he's the man who got you here! He never gave up. He flew to the embassy in Phnom Penh. The paperwork sat there for ages.

SAVATH Welcome to Los Angeles, Mrs. San.

THIDA *Los Angeles?*

KIM We're very relieved to see you. How was your trip? Comfortable? [*touches a plastic bag Thida is clutching; Serey has moved away*] Serey!... You have no baggage? Nothing?

THIDA [*pats something under her shirt*] It is all here.

KIM Just crackers from the plane? [*watches Thida*]

SAVATH The papers say she sat in the dark in the temple for years.

SEREY She didn't want to come to America.

As Thida pats her shirt, Serey becomes the young woman Oun. Lights shift.

THIDA Miracle. A schoolgirl who eats, she breathes, she goes to school. When she comes home, everything is normal. Her father teases her, "Will she be a doctor?" One day my daughter says, "No, I will be a midwife." "Why not a doctor?" he asks her. His pride hurt, perhaps. She shrugs her shoulders. She walks away, to her room. To study. She is stubborn... Stop.

Lights are restored to the airport.

KIM Let's go home.

Scene Two

Dr. Lynn Simpson, wearing eyeglasses, shows slides while addressing her residents. Behind her, squiggly, abstract shapes float. We remain with her in this strange world.

DR. SIMPSON [*facing the audience*] Everything is spectacularly ordered. [*pointing to first slide on scrim*] See, there's nothing on this retinal cell—it's clear. You wait for the oddity. It comes rarely. [*showing second slide on scrim*] There it is. In night blindness, you know exactly what to expect. The retina has this white, murky surface, sometimes like a floating string. This is a floating world, a world where there is no speed, no weight. It's all here in front of us. Every day you wonder what you will discover.

Lights cross-fade to Kim leading Thida to an altar in his apartment as Cambodian music plays.

KIM I've made a small offering at the altar for your well-being in America. Rest. We have prepared some food—fried shrimp, rice.

CHHEM* Welcome to Little Phnom Penh, Mrs. San. [*sets down dishes as Kim lights incense*]

*pronounced *Chime*

THIDA Little Phnom Penh? They have renamed an American city?

KIM Chhem will be your guide. She is Savath's grandmother. She will take you to the temple.

THIDA You said I could live there.

CHHEM Yes, I will show you how to take the bus.

THIDA The bus?

CHHEM I've added some extra sauce. We must be generous. This is your first meal! [*handing her a bowl*] Don't be shy.

KIM Please, take some food, Thida. I insist.

THIDA [*takes the bowl*] When I used to find food, I would cut off the smallest piece for me and give Oun the rest. This is for you. [*smells the food as Serey enters, holding a book bag*]

KIM Come, Serey, sit—eat with us. Thida, you will have your own room with Serey. She has put clothing for you in her closet. [*to Serey*] Come and talk to your aunt.

SEREY She doesn't talk.

THIDA [*eats*] Delicious.

SEREY [*to Thida*] I'm sorry, I have to go, I'm late.

KIM Your aunt has just arrived.

SEREY I know. She stole my room.

THIDA [*eating*] So flavorful.

KIM Stay, she has come from so far away. [*goes to a window, lighting a cigarette; Serey puts on lipstick*] Who is that outside?

CHHEM His name is Trouble.

THIDA [*smelling*] Smoking.

SEREY It's Lee Var, Father. He's helping me with an assignment.

CHHEM Have you asked Savath for help? He's very intelligent.

KIM [*following Serey; lowering voice*] That lipstick is very red.

SEREY "Karma-red"—for energy. I thought you'd like that, Dad. The "karma" thing.

KIM No, I don't.

THIDA *Karma lipstick? Is she this old? The age of Oun?*

CHHEM [*inspects Serey; speaks under her breath*] The short skirt.

SEREY This is short?

KIM Don't talk back to your elders.

SEREY This is the eighties, Dad. I'll be right back.

THIDA [*eats*] *One more taste. So delicious.*

KIM One hour. I'm watching the clock.

Serey exits.

THIDA *Alone, in my rice world.*

CHHEM [*to Kim*] You know, the young do the "slow dance" with the bodies pressed so close together. [*demonstrates the closeness with the palms of her hands*] I have seen it on TV. Skin-to-skin. The "slow dance."

THIDA *"Slowdance"? Is that an English word?* [*stuffs more rice in her mouth as Chhem approaches and picks up her bowl; jumps*]

CHHEM Come look, Kim! Your sister is eating all the food.

THIDA *The loud one!*

KIM [*to Thida, comfortingly*] When we first came, we were so tired we couldn't stop sleeping, couldn't stop eating. We'd look at the food in the grocery stores, and our stomachs would ache with longing. We wanted to eat, but then it would make us sick. We had to take it slow. [*leads Thida to the altar*] There is a green mango on the altar for you, and a few flowers from my garden. I want to tell you—here, above, there are photographs. The few I was able to hide. They're on the wall. Even here our ancestors protect us. [*Thida pats something under her shirt as Kim watches*] You're home now, I will take care of you. We'll bring you to an eye doctor, take you for a physical exam—we'll go to the herb market.

THIDA *They said you promised I'd go to the temple.*

KIM Sister, may I ask? I never knew—what happened to your daughter? What happened to Oun...?

THIDA [*patting something under her shirt*] Still here? Are the photos still here?

Lights shift as Oun appears in front of Thida. Oun is weak and malnourished.

KIM Why don't you talk? We've waited so long. I still have Serey. I wonder what happened...

Oun works in a rice field.

THIDA She is hungry. The soup—or so they call it—is mostly water now, with only a few grains of rice floating on the surface. We see ourselves in the grains of rice, disappearing. We count them every day. One, two, three. They barely color the water anymore. [*young K.R. Soldier appears, watching Oun*] Stop. Swimming. On a beach, there were magnolia trees. Clear aqua water. [*another memory intrudes*] Another magnolia tree. I want to die.

Scene Three

Thida stares off as Dr. Simpson studies a chart.

DR. SIMPSON [*speaking to Kim*] Before she came, they told you she was blind. It's true she displays all the outward symptoms. But her exam reveals no physical problem. She has normal visual acuity. Her vision should improve to normal.

KIM I don't understand.

DR. SIMPSON Her eyes are sending signals to her brain.

KIM [*motions to a printout in the chart*] May I see the results? Yes, it is very strange. Her eyes work, but she cannot see. She's not lying.

DR. SIMPSON [*waves her hand in front of Thida's eyes, but Thida doesn't react*] Can you explain how this might have happened?

KIM No. There are many others like her. [*Dr. Simpson looks at Thida for a moment*] She refuses to speak.

DR. SIMPSON All the outward signs of blindness, but her eyes are healthy.

KIM It defies all odds.

DR. SIMPSON Let me try something else. [*exits*]

KIM You're in America now, Sister. Perhaps you can explain to the doctor, and somebody can help. I've brought you to a specialist. If you could tell me when you lost your sight—what happened? You can trust me.

THIDA [*patting her shirt; Oun and the blue of ocean appear*] Swimming. We went only months before the schoolgirl photograph where all is normal. She was a fish.

Standing at the shore, calling to her, "You are a fish! You are a fish!" And when she finally walked out of the sea at Kep, unconcerned, vain in her unawareness, simply... Oun... we would laugh. Sipha and I would laugh. We were so mad. It was late, we were hungry, and she would force us to stand on the shore calling to her, screaming for her. Her black head bobbing up and down in the waves, against the line of the horizon. But when she came out, she was transformed. From so much time in the sea. And she would spray water through her teeth... a trick she learned... and we would laugh... We would laugh and walk under the magnolia trees... [Dr. Simpson reenters and tapes electrodes to Thida's forehead] *Stop. All because there were also magnolias on the shore at Kep... Swimming, swimming... Anything to turn the clock back... Because the moments after—they are all accounted for, every detail, every movement. In my head I want it to stop.*

DR. SIMPSON Now I'm going to tip back your head and insert this contact lens in your eye...

Kim watches Dr. Simpson tip back Thida's head. Thida flinches.

KIM I'm sorry—in Cambodia touching the head is considered very personal.

DR. SIMPSON Perhaps it would be better if you put in the lens. It has an electrode on it.

KIM Yes, I'll do it. Thank you.

DR. SIMPSON You may want to tell her not to close her eye, or the lens will come out.

KIM We know English, we were educated. She was a midwife, and I was a doctor. But she doesn't speak.

Dr. Simpson studies Thida.

THIDA *This doctor's quick—she has no time. Empty—without a soul. She drinks coffee, smokes. Sipha smoked.*

DR. SIMPSON So she can't tell me what she sees?

Thida stares off as colored lights flash in front of her. Dr. Simpson and Kim watch lines with jagged peaks dash across a screen.

KIM Thida? If you see something, can you nod your head?

THIDA [*does not nod*] Darkness.

DR. SIMPSON If she can't talk, it makes it difficult to examine her.

THIDA *Don't cry.*

DR. SIMPSON Ask her if she sees the lights.

KIM Sister, did you hear the doctor? Do you see the light?

THIDA *I see nothing.*

DR. SIMPSON [*consults Thida's chart*] How did she lose her sight?

THIDA *Don't cry.*

KIM I don't know. It was during the Pol Pot regime. We were separated.

DR. SIMPSON Did she have eye problems before that?

KIM I know she wore glasses. For far distances.

DR. SIMPSON But with the glasses she could see.

KIM Yes. The Khmer Rouge tried to eliminate all intellectuals. They killed people who wore glasses.

DR. SIMPSON Does she have any other kinds of physical problems?

KIM Not that a physical exam detects.

DR. SIMPSON [*untapes the electrodes as the flashing lights fade*] Her eyes are sending signals to her brain.

KIM Yes, I saw the ERG.

DR. SIMPSON Your sister may be malingering, Mr. Lok. Is she applying for disability? Benefits for blindness are higher in California than anywhere else. I'd like to check something. [*looks through charts*]

KIM [*touches Thida*] Are you there? What would happen if you spoke? Would it be so bad? They've taken the time to see you, they want to help.

Thida keeps her head lowered.

DR. SIMPSON Does your sister know Bina Prak? She also lives in Long Beach.

KIM No, why do you ask?

DR. SIMPSON Well, she came in to be tested. She was applying for disability benefits, too, and she had the same problem as your sister.

KIM Doctor, my sister just arrived from Cambodia. She's not applying for disability.

DR. SIMPSON Isn't it sort of strange: two women the same age, from the same country, living in the same city? It sounds suspicious.

KIM I said before, my sister would not lie. It's not strange. I've seen many other women like her. They are not making it up.

DR. SIMPSON How do you know?

KIM Because I've lived among them. Those of us who survived ended up in refugee camps in Thailand.

THIDA *Don't cry, don't cry or they will kill you.*

DR. SIMPSON How did you get to Long Beach?

KIM My friend's grandson worked to bring us here.

DR. SIMPSON Have you seen the blind women here, too?

KIM Yes.

DR. SIMPSON It's odd... Perhaps I could see more of them. Could you help?

KIM Why not? [*looking at her; curious*] If you are interested.

DR. SIMPSON Yes, yes, who knows? Clinically, it might prove useful. [*looks at him while taking parking stickers from her doctor's coat; cigarettes fall out*] I don't smoke.

KIM Me neither.

DR. SIMPSON [*nods, then scribbles*] Make sure you give this validation to the parking guy, or he'll charge you an arm and a leg.

Scene Four

In Kim's apartment, Thida sits by an open window as light from a streetlamp shines in. She unpins a plastic bag from under her shirt and takes out a photo. She passes her hand over it. Sipha, wearing a white doctor's coat, appears in the shadows.

THIDA *He stands in the back of the truck. With other doctors in white coats.* [*he mimes for her to be quiet*] *He puts his finger to his mouth, telling me to be quiet.* [*she nods; he gestures*] *He motions for me to take off my glasses.* [*she mimes*] *I take them off. He gestures to get rid of them.* [*she mimes*] *I throw them on the ground and I crush them with my foot. My sight is now blurred as I look at him. The man I love. He simply looks back. The truck starts to go. I look at him, but I cannot see him clearly. The truck begins to move away, a cloud of dust.* [*she extends her hand*] *Sipha.* [*the sound of gunfire comes through the window; Thida holds the photo to her breast as Sipha disappears; a siren wails, and she crouches down*]

KIM [*entering with Serey*] Sister? What are you doing? What's happened to you?

SEREY What's wrong with her? What's her problem?

KIM [*puts his arm around Thida as Serey takes books out of her bag*] Please don't be frightened. It is simply the police. I had to go outside and retrieve Serey from her own folly. You are safe.

SEREY You're not actually that safe. There are gangs.

THIDA Are there boys with guns...?

KIM Serey, don't tell her that.

THIDA Smoking cigarettes, Brother?

SEREY They live in our building.

KIM That was a police siren. You are fine inside. There is no problem. [*helps Thida to her seat by the window; Serey starts to go*] Don't think I have forgotten what I saw.

SEREY Forget it.

KIM His car is enough.

THIDA *His car?*

KIM If your mother was alive, she would agree with me about Savath.

SEREY You're the one in love with Savath.

KIM That isn't funny. You liked him, you told me so. He's very respectable.

SEREY Maybe too much. Have you seen how he dresses?

KIM Is it because I like him, suddenly you don't? You've been out with him once—was it so bad?

SEREY Yeah, I'm not ready. I need to have some fun.

KIM One thing you won't have is fun with [*pointing outside*] the guy with the car, I can assure you.

SEREY Oh, and you know this by telepathy?

KIM I know you are very clever, but in this case you are not seeing clearly. You are too American. Try again with Savath. He was friends with your brother. [*lights a cigarette*] My daughter has driven me to smoking.

THIDA *You always smoked.*

KIM Oh, God, why won't you say anything?

THIDA *You don't want to hear what I have to say.*

Kim exits as Serey gets some books.

SEREY We yell all the time. Sorry I said that about the gangs. It's scary, but it's not that bad. Besides a few bullets coming in through the front door—just kidding. No, there were some once, but it's okay. He hardly ever mentions my mother. You really think she'd want me to marry Savath? Sometimes I pray to her. Savath is good looking, but who wants someone your dad picked out? My father was different when my mom was around. We used to have some fun. We'd catch fish together. Sing songs. We were just crazy. But that was before Pol Pot. Now I'm supposed to marry Savath because he was friends with my brother? Everyone's dead. Good way to guilt people, huh? [*to herself*] Asking you? What was I thinking? [*passes her hand in front of Thida's expressionless eyes*] Can you see? He's wanted you to come here so bad. You were supposed to save us from something. [*takes off her mirrored sunglasses and puts them on Thida*] Hey, when you're around people, maybe you wanna wear these.

THIDA [*feels them, surprised*] *Are they eyeglasses?*

SEREY [*looks at herself in the mirrored glasses*] You can see yourself in them. They're sunglasses.

THIDA [*stares out, wearing the sunglasses*] *Words won't bring them back, Serey.* [*Serey exits; Thida sits by the open window; night slowly turns to day; she listens to the* *sound of construction vehicles, followed by the sound of a jackhammer; she takes out another photo from the plastic bag and passes her hand over it]* A cloud of dust. Sipha doesn't return. I dress myself and my daughter as peasants. We work in the fields, pray to the spirits that the soldiers will not see us, that we will disappear. They find us—try to force Oun to marry. [*sunlight shines in Thida's eyes, and she shields them from the glare; Oun appears with K.R. Soldier in the shadows*]

K.R. SOLDIER [*ordering Thida*] You, come here! You are the mother, you must watch!

THIDA *Sun shines in my eyes. I leave my hut, walk towards the tree.* [*stopping the memory*] Stop.

K.R. SOLDIER You must watch your daughter!

THIDA *The people watch, expressionless. I search their eyes for clues. Stone faces.* [*Communist propaganda music from speakers becomes louder and louder*] *Magnolia flowers fall. Oun is tied with rope. No.* [*lights are restored as Kim enters in gardening clothes*]

KIM You never sleep? I want you to come outside to my garden for a little fresh air—you must.

THIDA *Fresh? Where is this city that smells so bad?*

KIM [*giving her a lime*] Here is a lime from California. Take it. I have avocados, too. They will soon be ripe. I never tasted avocado in Cambodia, did you? [*a beat*] Sister, do you remember that fruit we had in our garden when we were young? With the milky white flesh and the black seed? *Teak dos ko?* So delicious. It doesn't exist here. It has no name. But with time, it will come. Some Cambodian will learn to grow it. And then it will have a name, Americans will learn to love it and they will mass-produce it. The fruit will become bigger and bigger, the colors more vibrant, and finally, it will lose all its flavor so that it tastes only like water. [*she drops the lime; he gives it back to her and sees the photos on her lap*] Can you see the photos, Thida? [*she finally responds by nodding*] Ah, you made a sign. Finally. You said yes. You can see the photos. I don't understand.

THIDA *I see Oun and Sipha.*

KIM [*sees Thida put her hands together and pray*] You want to pray. Yes, we will bring you to our new temple like I promised. [*lying*] It is much like the temples in Cambodia. Well, it is a haven for many, let us say.

THIDA *I want to become a nun. I have nothing to hope for but the next life.* [*hears construction sounds and looks toward them*]

KIM Do you hear? They are repairing the road outside. It's a bulldozer. The other noise is a machine to break up the cement. All the soil—they cover with cement here. Concrete. They want to seal away the earth.

Scene Five

Sounds of busy traffic. Chhem looks up at a bus-stop sign as she guides Thida. Underneath the sign is another sign, which reads NO STANDING.

CHHEM The bus stops here, but we cannot wait here, Thida.

THIDA I would prefer to go home.

CHHEM Don't worry. We'll wait on the next corner. It's safe on the next corner. [*leads Thida away*]

THIDA The city's loud, always a hum like rushing water, an electric current. Is the city breathing?

CHHEM [*stopping*] Here, we will wait here. Your brother is very worried about you. Poor man, he must work during the day and cannot take you to the temple. You are safe with me. No problem, I'm a good guide. Serey, she is driving your brother to madness. The boyfriend, the car! The car is called a "Trans Am"! Very, very big. Very white! New. When the sun shines on it, it gleams like a jewel in her eyes. [*sound of a bus approaching*] The bus is coming, Thida! Now we must run! [*tries to run and to pull Thida with her*]

THIDA Why must we chase the bus?

CHHEM Hurry, Thida! Please! [*Thida drops her cane; Chhem goes to pick it up; the sound of the bus pulling away; Chhem is upset*] Well, this is unfortunate. The monk is waiting at the temple, we'll be late. Don't worry, it is not your fault. Come. [*leads Thida back to where they were waiting*] The sign says we cannot stand there. "No Standing"! There is an arrow that points in both directions! [*points to something offstage near the bus stop*] Oh, I see a man is standing right next to the forbidding sign! Maybe we can stand behind him. This way if something happens, he will be punished first. [*leads Thida as lights cross-fade to Kim with Dr. Simpson in a teashop, sampling tea and smoking*]

DR. SIMPSON I drink Lipton.

KIM [*horrified*] In a tea bag?

DR. SIMPSON What else?

KIM I'll buy you some tea on the way out so you can enjoy it.

DR. SIMPSON What would I put it in?

KIM A pot?

DR. SIMPSON I drink coffee anyway.

KIM You need to take a little time—go ahead, sip it slowly. Sustenance. Of course, the cigarette doesn't help. But we can't have everything.

DR. SIMPSON No.

KIM The temple is an old union hall on Willow Street. Some of the blind women pray there. Afternoons are best to find them.

DR. SIMPSON They'll have to come to my office. When did you first see the blind women?

KIM Among the refugees, in the Thai camps.

DR. SIMPSON It couldn't be malnutrition, or they would have regained their sight.

KIM In our country, the head is considered the place where the soul resides. It's the window through which life enters and exits.

DR. SIMPSON Would you consider bringing your sister by my office again? I want to start by looking for an organic basis in the women. What do they have in common?

KIM That's what you have to find out. You know, doctors like myself, in Cambodia, are ... were more experimental. My sister knew much about herbs, and I used many of her remedies. I used to love seeing the whole world.

DR. SIMPSON What do you mean?

KIM Before Pol Pot, I looked at everything. From my head to my feet. My heart, my brain. And outward. The infinite. Now it's the opposite. I see only limits. I walk on a tightrope: how will I survive?

DR. SIMPSON [*looks at him a moment*] What is your answer?

KIM My family. If I can save them. That's all that matters. [*looks at her*] What about your family?

DR. SIMPSON [*does not answer the question*] If I can find the physical reason for the women's problem, I can help them. What would make them see again?

KIM You didn't answer my question. [*looking at her*] You're right. What would make them see again? [*asking about her*] What would help?

Chhem guides Thida into the darkness of a Buddhist temple. Above the altar is a faded sign: OIL–CHEMICAL AND ATOMIC WORKERS UNION LOCAL 1-128. *Thida kneels as Chhem exits. Sipha appears in the shadows.*

THIDA Sipha, you're here! I should never have forced her. I was always stubborn. Please say something. Say something to me. Come, sit. [*he sits next to Thida*] Tell me where you go.

SIPHA [*staring straight ahead*] I travel through jungles where the forest's so thick I can barely squeeze by. Swim in rivers where you can catch the fish in thin air. At the seaside, the sand is mixed with the bones and teeth of farmers.

THIDA The temples—tell me about the temples!

SIPHA I dance with the celestial dancers—and there are thousands—on the walls of the ancient city.

THIDA *Are you so popular?*

SIPHA Yes, in the nighttime, serenaded by the soft rush of the wind, so seductive with their necklaces of jasmine falling on their breasts. The thieves in the night cut off the statues' heads. They reappear in foreign lands, chopped off, eyes gouged from their sockets.

THIDA *The dancing!*

SIPHA Vines grow through the rock, strangling, squeezing the stone, cracking the faces, erasing the shrines. Soon the temples of Angkor will vanish.

THIDA *Dancing.*

SIPHA In the distance you can hear the snap of land mines—another little boy running home, too careless.

THIDA *Sipha.*

SIPHA Near Siem Reap in an empty schoolhouse there are rusted shackles from its days as a torture center. Bones piled high to the sky, mountains and mountains of bones. When the air is still, you can hear the skulls whispering to each other. [*whispers menacingly*] Sssssssssssss... Snakes...

THIDA [*speaking aloud for the first time*] Stop!

CHHEM [*reenters, shocked*] Thida? You can talk? You are finally speaking. [*Thida is silent*] Who are you talking to? Who is here?

THIDA [*watches Sipha slip away*] Sipha. He is not what I want him to be.

CHHEM Sipha?

THIDA [*stares at the place where Sipha was; to Chhem*] I cannot speak about it. I am sorry. It is too difficult. I...

CHHEM [*leads Thida out*] Come, you are haunted. You are speaking! At home I will coin* you to make you feel better. Are you glad you came to the temple today? [*there are street sounds and graffiti as Thida walks with Chhem, who looks up*] The sign is usually right here, but it has disappeared. Perhaps the wind blew it down in the storm.

THIDA What storm?

CHHEM All the buildings look the same. Ugly, so ugly. [*panicking*] No trees. Always the gangsters on the corners. One in my block has a tiger on his arm, a tattoo. Always smoking, just boys, painting the buildings all different colors, like children! [*Thida hears the construction sounds in the distance*] It is pitiful. We are lost, so lost.

THIDA [*soothingly*] I believe I know the right direction, Chhem. I do hear the sound of the road construction. My brother told me they are repairing the road. Cement. [*with vigor*] Yes, come now!

*a traditional dermal massage technique in which oiled skin is rubbed vigorously with a coin for healing purposes

Scene Six

Chhem coins Thida as Kim stands near the altar.

CHHEM And she told me to follow the bulldozer and got us home!

KIM She spoke to you? Truly?!

CHHEM Yes.

THIDA How else was I ever going to get home?

KIM Thida!

CHHEM She said you told her there was roadwork on the street—she heard it. And she was talking to ghosts at the temple. She's getting better.

KIM I hope.

CHHEM Your daughter, Serey, is getting older. She is very studious. [*ominously*] And very beautiful.

KIM Thank you. You are kind.

CHHEM [*teasing*] You know, without my grandson your sister would still be in Cambodia.

KIM We are very grateful.

THIDA [*muttering*] No, we are not!

KIM [*looking at Thida*] What, Sister?

CHHEM Savath is at the agency from dawn to midnight, never stops. Meetings with bigwigs from government offices, visits to shelters, casinos. He goes because other people lose their shirts—not him! You know that he and Serey had a date... I did not hear that it was a failure. They did not run in opposite directions.

KIM Perhaps we should adapt to the American way, encourage another date.

CHHEM My grandson is old enough to be a monk.

KIM Serey is younger. I worry...

CHHEM In a blink of an eye, all this will change. [*threateningly*] In a car.

KIM You don't need to tell me. But she is a good daughter. We have lost so much, I want to protect her.

CHHEM Exactly! We're all that's left. Our families knew each other. Savath is the right choice, the best insurance a father could buy. He is Cambodian. A good man. College educated. We will bring two families together. I will consult the astrologer, and we can arrange a marriage.

KIM Go ask him. [*exits with Chhem*]

THIDA *I am in between a tiger and a crocodile. Please let me out of here—I need to go home.*

Dr. Simpson alone, exhausted, drinking coffee, clicks through slides of healthy retinal cells. She shuts off the machine and gets up, searching the darkness.

DR. SIMPSON Tom, are you there? [*lets down her guard to someone in the darkness*] Can you see me? [*searches a moment longer, then puts her guard back up*] I don't believe in ghosts.

Lights shift as she clicks through slides of healthy retinal cells, addressing her residents.

[*facing the audience*] Sovandy Meng: her job was to carry bodies to mass graves. Fifty-two years old. Blind in 1977. [*referring to slide*] Healthy retinal cell. Chantha Li: last child died of starvation. Age sixty. Blind in 1978. [*showing slide*] Healthy retinal cell. Ang Malay: saw a baby thrown against a tree. Age fifty-four; 1976. [*showing slide*] Healthy retinal cell. Navy Hun: saw her sister killed—because of her white skin? At the beginning of the genocide. In her fifties; 1975. [*showing slide*] Healthy retinal cell. Thida San: she won't talk about what happened to her family... All of them should be able to see.

Scene Seven

Thida listens to a siren as she sits at her usual place by the window. At the altar, Kim smokes, showing Serey astrological charts.

KIM The stars say yes, Serey. Chhem has made a very substantial offer, but more importantly I want to join Savath to our family. This will please our ancestors and tie us to our lost country.

SEREY I'm not in love with him, Father.

KIM You will grow to love him, as I grew to love your mother.

SEREY But that's not the way things are here. People date before they get married—they fall in love!

KIM We do, too. Simply in reverse. Since you were a little girl, you have known that your mother and I would arrange your marriage. Now that she is gone, it is up to me to make the right choice, to honor her. It is the single most important way you can show her your respect.

SEREY Everything has changed. We aren't in Cambodia.

KIM We must honor our dead and preserve our traditions.

SEREY But we live in a new country.

KIM It is very important. Please don't contradict me, Serey. I am your father. You will thank me later.

SEREY I can't start having babies now. What if I want to go to college?

KIM Then you will go. You are no longer a girl. Savath is a sensitive soul—refined and ethical. He will make a good husband for you.

SEREY I won't marry him.

THIDA [*haunted, hears the Communist propaganda music; addresses Kim*] Yes, she will, she will. Give me a moment. Let me speak to her. Say yes, Oun—my girl. You must say yes.

KIM [*touches Thida*] Sister, what are you saying?

THIDA [*pushes him away, continuing out loud*] Rays of sunlight shine into my eyes. The loudspeakers are hanging in the tree. There are flowers on the tree. She is tied. Water drips from a tiny hole in a bucket, on her head. The drops of water mix with her tears. They tied Oun to a tree. A magnolia. They're forcing her to marry.

SEREY [*to Kim, softly*] Her daughter, Oun?

THIDA The official, he unties her. He points to a young soldier. "Will you marry him?" She shakes her head no. She is stubborn. *Will not accept.* The official takes out his blade. He grabs Oun by the hair. They cut off her head.

KIM Sister...

THIDA He looks at me. He holds her head. He throws it into a fire where a pile of corpses and body parts burn... Smoke got in my eyes... Don't cry, don't cry, or they kill you. [*to Kim*] Please. Let me die.

KIM No, it is important to live. [*holds her*]

Lights black out.

Scene Eight

Morning. Thida wears the mirrored sunglasses. A Punk barber watches as she enters the barbershop with her cane. Rock music plays.

THIDA There is very loud music in the barbershop, but the place is cool. It smells of smoke and soap.

BARBER [*spins around a chair for her*] Whoa, first customer. You're an early bird. Sit.

THIDA He ties something around my neck.

BARBER Hey, how'd you want it cut?

THIDA Shaved, please.

BARBER Sure you want it shaved?

THIDA Yes. Please. I am going to the temple. Now I must become a nun.

BARBER What's your name?

THIDA *It is not the practice in my country to ask the name of the customer.* [*to barber*] My name is Thida San. [*politely*] What is your name?

BARBER The Spider.

THIDA Hello, The Spider. *Am I wrong in remembering that the spider is an insect?* [*stands with her cane; the barber reveals her scalp, now entirely shaved except for a spot with her initials, TS; she touches the letters*] Thank you.

Lights rise on Kim's apartment. He is near the altar, frantic and on the phone, waiting with Serey and Chhem.

KIM You call the police, you get put on hold...I trusted you to watch her, Serey!

SEREY Dad, I stayed up until five a.m. with her. She was asleep.

KIM You promised me you'd stay awake. We said we'd take turns.

SEREY I dozed off!

KIM I can't trust you. [*on the phone*] What is taking so long?

SEREY It was terrible what she told us. What do you think she'll do, Dad? I'm scared.

CHHEM [*confused*] Nowhere in the neighborhood. Perhaps she took the wrong bus.

SEREY She kept on saying she wanted to be alone.

KIM I can think of nothing scarier for her than to be alone outside in Long Beach. [*to Serey*] How could you let this happen?

SEREY It's not my fault. She hates it here, she can't rest. We yell too much.

KIM She's been keeping Oun's death inside all this time. I didn't know what to say. I've tried so hard to forget. [*listening on the phone*] Yes...I'll repeat it again. Thida San, Cambodian, blind...T-H-I-D-A...245 Seventh, Little Phnom Penh...And please, I'll be right over. [*hanging up*] I'll go to the police station, then check back with the doctor.

CHHEM We will find Thida. She knows more than she pretends. We will look everywhere. Savath always knows what to do.

KIM Chhem, will you go back to the temple and check again? And go with Serey so you don't get lost, too!

Lights shift to Thida, wearing the sunglasses and walking with her cane. Street sounds.

THIDA *I walk in a quiet place, the sun is so hot—hear only an occasional car. The wind blows sharply, as if through a tunnel.* [*Mugger appears behind her*]

MUGGER Hey! Your money, man. Hey!

THIDA *Grabs my arm so tight.*

MUGGER [*spins her around, knocking her glasses to the ground*] Your money! [*pulls a knife*]

THIDA [*unpins the plastic bag under her shirt*] My brother tells me to carry it always.

MUGGER Whatever, lady.

She pulls American bills from among her photos. Sound of a car approaching. Mugger grabs the plastic bag with photos and exits, crushing the sunglasses. Thida kneels and feels about on the ground.

THIDA Sipha. Oun. [*her fingers find the discarded plastic bag, the glasses*] I feel only crushed eyeglasses. [*stands, putting her hand to her shirt where her photos were pinned; sound of cars speeding by; against the blue, she bends down and feels the ground with her fingers*] I am now walking on earth, not on cement. In the distance I can hear the sound of strong wind in the trees... or perhaps it is the sound of waves. [*sound slowly becomes crashing waves*]

Lights shift to Savath, holding a map and hurrying to Serey and Chhem, who are waiting outside Kim's apartment building.

CHHEM What took you so long? We've searched every street...

SAVATH Everyone's looking: my agency, the temple, the community center—I've broken up the area into sections on the map.

THIDA [*walking*] Yes, I must be walking near the sea! Soon I will reach down and feel the sand. White. I say to Sipha as we walk, "Look at the sand, not the bones."

SAVATH [*to Chhem*] I want you to go to every neighbor and ask what they saw. She could be hiding right around here—that can happen. [*to Serey*] You go with her, page me on my beeper. What was she like last time you saw her?

SEREY I think she probably wanted to kill herself.

SAVATH You should've told me that on the phone.

SEREY She told us something bad about her daughter.

SAVATH That makes a big difference for the police.

THIDA [*continues to walk*] I'm going to the sea. Back to Cambodia.

SAVATH [*to Serey*] Where would she go?

SEREY Rushing traffic, the ocean? I don't know. It was a shock for her to let it out. I can't believe I let her run away.

SAVATH It's okay, we'll report that, too. We've got about a hundred people looking—even the monks. Your father is out with the detective.

SEREY What she told us... it makes me feel so empty. Like the worst part of the Thai camps.

SAVATH I know... that's how I felt when I lost my sister. [*calm and optimistic*] Hey, she survived the killing fields—she'll survive this.

THIDA [*sits cross-legged as the sun colors her face fiery orange; hears the rhythmic sound of oil pumps; lifting her head*] Ah, sun. Was it waves I heard, lapping on the shore? No, I was tired, from walking. [*listening*] But what is that strange whir, whir, whir? I don't recognize that. It comforts me...I'm floating. Below are the trees. And blue-green as far as I see. [*a beautiful vision*] The beach at Kep! [*meditates as light fades to night; hears the oil pumps*]

SAVATH [*holding a flashlight, walks over to Thida and leans down, touching her gently so as not to frighten her*] Mrs. San? It's Savath. Your family is here now. We've been looking since yesterday. The police that found you said you didn't want to talk.

Kim and Serey rush in, exclaiming in relief.

KIM Thida! Thida! [*laughing from panic*] I'm about to have a heart attack, and you're calmly meditating. You shaved your head?

THIDA I tried to walk to the sea.

SEREY You went in the wrong direction. If something had happened, I never would've forgiven myself.

KIM You shouldn't have run away.

SAVATH L.A.'s a dangerous place.

SEREY [*touches the initials on Thida's scalp*] Where did the letters on your head come from?

THIDA The Spider.

KIM I am more and more astonished.

SEREY [*touches Thida's ripped clothing*] What happened to your shirt?

THIDA [*feels where the plastic bag was pinned to her shirt*] They robbed me of the photographs of my family.

SAVATH She got mugged.

THIDA After that, I felt I must finally return.

KIM Return where, Sister?

THIDA To the beach at Kep. I am not alive.

KIM Of course you are. We see you right here in front of us. Living, breathing.

THIDA My soul left my body and traveled to Kep.

KIM I was mistaken to leave you alone with Serey. Now I understand why you wanted to hide in the dark for so long in our country. I wish I could've been there to comfort you.

THIDA You promised I could go to your temple to live. Now I've waited long enough!

KIM You wouldn't be safe at the temple. It's with your family that you'll finally get better, surrounded by those who care for you.

SEREY My dad's right. We want you to get better now, Auntie.

THIDA Without my vision, I am useless.

KIM I sometimes feel that I can't live, but we go on for our ancestors. The doctor got money from the university to study your case. Here's someone who wants to solve the problem. Of course there's a scientific answer. And one day you'll see again. You will see Serey's children.

SEREY I may not have children. [*Kim gives her a dirty look*] But if I do, sure, you can see them. Or not. Whatever. We just want you to be happier. We meant no disrespect.

KIM [*holds Thida to him*] We're the last survivors of our family. You have to trust me.

THIDA I want to become a nun. That is final!

SEREY The temple is a warehouse with peeling paint. You wouldn't want to live there.

THIDA He said it was like the temples in Cambodia.

SEREY He lies sometimes.

KIM Serey.

SEREY Sees things through rose-colored glasses. I'll take you to the temple more often, I promise.

THIDA [*listening to oil pumps*] Where am I?

SAVATH You're in an oil field.

Scene Nine

Thida taps her cane impatiently as Dr. Simpson shares her research with Kim in her office.

DR. SIMPSON There are about 150 survivors: a cluster of women in Long Beach who don't know each other. I can't find any anywhere else. We're testing blood pressure, heart rate, doing neurological tests. My colleagues are looking forward to meeting you, Thida.

THIDA I am not here.

KIM You need to stop saying that now. You are clearly here in front of us. [*to Dr. Simpson*] She says her soul left her body and traveled to the beach at Kep. [*to Thida*] A soul is a mysterious thing. It wanes like the moon, but it comes back to full, you'll see.

DR. SIMPSON We'll do an ERG and an MRI, so we can look at your brain.

THIDA Do so at your own risk.

KIM Stop that with your cane. They want to ask you some questions about your background.

THIDA She doesn't listen.

DR. SIMPSON What kind of suffering could be so great that it would blind someone? It's the grief that interests me and how that affects the eye.

THIDA You do not understand.

KIM What?

THIDA I see the same things over and over in my head. At night I cannot sleep. My head, it pounds, as if a nail is being twisted into it.

DR. SIMPSON We need to give you some medicine for your headache, Thida. That will help.

KIM Of course. Why didn't you tell me this?

THIDA [*to Dr. Simpson*] I do not want the medicine. It's bad for you. [*to Kim*] I want to go to the temple. Plan a ceremony for Sipha.

KIM What are you talking about now?

THIDA Release him.

DR. SIMPSON Who is Sipha?

KIM Her husband.

DR. SIMPSON Medicine will help for your headache. [*to Kim*] I'll need her to come with me to the resident presentation, and if she could come back for more tests, I have the women scheduled all week.

KIM I'll be interested to see if you can find any organic basis for this.

DR. SIMPSON Yes, the funders were generous with something that could easily be interpreted as psychosomatic. [*joking*] It also helps my reputation for not being a "people person."

KIM I see. I loved doing research. Here, in this country, I'm a lab technician. This is more exciting than doing blood work.

DR. SIMPSON I'm sure you were a good doctor. I'm grateful to you.

THIDA I feel sick.

KIM You must go with Dr. Simpson.

THIDA [*muttering to herself*] The walking dead. [*to Dr. Simpson*] Can you make yourself useful and bring me to the temple, Doctor?

KIM Thida!

DR. SIMPSON [*to Kim*] I'll make sure someone gets her home, about five. Will someone be there?

KIM Yes. Just don't lose her. [*exits*]

Lights shift as Dr. Simpson addresses her residents, who are in silhouette, examining Thida.

DR. SIMPSON No country has lost such a sizable part of its population in such a short time and was stripped of an entire generation of people with education. [*staring off*] I'm sorry... The earth leaves me sometimes... Who had a question?

The residents interrogate Thida.

RESIDENT 1 [*voice-over*] You see nothing at all, Mrs. San?

THIDA No.

RESIDENT 2 [*v.o.*] Did the insomnia and headaches come with the onset of the blindness, Mrs. San?

THIDA I can't remember.

RESIDENT 3 [*v.o.*] Can you describe the nature of the forced labor, Mrs. San?

THIDA Leave me alone.

RESIDENT 1 [*v.o.*] How long were the periods of starvation?

DR. SIMPSON Trust in society was eroded; the perpetrators were often victims—many young boys were forced into the Khmer Rouge during the instability of the Viet Nam War bombings and the country's own civil war...

RESIDENT 2 [*v.o.*] Did you experience shell explosions, Mrs. San?

RESIDENT 3 [*v.o.*] Did you suffer injuries to the back of your head?

RESIDENT 1 [*v.o.*] Do you have a history of cataracts, glaucoma, Mrs. San?

RESIDENT 2 [*v.o.*] Can she speak?

RESIDENT 3 [*v.o.*] Were there remnants of Agent Orange in that area?

RESIDENT 2 [*v.o.*] Is this a symptom of PTSD?

RESIDENT 1 [*v.o.*] Does her culture somatize illness?

RESIDENT 3 [*v.o.*] Has she worn a halter monitor while she's been questioned about trauma?

RESIDENT 1 [*v.o.*] Have you repeated the MRI, Mrs. San?

ALL THE RESIDENTS [*v.o.*] Mrs. San?

Scene Ten

Thida sits by the window.

SEREY [*enters*] You're really *pissed* at my dad. [*explaining*] Angry.

THIDA Correct.

SEREY He has that effect on people. When you ran away, it made me think of the camp. We lived in a hole, Aunt, before we got assigned a refugee number in Thailand. It was just he and I, and a jerrycan of water. He'd stay up at night, wouldn't let me stray anywhere. I found out later it was 'cause the Khmer Rouge from the next camp raped girls.

THIDA On the day the Khmer Rouge came into Phnom Penh, a statue of the Buddha cried real tears.

SEREY I'd ask him to show me my mother's photograph over and over. The only thing pretty. I'd ask, Where was she in the photo? At home? Where would she go after the picture was taken? The color of the blouse? The little scarf? If I could just get back to where she was in the picture. He'd never say anything, just stare off. He'd put the photo back in the plastic bag, fold it in a square, and pin it back to the inside of his undershirt. I miss her so much, but I didn't even really know her. [*filled with grief for what she can't have and won't ever know*]

THIDA Serey? The photo as you describe it would not be taken in her house. She would be in the studio at a photographer's—a room with a red-velvet drape. After the picture was taken, she would accompany your father for tea at an outdoor café with white tablecloths and silver. They would hold hands and watch the sun setting, the villas changing color. There would be a soft wind. They would have sandals, which they would slip off under the table. Their feet would touch. Her blouse is pink, I'm certain, and the scarf blue.

SEREY I'm sorry about Oun.

THIDA You are a stubborn one, like her. She was a fighter.

SEREY Did you choose your own husband?

THIDA No, it was my parents who chose him.

SEREY Did you love him?

THIDA He saved my life, warning me to take off my glasses. Our last moment together, I understood what love was. [*Serey kisses her and exits*] I stand in the blue-green water, feel my baby kick. Hear the sound of waves breaking, smell the salt air. At Kep, I waded in the aqua water, lay on the white-sand beach. Sipha would rub my shoulders…

Scene Eleven

Serey and Savath sip espresso after dinner in a restaurant. The room is revolving.

SEREY I like the way this restaurant spins. So you can see different parts of the city all the time. Not that the smog makes it possible. I'd like to live in a house that spins.

SAVATH Why?

SEREY So you could see the world from all different sides. It's boring to look out a window and see the same thing. In my case, a trash dumpster, thank you. But think if you saw a waterfall, a volcano, a cabana, and a child playing. If it was always changing.

SAVATH A cabana?

SEREY Like in Hawaii. I really want to go there. I want to scuba dive.

SAVATH So do I. Think of how good you'd feel if you breathed underwater. Like a fish. Want to go to Hawaii?

SEREY Isn't that the big "honeymoon place"?

SAVATH [*noticing*] Are you hyped on coffee?

SEREY My head's spinning a little. It feels good. I thought you were the big Buddhist-of-the-Year. You drink double espressos?

SAVATH Of course. With my job, I need all the help I can get. Living in courtrooms, the DMV? Writing petitions so Khmer people don't get arrested for child abuse when they "coin" their kids? Plus, this espresso is good.

SEREY We should go dancing. Except not that corny Khmer stuff. We should go to a club. Get all sweaty. It makes you forget.

SAVATH I love the Khmer stuff. Sin Sisamouth.

SEREY He died at Tuol Sleng, you know. It's like if America sent Elvis to a concentration camp. Why would anyone do that?

SAVATH You're right. I don't know why anyone would do that.

SEREY Okay. [*gulps her espresso*] So we've been on their "second date." I like this place. I like the tablecloths and the silver.

SAVATH I'm glad you like it so much.

SEREY My aunt would like it. She's classy. I used to lust after her makeup when I was little. I wished I could steal her lipstick.

SAVATH You look very classy in that silk.

SEREY My dad's never seen this. [*shows him a tiny tattoo above her breast*]

SAVATH A lotus. It's sexy.

SEREY You found my aunt. You know everyone. It's good the way you never get freaked. [*he touches her hand*] So. I have an idea. It's bold. These two weirdos are breathing down our necks. [*quoting*] "We want to adapt to the American ways; go on a date." They think they're trying to be so smart. So we one-up them.

SAVATH I think I may know what you're talking about. But I may just be dreaming.

SEREY I mean, I hate to say this…It sounds, I don't know, but doesn't it always come down to…? I mean if that doesn't work, if that part's not happening, then it's a kind of a big commitment to make for an entire lifetime.

SAVATH [*teasing her*] I like that you're bold. I really like that.

SEREY I thought… [*he leans over and kisses her*] I think you're really good looking. Sometimes I worry you're too serious.

SAVATH I am serious.

SEREY [*making up her mind*] Okay. Let's check in to the spinning hotel.

SAVATH Get the biggest, most expensive room, with a tape player. Make it beautiful. I have my credit card.

SEREY You know the hotel part doesn't spin.

SAVATH We might be able to make it spin. I'm not as square as you think.

SEREY [*looks at him*] It's my first time.

SAVATH Me, too. [*protectively*] It will be our secret.

Scene Twelve

Dr. Simpson talks to Kim near the altar as Thida sits by the window.

DR. SIMPSON Has she spoken since the residents' presentation?

KIM No.

DR. SIMPSON They were asking her questions, and she stopped suddenly. She wouldn't say anything.

KIM Sister, Lynn needs you to answer when people ask questions. If you see, then perhaps it will stop the memories in your head. They will be replaced by new ones.

THIDA She knows nothing.

KIM Thida!

DR. SIMPSON I had to reschedule. We'll see if she can do it next week. It's hard to get all the doctors in the same room.

KIM Yes, she'll be better next week.

DR. SIMPSON And she refused to have another MRI so we could look at her brain.

KIM Perhaps she got overly tired. How did the MRI research turn out?

DR. SIMPSON They do have similar problems—high blood pressure, heart palpitations—but it's still somewhat of a mystery. I should go.

KIM May I ask... Do you eat, Doctor? You look thin.

DR. SIMPSON I drink too much coffee and smoke. [*ironically*] In some ways, it really functions almost better than food.

KIM Did I tell you? I'm quitting.

DR. SIMPSON Really?

KIM Soon, very soon.

DR. SIMPSON Just about the time I do.

KIM Perhaps stay for dinner? Any good doctor knows one must eat. Shrimp with lemongrass and pepper, squash soup. Chicken in coconut milk and lime, with Chinese broccoli?

DR. SIMPSON I better run. I'll check in with you tomorrow and see how she's doing.

KIM We received good news. My daughter just got into college.

DR. SIMPSON Congratulations.

KIM But I ask myself over and over: what can happen in four years?

DR. SIMPSON I think by then we'll find a cure for your sister.

KIM Yes. I always cook too much food, and my sister eats none of it; Serey's always at the library. Can I put some food in a container for you? I hope you don't stay up all night with that research. You need to sleep, too.

DR. SIMPSON It's a fantastic project. There has to be something—I just know it.

KIM Sit and have tea, while you wait for the food. Take a breath. Enjoy yourself. You're so lucky.

DR. SIMPSON Lucky?

KIM You have everything.

DR. SIMPSON Everything?

KIM I miss my work. I miss a lot of things.

DR. SIMPSON I'll stay and eat. It smells good.

KIM [*touches her hand*] Just sit, I'll serve you—don't worry about anything. [*starts to exit and runs into Serey; Kim and Serey try to keep their voices down as Thida sits* *in her chair by the window and Dr. Simpson waits*] Chhem has already rented an entire restaurant!

SEREY So what?! I'm not doing it. I told you that already. We both told you.

KIM I wish your mother was here. [*putting his hands together*] I wish to Buddha and all the gods in the sky and all the gods in the Long Beach cement that she was here.

SEREY What's gotten into you?

KIM [*to himself*] Why do I have to be the one to do this? Why?!

SEREY Do what? Cool out. Take a breath.

KIM Cool out?

DR. SIMPSON [*starting to leave*] I'll go.

SEREY [*to Dr. Simpson*] Sorry he's acting so strange.

KIM Forgive us, this is poor timing. Please come back for dinner.

DR. SIMPSON Yes. [*exits*]

SEREY Savath's grandmother is having a bad influence on you, Dad.

KIM [*trying to gather his courage*] Okay, okay, okay.

SEREY Jesus.

KIM Don't swear.

SEREY "Jesus" isn't swearing; plus, we're not Christian.

KIM So why do you talk about Jesus? We're off the subject. If you do what the Americans do... you know... the... [*trying to explain sex; partly using the palms-pressed-together-slow-dance-analogy Chhem used*] You know... I can't say it.

SEREY Dad, you are so goofy.

KIM Don't call me goofy! Have you had conjugal relations with a man?!

SEREY Look... it's different here.

KIM What are you saying?

SEREY I had to "check it out"...

KIM "Check it out"?

SEREY [*a beat*] I've had sex with Savath.

KIM Oh no, God! [*an aside*] Do you think your aunt can hear?

THIDA Every word.

SEREY I don't want a marriage where in ten years we hate each other.

KIM *Serey, you are a fallen woman! Why did you do this? What is wrong with you?*

SEREY It's fine.

KIM *No, it's not fine!*

SEREY It was good...

KIM You've ruined my life. [*deadpan*] "It was good." [*to Thida*] America has turned her into nothing!

SEREY I can't help who I am... He's a lot different than I thought.

KIM Oh. [*deadpan*] Wonderful. [*freaking out about what they are discussing; to Thida*] Why me, Sister?! [*to Serey*] You are worthless! What will people say?!

SEREY It's none of their business.

KIM It's everyone's business! You'll see! You have to get married right now, Serey.

SEREY Thanks for trusting me.

KIM I don't. And now I don't trust Savath.

SEREY He loves that I'm going to college first; he wouldn't care if I went to graduate school.

KIM Graduate school? No! What am I saying? Yes, go to graduate school, get your Ph.D. [*to Thida*] I don't care what she does anymore.

THIDA [*to Kim*] Maybe you picked the right man for her after all.

KIM [*takes a pen from his shirt pocket*] You want me to undo all the plans with Chhem? Cancel everything? Pay her back for what she has bought?

SEREY You're not listening. You never do.

KIM I did listen, and it was a disaster.

SEREY Well, too bad my mother isn't here. Too bad there isn't anyone here who gets it. It's hard. You think I like being the only child left? We're supposed to look to the future—that's what you say—but all you do is live in the past. I'm going to college and maybe I'll transfer. Transfer right out of here.

KIM Fine, transfer. Be like all the other American families, *separated* and alone.

SEREY [*looks at the pen*] Why do you steal pens, Dad? You take them from everywhere—banks, gas stations, stores. [*takes another pen out of his pocket*]

THIDA The officials killed us because we could read and write. Then they kept pens in their pockets to show us their power.

KIM I guess I can't help myself.

Scene Thirteen

Chhem is in Kim's garden. Thida sits inside.

CHHEM [*calling to Thida*] What were you thinking to get those initials on your head?

SAVATH [*entering*] Grandma?

CHHEM His sister is slowly going crazy. Kim is so patient, but we have to watch her every minute. [*gathers some fruit*] My mother used to give me a hook and let me climb the ladder to gather the ripe ones. How I loved to see the trees from above.

SAVATH Grandma, I need to talk to you. Don't bug Serey anymore. [*taking out a letter*] Listen, and try not to talk.

CHHEM I should go inside and attend to Thida.

SAVATH This is Serey's college acceptance letter. She showed it to me...on our "date." She's very proud.

CHHEM But the wedding will be next month. We have already purchased the bedroom set.

SAVATH Look, it's generous to get the bedroom set, but that's not really what we need.

CHHEM She will have children! When your mother died, I prayed that you would stay with me and promised in return I would do good.

SAVATH You're seeing all this in your head, but it's not going to happen that way. She'll go to college for four years. Then, if we want, maybe we'll get married.

CHHEM Four years? Who will cook your food?

SAVATH I eat out.

CHHEM Who will do your laundry? Clean your house? You will wait for four years to be together? To have children?

SAVATH It's a whole different thing here, Grandma...

CHHEM No engagement? No party? No announcement? No invitations? No prayers? I want to give back to the monks.

SAVATH None of that. We'll date, maybe take a trip to Hawaii on her break, go out dancing.

CHHEM Slow dancing?

SAVATH I think she likes rock.

CHHEM [*hearing "rock"*] I will go buy her a ring tomorrow!

SAVATH I already bought one. [*taking out a box*] You want to see it?

CHHEM Ah, why did you not let me pick it out?

SAVATH I think our tastes are at opposite ends of the planet.

CHHEM I want to pay for it. The rock is too small, the band too thin.

SAVATH She likes it.

CHHEM No! She cannot see it before the wedding!

SAVATH I showed it to her in a window. I didn't say it was for her. It's a double thing: college, engagement. And actually, something else...Love.

CHHEM Love? You must get married now, Savath. I have already made the invitations and reserved the temple.

SAVATH Well, unreserve it! Tear them up.

CHHEM You are disrespectful.

SAVATH *I* need to respect Serey.

CHHEM All the evil we saw, we must preserve our customs. The astrologer is very optimistic.

SAVATH We're not getting married because of the stars!

CHHEM Think: the gold I hid in the soles of my shoes, the chains in my clothing's seams. *They* did not find it. It is for you and your new family. She is "easy," she'll sleep with anyone.

SAVATH *I won't listen to that!*

CHHEM You will make me lose face with Serey's father.

SAVATH It's not about you. [*vulnerable*] Look, it may not work out, okay? We don't know. It's a risk I have to take.

CHHEM You'll see, everything good about our country will disappear!

Scene Fourteen

Dr. Simpson and Kim smoke in his garden. Sirens sound in the distance.

KIM Now the three women in my life aren't talking to me. My sister is angry at me, my daughter hates me, and my daughter's fiancé's grandmother has taken out a contract on me by now.

DR. SIMPSON You're very funny.

KIM Why?

DR. SIMPSON I don't know. You just are.

KIM My daughter says "goofy." Thida refuses to see you. I wonder what happened. Ever since the meeting with the residents, she seems worse.

DR. SIMPSON Let me talk to her.

KIM Anything new on the research?

DR. SIMPSON There are no links. The women have some of the same symptoms—that's the best conclusion. I won't be able to get the second part of the funding if I can't prove more. There may have been something I missed. The other women are reacting like your sister: they're withdrawing, don't want to be tested more, don't want to be seen. It's hard to do a study when the subjects don't want to get better.

KIM Why not visit the temple on Willow Street? Take a look.

DR. SIMPSON I ask myself this question: you saw trauma, but why didn't you go blind?

KIM Have you ever had a moment when medical science doesn't help?

DR. SIMPSON [*a beat*] Yes.

KIM We discovered recently that Thida's daughter refused to marry a Khmer Rouge soldier and was killed in front of her. We did not know this before. Her daughter was beheaded. Thida saw her burn.

DR. SIMPSON You can't reverse that.

KIM I promised my wife I'd take care of our children. As a doctor, I was a marked man. I pretended I was a farmer, rubbed my hands in the dirt until they had calluses. [*looking at his cigarette*] You know the Khmer Rouge rolled their cigarettes with pages from books and plays. Serey is all I have left. You're lucky your eyes have not seen such horror.

DR. SIMPSON This is a beautiful garden.

KIM Thank you. Sometimes, solutions are found outside. Prayer, food, family... growing beans... a nap?

DR. SIMPSON A nap would be good.

KIM Sitting around and doing nothing at all.

DR. SIMPSON Laughing a lot.

KIM Who knows?

DR. SIMPSON I don't.

KIM Go talk to Thida. Let me get some food for you to bring home.

Lights up on Thida, who sits as Dr. Simpson approaches.

DR. SIMPSON In this country, we get so carried away with the diagnostic procedures that we lose sight of the patient.

THIDA You smoke too much.

DR. SIMPSON I'm sorry.

THIDA I will never again have a test.

DR. SIMPSON Were they uncomfortable?

THIDA Everything is uncomfortable. I am a prisoner.

DR. SIMPSON Let me ask you this: you said your soul left your body and traveled to the beach at Kep. How does a soul leave a body?

THIDA How does it, Doctor?

DR. SIMPSON Yes, that's what I asked.

THIDA What do you think?

DR. SIMPSON Well, perhaps because the pain is too great?

THIDA Yes. What do you do with your day?

DR. SIMPSON Work.

THIDA Do you ever go to sleep?

DR. SIMPSON Not much. What was at the beach at Kep?

THIDA Such beauty. Do you have a family? Are you married?

DR. SIMPSON Yes. My husband, Tom, is dead.

THIDA How did Tom die?

DR. SIMPSON [*sees Thida is waiting*] He had an illness.

THIDA What type?

DR. SIMPSON I can't talk about it.

THIDA I know.

DR. SIMPSON A disease of the nervous system. It was like a bomb that went off in his body. And in mine.

THIDA Where did your soul go?

DR. SIMPSON Nowhere beautiful. [*takes a photo from her wallet, then takes Thida's hand and passes it over the photo*] We were everything to each other. I lost my only family. It happened fast... I don't know. [*breaks down*] I couldn't bear it. That kind of illness can't be explained—it's too cruel.

THIDA You see: telling the story is very difficult. Almost like being strangled.

Kim enters with a food container. Dr. Simpson puts away the photo, then takes the food container and exits.

KIM What happened to the doctor?

THIDA She lost her husband some time ago.

KIM She wears the ring. Why did you talk to *her* if you are so unwilling to talk?

THIDA I must find you and her some herbs. Margosa, coconut milk... Release of stress for you, sleep for her.

KIM [*puzzled*] Why did the doctor make you feel better?

THIDA I felt useful. She did not know something, and *I* knew.

KIM I need your help, too, Sister. You're useful to me. I need you to live.

THIDA Why not take me to your garden? I'm sorry I've always refused your invitations.

KIM Really, you'd like to come? [*starts to take her to the garden*]

Lights shift to Dr. Simpson slowly entering the temple. She speaks her thoughts aloud, using a microphone.

DR. SIMPSON I add my shoes to the mountain of shoes. The temple is crowded with bright silk, an American flag, a stray skeleton from Halloween. Monks in orange robes sit cross-legged on dainty satin pillows eating from an array of bowls. People kneel, talking. The altar is filled with baskets of tea, money, cigarettes, Oreos. A statue of Buddha is cloaked in the same robe as the monks. Blind women, shoulders slumped, staring off, expressionless, holding canes. Life whirls around them, but they aren't there. Where? How can they come back? [*a realization*] You almost have to die first before you can live again.

Scene Fifteen

Kim takes a photo of Serey and Savath. Dr. Simpson sits in Kim's living room with Thida; Chhem serves dessert.

CHHEM [*to Dr. Simpson*] After this engagement party, I have four years to wait for my grandson's marriage. I have taken up embroidery, Doctor. A very long project. I hope I don't die before the wedding.

DR. SIMPSON I'm sure it will be okay.

CHHEM Okay? The tradition is ruined.

Kim, Serey, and Savath enter the living room as Dr. Simpson gives Thida a box. Sound of sirens outside the apartment.

THIDA [*opening box*] I would like to preserve the wrapping. [*showing a skirt*] It is a *sampot*.

DR. SIMPSON Red and yellow. Serey told me about the shop.

SEREY The lady gets the silk from a co-op in Takeo. It's pretty...

CHHEM And I helped pick it out.

THIDA [*to Dr. Simpson*] You must take it. I will never again have the occasion.

DR. SIMPSON It's for you. I wanted to thank you. The tea helped me sleep. I started thinking.

THIDA About what?

DR. SIMPSON Memories.

THIDA You've changed. You seem lighter. [*feels the fabric*] You have good taste. Why do you not try it on? It would give me so much pleasure to see you dressed in something different for once.

DR. SIMPSON You can't see me.

THIDA I do know what you wear. I asked my brother to tell me.

KIM I said you dressed very well. [*to Thida*] Why don't you try it on?

THIDA [*to Dr. Simpson*] I do not feel like changing.

DR. SIMPSON Serey says you were a city lady. I'm sure you were very elegant.

THIDA I adored clothes. It was another life... I cannot imagine. It would give me pleasure if you would try it on... just to see. [*holds out the long skirt*] Take it. [*Dr. Simpson tries it on*] It is from my country. Let me feel. [*feels and adjusts it; Dr. Simpson stands in the skirt*] You have given me something very beautiful.

DR. SIMPSON What?

THIDA A way to imagine something different. I always admired doctors. And now there's you.

SEREY It's nice. [*to Savath*] You should buy me one! [*Savath puts his arm around her*]

CHHEM They show the world. They are a mystery to me.

THIDA [*touches Serey, speaking softly*] You know, I was a midwife. I will be able to help you someday.

KIM [*listening to sirens*] Why don't these gangs stop? War follows us everywhere.

THIDA It's always that way. A little girl drops a grain of rice on the floor, and a lizard grabs it. A cat sees the lizard and pounces, which brings the dog. The cat's owner starts to beat the dog, and this angers the dog's owner. The two men start to fight, and the families, neighbors join in until everyone is fighting. Word reaches Angkor that a fight is raging. The king thinks it's an attack by a foreign enemy and rushes out with ten thousand men and elephants. The king of Siam thinks the Khmers are mobilizing to attack him and rushes out with his men and elephants. All because a careless little girl drops a grain of rice, a war breaks out. I never thought war could touch a place like Kep, but we've always had fighting. Siam. Viet Nam. The U.S. We are a small country.

KIM I'm so happy you told us that story. My sister was always an excellent storyteller.

SEREY You know, Aunt, maybe only big countries survive? A simple law of size.

Savath puts on some Willie Nelson music.

CHHEM Ah, now is the time! Would you like some more to eat?

THIDA [*listens to the music*] Sipha loved him.

KIM Who?

THIDA Willie Nelson.

DR. SIMPSON Your husband loved Willie Nelson?

Savath puts the ring on Serey's finger.

CHHEM Finally, the ring.

SEREY [*looks at the ring*] Okay, we've made a commitment to each other. We think we want to have children, but I really need to go to college. We'll probably have a traditional wedding, but we also want to help plan it. [*taking something out*] I have a ring.

CHHEM Another?

SEREY [*puts it on Savath's finger; to Kim*] I want to honor you. And my mother. I know we can never forget what happened, Dad. [*to Thida*] You know, maybe big countries like this survive because of the stuff from the little countries? We're family. We have to stay together, and we have to grow up.

KIM I don't know. Fate has put part of you here and part of you there. [*looks anxiously at Serey*]

THIDA [*turns in Kim's direction*] She's intelligent. A fighter. You must trust her.

KIM Yes.

Scene Sixteen

Blue of ocean and sounds of waves. Thida sits with Dr. Simpson.

DR. SIMPSON [*looking out to sea*] Do you see colors?

THIDA Yellow powder spread on a woman's body after giving birth. Green lemon leaves steamed for the new mother to bathe in. Brown star anise with its delicate flower. Cook it in a curry and take her to the sea. Let her play until she gets hungry, then feed her the dish. When she is finished, tell her your stories, take her to the top of the mountain, and show her how beautiful when the sun goes down. [*points*] Look... [*turning to Dr. Simpson*] Thank you for bringing me here. What is the color of the water?

DR. SIMPSON It's blue-gray, darker in the parts where there's seaweed. The shore is flat all the way to the sea. The sand is brown. The waves—you hear them?

THIDA Yes.

DR. SIMPSON They break in one place, then ripple in a straight, white line.

THIDA [*hears the sound of a wave breaking; wades into the water, holding up her skirt*] Colder than Kep.

DR. SIMPSON Blindness. That's how you survived.

THIDA There was once a lady who poured out all her misfortunes to the Buddha. He told her these miseries would go away if she obtained a seed from a house that had never known sorrow. When the Buddha asked the woman if she had found the Seed of Happiness, she replied, "No. I went to every house seeking it and found no house that had not known sorrow." [*the two women stand in the water*] In my country, we believe your husband's spirit will always protect you. [*peering far out*] Lynn?

DR. SIMPSON Yes?

THIDA I still see her head bobbing up and down against the line of the horizon. I still hear Sipha and myself calling her name. She said no to them.

Oun appears against the blue. She slowly walks out of the sea. Lights fade.

A PROJECTION READS: "AT LEAST 150 CAMBODIAN WOMEN LIVING IN SOUTHERN CALIFORNIA HAVE FUNCTIONAL BLINDNESS, A PSYCHOSOMATIC VISION LOSS LINKED TO WHAT THEY SAW IN THE YEARS OF KHMER ROUGE RULE." THE NEW YORK TIMES, AUGUST 8, 1989.

A Conversation with Catherine Filloux

For twenty-five years, Catherine Filloux has been writing plays about human rights and social justice. She has also been a spokesperson for the value of theater as a force for social change. She has given readings and workshops and overseen productions in Cambodia, Sudan, South Sudan, Iraq, Morocco, Northern Ireland, Italy, Belgium, and Bosnia. Her more than twenty plays and librettos have been produced in New York, across the U.S., and in Europe, Asia, and the Middle East, and her essays have appeared in such leading theater magazines as *American Theatre* and *Drama Review*.

Most recently, she was honored in New York City with the 2017 Otto René Castillo Award for Political Theatre. Her new play *Kidnap Road* was presented by Anna Deavere Smith as part of NYU's Institute on the Arts and Civic Dialogue in 2016. For her long career of activism in the theater community, Filloux received the 2015 Planet Activist Award. Her play *whatdoesfreemean?*—about women and mass incarceration in the U.S.—will premiere in 2018, produced by Nora's Playhouse. She is also the librettist for three produced operas—including *Where Elephants Weep,* which premiered in Cambodia—and has been commissioned by the Vienna State Opera to write the libretto for composer Olga Neuwirth's new opera, *Orlando,* to premiere in 2019.

A former Fulbright senior specialist in Cambodia and Morocco, Filloux is an artist-in-residence at La MaMa Theatre, a member of the Vassar College faculty, and a cofounder of Theatre Without Borders.

The following conversation took place in July 2017.

MĀNOA You've been writing plays for a long time. What in your background led you to concentrate on issues of human rights, social justice, and equality?

CATHERINE FILLOUX French was my first language, and when I learned English I consumed it with joy. I grew up on the border between San Diego and Tijuana, and was very familiar with that border and with Mexico. My father grew up in France during the Nazi occupation when the country was split into zones. My mother's French-Belgian-Corsican family lived in Algeria, North Africa, for three generations before her. I inherited the privilege of being a citizen of the world. And we were strangers in a strange land.

When I first went to Cambodia in 2001, it was almost a decade after I had begun writing about the genocide. What Cambodian women refugees had told me for years made it seem as if Pol Pot—his real name Saloth Sar—was in the room with us, though we were in Bronx, New York. Why did he do it? I wondered. Why were they now here, these women whom I grew to love, in this strange land, where they told me Spanish would be a better language to learn than English, since the Bronx was a Dominican neighborhood. And also Dominican were the Sisters who ran St. Rita's Refugee Center in the Bronx, where we all met.

When I landed for the first time at the airport in Phnom Penh, I could feel the wandering ghosts, *kmauit,* as I got on the back of a moto and entered the sea of motos that formed the most extraordinary Zen flow of traffic I'd ever seen.

MĀNOA   You have had plays produced, held workshops, and spoken about theater and human rights all over the world. And Theatre Without Borders, which you cofounded, is devoted to supporting theater worldwide. How would you compare the ways that socially aware theater such as yours—dealing with very difficult social and legal issues—is received in some of the countries you've been to? What has been the reaction to these kinds of plays?

CF   I've experienced productions of my plays translated into languages including Arabic, Bosnian, French, Guatemalan Spanish, Khmer (Cambodian), and Kurdish, in a variety of international venues. I'm always struck by the flexibility that is required when a playwright crosses borders. In the U.S., a playwright's words are not to be altered; however, I've found that compromise and having an open mind are key attributes. One lives in between languages, always hoping to find better connections and associations for translation and not always succeeding. However, this itself is part of that artistic process.

MĀNOA   Most of the plays in *Eyes of the Heart* deal with the unequal status of women, who are the main characters in all the works except *Lemkin's House*—and there, women also figure prominently. Do you feel a responsibility to portray the global condition of women in your work, and do you think that too little attention has been given to women in theater, especially with regard to human rights?

CF   I wrote the play *Mary and Myra* in the year 2000, and in 2016 I saw a production in Salt Lake City, right before the presidential election. The timeliness of this story was apparent. History repeats itself. Plays may influence and offer the tools to help people make distinctions between truth and lies, and to nurture intellectual and emotional freedom. Myra Bradwell was written out of history by her adversary, Susan B. Anthony, and needed to be resurrected. And Mary's reputation was maligned by biographers. Theater places stories in front of hearts and minds, as a sentient being, as an experience that is living and transforming. In my play, Mary Todd Lincoln says to Myra Bradwell, "I believe you mean well with your causes. But you fight so often with the opposite sex you've become it." And Myra responds, "I have fought endlessly for justice, placing the law ahead of myself on every occasion, and they have ignored me, trampled on me, placed obstacle after obstacle in my path. I am furious! Give me the secret about your son." When I saw *Mary and Myra* recently, I remembered how its first director commented that Myra's lines sounded perhaps a bit too much like the playwright. I smiled to myself when I heard the play so many years later.

I read that Raphael Lemkin was home-schooled by his mother. This inspired me in writing the end of my play *Lemkin's House*. Plays and theater can raise awareness regarding challenging subjects—creating a space for dialogue—and a commitment to the power of language and the power of healing. Theater can have a responsibility to foster civic discourse and to spark people to think critically. It can offer ethical queries and put marginalized communities onto center stage.

MĀNOA   War and violence are important issues in your plays. How are you able to put such large, difficult subjects on the stage, especially using so few actors? How does your passion for these subjects affect your daily life?

CF   I see myself as a witness in my theater work. In terms of theatrical language, I like to design a kind of poetry, which lives and breathes through action and characters onstage. The poet Wallace Stevens says, "The poem must resist the intelligence / Almost successfully." The language of theater onstage and the audience are involved in a collaboration—a co-creation. I believe theater as an art form exists every time differently—it lives and breathes in a community. When Albert Camus, the French and Algerian author, says theater is, "The night when the game is played," he means each time with a different outcome, like a sports match. And for me, theater pieces are prisms, which cast different lights for each audience member: everyone imagines and interprets the plays differently, which allows a shared personal experience.

MĀNOA   Thank you for your work.

ABOUT THE ARTIST

Camille Assaf is a French and American costume designer for theater, dance, opera, and film, and a lead design editor at *Chance,* a photography magazine that looks at the world through the lens of theatrical design. Recent work in the U.S. has included designs for productions of the Santa Fe Opera, Juilliard Opera, Metropolitan Opera's Lindemann Program, and McCarter Theater. She has also created costumes for productions at Wolf Trap, the National Gallery in Washington, D.C., New York City Ballet, and many regional theater companies across the U.S.

Internationally, her designs were included in "Costume at the Turn of the Century, 1990–2015," a major exhibition in Moscow. In 2008, she was part of a team, led by Eiko Ishioka, that designed costumes for the Beijing Olympic Games' opening and closing ceremonies. She has also produced designs for the Palais de Tokyo (Paris), Opera Holland Park (London), Shanghai Performing Arts Academy, Hong Kong Fringe Club, and Théâtre Municipal de Castres in France.

Her honors include the Leo Lerman Fellowship award and selection for the Theatre Communications Group Career Development Program. She has collaborated with Catherine Filloux since 2004, designing costumes for the plays *Lemkin's House* and *Killing the Boss,* as well as Filloux's Cambodian rock-opera, *Where Elephants Weep,* which premiered in Phnom Penh.

COPYRIGHT AND PERMISSIONS

Selma '65 © 2016 Catherine Filloux
Lemkin's House © 2007 Catherine Filloux
Eyes of the Heart © 2007 Catherine Filloux
Mary and Myra © 2005 Catherine Filloux
Reprinted by permission of Playscripts, Inc.
To purchase acting editions of *Lemkin's House, Eyes of the Heart, Mary and Myra,* and *Selma '65* or to obtain performance rights, contact Playscripts, Inc., www.playscripts.com
info@playscripts.com.

Kidnap Road © 2017 Catherine Filloux
Silence of God © 2007 Catherine Filloux
To obtain performance rights to *Silence of God* and *Kidnap Road,* contact Elaine Devlin Literary, Inc., 411 Lafayette St., 6th Floor, New York, NY 10003
edevlinlit@aol.com.

WWW.UHPRESS.HAWAII.EDU/JOURNALS

UNIVERSITY of
HAWAI'I
PRESS
JOURNALS

OTHER MĀNOA TITLES PUBLISHED BY UH PRESS

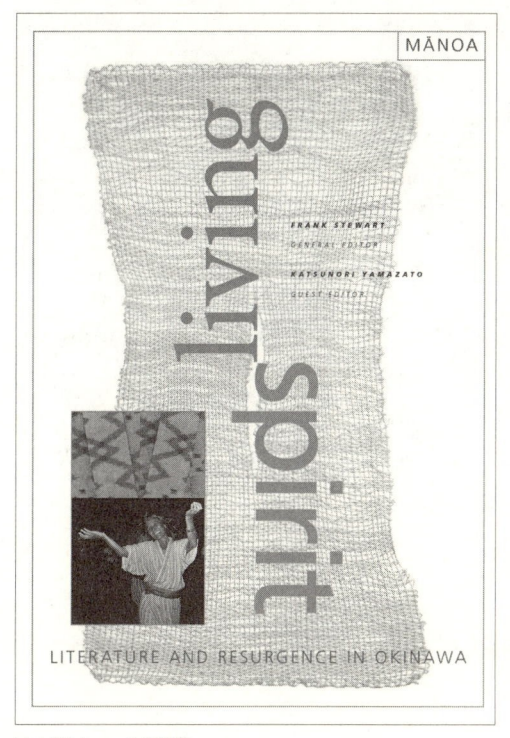

Vol. 23, Issue 1 (2011)
Editors: Frank Stewart, Katsunori Yamazato

Vol. 26, Issue 2 (2014)
Editors: Frank Stewart, John H. McGlynn, Cobina Gillitt

LIVING SPIRIT
LITERATURE AND RESURGENCE IN OKINAWA

Living Spirit includes two plays by Ōshiro Tatsuhiro, one of Okinawa's most revered writers. Never before published, *The Cocktail Party* is adapted by Ōshiro from his 1967 Akutagawa Prize–winning novella. Written in 1995, it examines the troubled relationship between the U.S. military and Okinawans. *Gods Beyond the Sea*, a modern *kumi odori*, retells the tragic love story of King Shō Toku and the priestess Kunikasa.

ISLANDS OF IMAGINATION
MODERN INDONESIAN DRAMA

This title contains seven plays written between 1933 and 2009, all united by the literary artistry and treatment of social issues that characterize modern Indonesian drama.

Contributors include Rita Matu Mona, Armijn Pané, N. Riantiarno, Ratna Sarumpaet, Iwan Simatupang, Luna Vidya, and Putu Wijaya. *Islands of Imagination: Modern Indonesian Plays* is published in cooperation with the Lontar Foundation of Indonesia.

UNIVERSITY of HAWAI'I PRESS JOURNALS

WWW.UHPRESS.HAWAII.EDU/JOURNALS

OTHER MĀNOA TITLES PUBLISHED BY UH PRESS

Vol. 19, Issue 2 (2007)

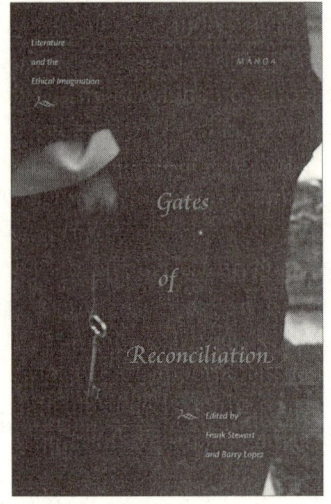

Vol. 20, Issue 1 (2008)

Vol. 20, Issue 2 (2008)

MAPS OF RECONCILIATION
LITERATURE AND THE ETHICAL IMAGINATION

In this collection, the editors turn to some of the world's most thoughtful authors — in fiction, essay, poetry, drama, and parable — to ask important questions about the future, to give us moral direction, individual courage, and a map toward reconciliation. In many voices and dialects, they urge us to be attentive and compassionate — somehow, as guest editor Barry Lopez writes, to bring hope to bear on the things that confound us. Contributors include the playwright Catherine Filloux; poets Kazuko Shiraishi, Ann Hunkins, Chris Merrill, and Luis H. Francia; fiction writers Yan Lianke, Tony Birch, Wang Ping, Prafulla Roy, and Galsan Tschinag; and others.

GATES OF RECONCILIATION
LITERATURE AND THE ETHICAL IMAGINATION

A diverse group of writers explore the role of literature in confronting the most pressing issue of our time: how individuals, communities, and nations can reconcile differences and grievances and forge a future with a renewed sense of dignity and mutual respect. In these works, past and present conflicts — some resolved and some not — are illuminated by literature, uncovering the complexities, subtleties, gestures, and necessary deliberations of forgiveness and healing. The urgency of such deliberations is captured by guest editor Barry Lopez when he asks, "Who will heed the plea of Everychild for a less brutal future?"

ENDURING WAR
STORIES OF WHAT WE'VE LEARNED

The stories, essays, and poems in this volume render the effects of war in our time and the shadows they cast, from the Pacific campaigns of World War II to genocide under the Khmer Rouge to hostilities in the Middle East. Soldiers, however, are not in the foreground in most of these works. More often, the writers depict war as a destructive force on the lives of children, women, and other civilians, and capture the lasting, complex ways in which innocent individuals and communities are harmed. Works such as those in *Enduring War* tell the truths that history and politics hide. We see that wars brutalize victors and vanquished alike, thus sowing the seeds for future conflict.